OTHER BOOKS BY PETER M. BOURRET

THREE JOSS STICKS IN THE RAIN

THE PHYSICS OF WAR

LAND OF LOUD NOISES AND VACANT STARES

SNOWFLAKES FROM THE OTHER SIDE OF THE UNIVERSE

All these title are available @amazon.com

Also available @barnesandnoble.com

Jello's Nam:
A Memoir

Peter M. Bourret

Jello's Nam: A Memoir
Copyright © 1999 Peter M. Bourret
All rights reserved.
This includes the right to reproduce any portion of this book in any form unless given permission. No part of this publication may be reproduced, stored electronically, or transmitted in any form without the prior written permission of the author, except brief quotes used in reviews.
Printed by CreateSpace in the USA
Memoir / Nonfiction / Vietnam War / PTSD / Marine Corps / Education
First Edition (July, 2018)
First Printing (July, 2018)
ISBN:10-1986448460
ISBN:13-978-1986448468

DEDICATION

A special dedication to Sgt. O'Conner and LCpl. Vargas, two forward observers for mortars, for making the ultimate sacrifice.

For the members of 81s Platoon, especially, Bravo Section, 81s, H & S Company, 1st Battalion, 7th Marines during my tour of duty from June 1967 to July 1968; and in particular, the members of the JELL-O Squad. Jerome Cockerhan, aka Sugar Bear, Walter Kolomyjec, aka Cossack, Michael Oleniacz, aka Pink Rat, ADB Brown, Aaron C. Legget, Paul Ignash, Bill Witting, Mike MacIntire, aka the Hippie Kid, Mike Rae, Skip Sullins, Doug Havalin, Hud Gillis, Cpl. Brown, Cpl. Johnson, Cpl. Clark, Roger Sexton, Jim Drayton, Roger Mainville, Frantz, Meyers, Kelley, Yingiling, Hutchins, Harris, Hunt, Sgt. Huffmeister, Rodick, Waggoner, States, Boksa, Cheatan, Eatmon, King, Ski and Stan. If I failed to remember your name or if I misspelled it, please forgive me. I'd love to hear from anyone from my Nam days. You can find me on Facebook.

I would be remiss if I failed to include Dave Stewart, my neighborhood friend who joined the Marines with me and served with the 1st Recon Battalion in Vietnam; Jim Shott, a fellow Tucsonan and Boot Camp buddy, who also served on Hill 10 with me; Mike Rae, a radio operator for 81s and was my roommate after he finished his enlistment; and Dale Witzman, who served as a 60mm mortar squad leader with Charley Company. Thank you for your fifty-plus years of friendship, born in the Nam.

Semper Fi and welcome home.

PETER M. BOURRET

"Those who go to fight monsters should see to it that in the process they do not become monsters; and when you look long into the abyss—the abyss also looks into you."

Friedrich Nietzsche

CONTENTS

Chapter   **Title**   **Page**

ACKNOWLEDGEMENTS

MAPS: HILL 10 & MAMELUKE THRUST AREA

PREFACE

PROLOGUE

Chapter	Title	Page
1	Oh, Youth!	1
2	Four-Year-Old Tree Climber	2
3	Nam Numbers And A California Cup Of Coffee	3
4	JELL-O's Magic	9
5	Class Of '65	20
6	Thank You For Your Interest, But…	25
7	Sir, The Private's Name Is Pronounced Boo-ray	27
8	The Problem Of Going From Level Four To Level One	43
9	Cruising Sunset Strip In A Shopping Cart	46
10	A Star-Spangled Thank-You	56
11	Too Busy To Write	62
12	I Kind Of Lied To The Recruiter	64
13	Got Those Blindfolded Blues	71
14	Dying In The Darkness Of The New Year	78
15	No Longer Killing The Problem	93
16	A Triangle-Flag Month	96
17	Some Orders Beg To Be Disobeyed	107
18	Job Skills Blues	122

Chapter	Title	Page
19	Crimson Claw Marks Comin' Our Way	124
20	The Price Of Lunch	131
21	They Promised God Anything	132
22	*Only*	134
23	From Antics To Enlightenment	135
24	Levity	140
25	Mickey Mouse And The Art Of [sic] Writing	142
26	Rockets!	144
27	Outside The Killing Radius	148
28	The Iowa-Farm-Boy Methodist	149
29	Chicken And Noodles With Mortar Round	152
30	The One-O'clock Sun Knew	163
31	Ponchos Full Of Silence	171
32	Two KIAs And Their Hungry Flies	172
33	Ho Chi Minh's Boys Visit Cossack	174
34	Death Lurks Down By The Water Bo	177
35	Hold The Paris Peace Talks At Hill 52?	181
36	Someone's Tryin' To Kill Me	183
37	I Thought We're Supposed To Do The Killing	188
38	Letters From The World	193
39	Doc Saves The Jello Kid's Butt	202
40	The Last Shitty Beer	213

Chapter	Title	Page
41	The Downside Of Being A Short-Timer	225
42	The Nam Without JELL-O's Magic	231
43	Mike Rae's "Corpsman-Up" Moment	235
44	The Overpaid Marine	242
45	Fate, Guilt and Growth	246
46	The Question	251
47	The Jello Kid Goes to Michigan	252
48	Eddie Plays Socrates	258
49	Jack Daniels, Guns, And Backgammon	265
50	A Kubler-Ross Moment	274
51	The Five-Year Old Magician	278
	EPILOGUE	281
	PHOTOS	283
	ABOUT THE AUTHOR	303

ACKNOWLEDGEMENTS

Although writing is a solitary venture, a number of people have helped me on this journey in a variety of ways. In addition to their support, Mary DeSantis, Cheryl Watters, Bill Black, Tina Carbo, Dave Barger, Mike Fitz and Ann Reaban have been invaluable, helping me fine-tune my memoir with their insightful observations and/or editing. Bill Black has also been especially helpful with his technical assistance. Working tirelessly, Tina and Dave made my cover happen. A number of people have been tireless in their support of my effort to tell the story of my Nam experience: Jeremy Bourret & Paul Bourret, my sons; Mike Hermes, Bob Kish, Candy Meyers [typed up the original *Jello's Nam* manuscript in 1980], Carolyn Kittle, Chuck Simms, Vicki and Howie Hibbs, Jeff Stensrude, Karen Schwabacher,, Steve Johnson, Wendy LaFave, Dale Witzman, Mike Rae, Ron Whiteman, Michael Brewer, Danetta Mecikalski, Mary Pat Sullivan, Sue Peters, Lynda Gibson, Marcus Conway, Megan Hughes, Morris & Sharon Barkan, Mary Bourret, my sister, & Rudy Saldivar, Wendy Newell, Melody Murray, Sarah Doshe Webb & Jason Hollander, five of my former students. Rose Pearson, the creative director and founder of The Writers' Circle, Inc., believed in me and published *WAR: a memoir* online. I cannot forget to mention my mom, a gifted writer, who was enthusiastic in her support of my writing. If I've forgotten someone, please forgive me. There will be more books; I'll make sure I'll remember for the next one.

I would be remiss if I failed to acknowledge the importance of all the people whom I've met along the way. You are essential pieces in the puzzle that is my life. John Donne was on target when he wrote that 'No man is an island, Entire of itself.' You've influenced and impacted my life although you might not have realized that. I believe that we meet the people whom we need to meet. Over time, I have discovered that my life has played out perfectly although it hasn't always been comfortable or enjoyable. I have no regrets, and I like the person I am. My fellow travelers, I appreciate you more than you will ever know.

Pete Bourret, aka The Jello Kid

PETER M. BOURRET

Hill 10 Area

Operation Mameluke Thrust Area

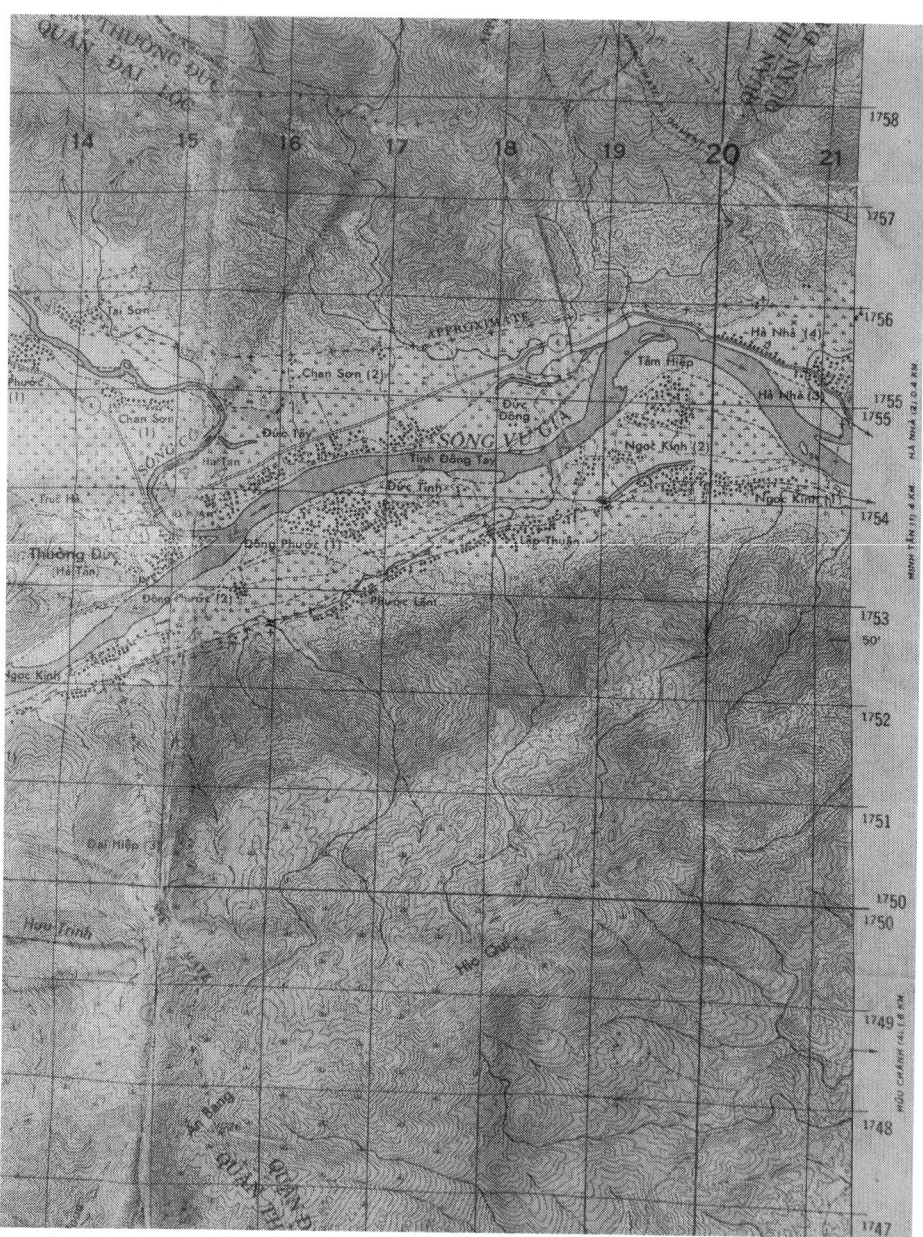

PREFACE

This year is the 50th anniversary of my departure from Vietnam. My tour of duty in the area southwest of Da Nang began on June 18, 1967 and officially lasted until I hopped on the sweet silver bird on the Fourth of July in 1968.

I began writing my memoir in 1970, two years after my return from Vietnam. During my tour of duty as a Marine 81mm mortarman, I occasionally found time to click away with my Instamatic camera, recording a visual record of certain aspects of life in the Nam. I have included some of these photos after the Epilogue. Enjoy. Additionally, I faithfully maintained a diary, on which I have relied to present a portrayal of my Vietnam War experience that is as accurate as possible. Occasionally, I have blended aspects of several events to expedite the narrative; when I did this, I was following my instincts as a writer as opposed to those of a historian. I have attempted to be as fastidious as possible, but if I fell short, please forgive me. I want the reader to be aware that my primary goal in *Jello's Nam* is to offer my recollection—a remembrance—and not a reflection about the events that create the tapestry of my memoir.

There will be those that find the crude language, pejorative terms and racial slurs to be offensive, which I understand; they are indeed. I, however, have chosen to present an accurate portrayal of the language that many young Marines in my memoir used in 1967 and 1968.

I ask much of the reader concerning military terminology, so I am providing a quick course in Vietnam War lingo: *the Nam* is Vietnam, more the experience than solely the geographic location; *Charlie* is the name American troops gave to the Viet Cong, aka the Cong, but these South Vietnamese Communist forces referred to themselves as the NLF, or National Liberation Front, which was modeled after the Viet Minh, who defeated the French in 1954; the *NVA* are the North Vietnamese Army or the PAVN, the People's Army of Vietnam; the *ARVN* are the South Vietnamese Army [American allies]; *gooks, dinks* and *slopes* are pejorative terms for the Vietnamese; *mamasan and papasan* are an older woman and an older man; *Uncle Ho* is Ho Chi Minh, the leader of North Vietnam;

the *Tet Offensive* is the surprise attack by Communist forces [VC and NVA] throughout South Vietnam during the Tet holiday [Vietnamese New Year] at the end of January 1968; the *grunts* are American infantry; *corpsman* are Navy medics, beloved by the Marines because of their courage under fire; an *FO* is a forward observer who uses the grid coordinates on a topographical map to call in 81mm mortar or artillery fire missions on the enemy; *arty* is artillery, which fire various sizes of shells/rounds: 105mm, 155mm, 175mm and 8 inch shells; *122s* are 122mm NVA rockets with a range of five about miles; *81s* refers to 81mm mortars, with a range of almost three miles; *HE* are High Explosive shells or rounds; *illum* are illumination rounds used to light up the night sky in a specific area; *PRC-25* is a field radio used to call in fire support or assistance; *FDC* [*Fire Direction Cent*er] is a bunker where the calculations for fire missions are created; a *topo map* is a topographical map used as reference by a forward observer to request a fire mission from the Fire Direction Center; a *klick* is 1,000 meters on a topo map; the *M14* rifle and the newer *M16* rifle are Americans assault rifles; the *AK-47* assault rifle is mainly used by the NVA but also by some VC; the *SKS* is a 7.62mm rifle used by the VC; the *M60* is an American 7.62mm machine gun with a cyclic rate of fire of 550 rounds per minute; the *RPD* is 7.62mm machine gun used by the Communist forces; a *Chicom grenade* refers to a Viet Cong or NVA grenade; a *Claymore mine* is an American anti-personnel device that fires a blast of pellets toward the enemy and is primarily used to prevent infiltration; *C rats* are C rations, carried on patrols and consist of several cans of food; a *water bo* is an abbreviation for two very different things: a water buffalo and a metal container on wheels that carries about 200 gallons of drinking water; *782 gear* is the military name for all of a Marine's equipment for the field; a *Marine squad* consists of 10 to 12 men; *spider holes* are camouflaged surface openings in a VC tunnel system that helped the VC fire and then disappear quickly; *R&R* is a 5-day break in which troops unwind outside the war zone; *KIA* stands for Killed In Action; *WIA* stands for Wounded In Action; *MIA* stands for Missing In Action; *AWOL* stands for Absent With Out Leave; POW stands for Prisoner Of War; piasters are Vietnamese currency; *Indian Country* and *Dodge City* are names given by Marines to dangerous locations in Vietnam with heavy concentrations of enemy forces; *sông* is the Vietnamese word for river, as in Song Vu Gia; a *ville* is a rural village or hamlet, which, based on a French mapping system, is followed by a number inside a set of parentheses, designating that the village is broken into various sections or annexes; *Ha Nha (3)* [near Hill 52 and Song Vu Gia]; *Khuong My (2), Tuy Loan (1), Dong Bich (1), Phuoc Ninh (7), An Nhon (1)* and *(2) and Phuoc Nhan* (2) are villes near Hill 10 and between five and nine miles southwest of Da Nang; *Hill 55* is our regimental hill; *Hill 10* is the battalion hill for the 1st Battalion, 7th Marine Regiment, 1st Marine Division, aka 1/7; *Hill 41* and *Hill 22* are each manned by a Marine company; *Hill 270, Hill 502, Hill 310* and *Charlie Ridge* are NVA strongholds 10-12 miles southwest of Da Nang [second largest city in Vietnam and is the location of a large American airbase]; the following NVA and VC units fought against 1st Bn., 7th Marines in late 1967-1968: the *Q-14 and Q-16 Companies* [Viet Cong units with a guerrilla cadre, or force, of approximately 100 each, the *368B* and *386B Artillery Regiments* [North Vietnamese 122 mm rocket regiments], the *T-3* and *402nd Sapper Battalions*, the *R-20 Battalion*, the *31st NVA Regiment*; a *cadre* is a small military group trained for a particular purpose; the *Purple Heart* is a medal given to those wounded or killed by hostile fire. Hopefully, I have clarified enough terminology to make my memoir more understandable. When in doubt, 'Google' any unfamiliar terms.

While in Vietnam, I promised myself that if I survived, I would become a teacher with the purpose of helping my students to think critically; additionally, I made a commitment to write and to talk about my war experience to help enlighten people about the realities of war, which includes Post-Traumatic Stress Disorder. I spent 30 years of my adult life teaching middle school and high school students, and for 25 years I have spoken in high school classes about my war experience. *Jello's Nam: A Memoir* is my fourth book that deals with the topics of the Vietnam War and PTSD. Because death stared me in the eyes at least a half-dozen times, I realize that I have been blessed because I was given the gift of life. I share my experience in the hope that people will listen with their hearts and come away with a clearer understanding of the insidious nature of war.

PETER M. BOURRET

PROLOGUE

So long ago, I desperately wanted only one gift for my twenty-first birthday: to be alive was my simple wish. Only thirteen months earlier I never expected, nor did I care, to be alive to celebrate the big two-one. July 16, 1968 was a non-hoopla day as far as twenty-first birthdays go: a lonely taxi ride from the airport in Tucson; then, a bottle of Budweiser handed to me by my father as I walked through the front door for the first time in more than a year.

As the mahogany door closed behind me, I was certain that I had shut the door on Vietnam; after all, it was over eight thousand miles away, so Tucson was out of range of North Vietnamese rockets. Better yet, the Pacific Ocean was a major obstacle for even the most tenacious NVA sappers, known for their commando-style tactics; I was certain they wouldn't waste their time on me, an insignificant cog in the great American war machine: I was a mortarless 81mm mortarman who was out of range, and gladly so.

To this day I have no memory of a birthday cake, the off-key singing of "Happy Birthday" or the blowing out of the magic number of candles. The birthday trappings and the rituals really didn't matter; being alive did. To this day I am the reluctant owner of a myriad of memories of the Nam, each one too fresh, too clear, too real.

The whitewashed, burnt adobe walls of my parents' house would insulate me from the heat of the Arizona desert; the solid, mahogany front door would protect me from unwanted intruders; however, I would discover that all walls and doors, regardless of their thickness or strength, are penetrable.

Twenty-one-year-olds have much to learn, so I ignorantly built a sandbag bunker around my young heart. I was officially an adult; however, the previous year my childhood had been killed in action; it was dead and buried, food for the worms; moreover, my soul had been captured by the forces of guilt. The NVA's shrapnel, booby traps and bullets had failed miserably, always missing me, their target; my body survived the Nam in spite of me, but the repatriation of my soul, a prisoner hidden deep in the dense jungle of my grief, would become a lifelong mission, one that continues even today.

Coming home from Vietnam is a simple exercise in movement through time and space, requiring only a troopship or an airplane; on the other hand, coming home from the Nam requires more than a twenty-one-year-old could ever realize.

Chapter 1
1967-1968

Oh, Youth!

When I was twenty, a war happened to me.

Chapter 2
Summer 1951

Four-Year-Old Tree Climber

The grey skies of winter are gone. He no longer pulls the snow sled up the hill for his older brother. Their snowman has gone away. He does not shiver anymore because of the lack of coal to warm their century-old house. It is summer, and his dad is working again. There is no TV to be watched, so he catches fireflies with his older brother. The fireflies in the Ohio night are magical creatures. He is positive of this.

Four-year-old tree climbers are usually certain, but tonight is different. It is seven o'clock, and he knows he should be sleeping, but there is the monolog of the clock with its steady ticking, its monotonous melody. A stomach full of boisterous lions are growling and howling his night away. His bedroom window is bending and swaying in the surreal almost black night; the nocturnal wizard is winning another round. His tired eyes nervously applaud the trick. The monster willow tree is slapping the panes of his bedroom window, but he knows it's really Jules Verne's giant octopus trying to get him.

Before he can pull the covers over his face, his mother walks into the room. She sits on his bed and hugs him. He feels safe when she assures him that the thunder and lightning of the August night are only Saint Peter moving furniture in Heaven. He smiles because he knows the boogeyman cannot get him.

His mother, like the fireflies, is a magical creature making sense out of a stormy Ohio night. The branches of the willow tree are still whipping his window, but he sleeps.

Four-year-old tree climbers grow up. Some of them become Marines going off to war.

Chapter 3
4 July 1968

Nam Numbers And A California Cup Of Coffee

The 707 was a day late, but it was finally ready to take us back to the World. Thirteen months of fantasies would soon become beautiful realities. For the plane full of the best kind of Marines, the going-home-alive kind, July 4, 1968 would truly be Independence Day.

I made sure I had a window seat. I wanted to see the Nam one last time. That magical silver bird climbed away from Da Nang air base: the airstrip getting smaller as the coastline came into view. It was all becoming just a topographical map. Someone else down there would have to worry about the ambushes, the punji sticks and other assorted booby traps, the North Vietnamese sappers, and the mortar and rocket attacks. I was drunk with the beauty of the sunset, crimson frosting on Earth cake. The plane was flying over the South China Sea and heading for Okinawa.

Before the Nam could shrink away and become thirteen months of memories, I had one final message for that place. Sister Luella, my second grade teacher, would not have approved. She had not been to the Nam, so I did not care. It felt good flipping the bird, the infamous and often used middle finger, at the Nam and all that it stood for. "It's been fun, Nam. A real cheap thrill. Catch you later, a whole lot later. A fucking drag to say the least. Goodbye!"

With only the ocean below us, I became bored with sightseeing. There would be etceteras of ocean between the Nam and the California coast. It was time to finally relax. The soft, sensuous voice of a stewardess welcomed us aboard. She made the mistake of asking if there was anything she could do for us. A plane full of Marines were whistling and cheering. Lust was the order of the day. The two Marines next to me were still grinning passionately when I decided it was time to attempt to catch some sleep, and not the Nam type but deep restful sleep.

damn...we lucked out...sure glad the North Vietnamese dropped their rockets on the chopper base instead of on the airstrip last night...bad enough having the plane delayed for a day...would have been a real bummer getting killed on my last day in that suck hole...lucked out once again...just like the time Andy wanted me to go to Da Nang with him...sure glad I was too broke...probably would have been blown away when his truck hit the mine...goddamn...skated once more...it'll be so nice to sleep at night...no bunker watch...no mortar attacks...no one out there trying to send my ass home early...back in the World I'll finally get to see a movie all the way through...no waiting for some klutz to change the reel...cold beer...ice cold Coors...no more warm tiger piss...the real thing...yeah the real thing...female types...all those crazy girlfriends...Sherry Cathy Liz Pam Wendy...my god...Wendy...what bizarre trip will she lay on me...interesting for sure...weird but not as strange as the Nam...at least she won't be shooting at me...I hope...best of all I'll get to rap with Fitzie and my family...Mom'll be all smiles...her number-two son actually beat the bullets...no sweat super mamasan...your Jello Kid faked you out...I'm coming home.

Several hours later, the plane got tired of flying and decided to land in Okinawa. For three days, we spent time doing activities that the Marine Corps thought were important for us. After we had taken bunches of showers and had lost what we had thought were suntans, we began our flight to Hawaii.

I wanted to think beautiful thoughts of the World, but the Nam ambushed me.

wonder if that corpsman really swished his broken syringe needle in the rice paddy water before he gave that NVA prisoner a shot of morphine...hope he didn't...but the Nam's a weird place...really messes with your head...like that dude in the other squad who tried to kill Boksa...damn...they were both on our side...ha ha...weird watching everyone sit there doing nothing when Boksa was being choked on his cot...sure lucky that dude didn't kill me when I tried to stop him from killing Boksa...if our section leader hadn't come in the tent I would have been a

KIA...damn...scared shitless...didn't go to the Nam to save us from us...glad I am out of that shithole...could do anything over there...no respect...a piece of ass was worth a carton of Salem cigarettes...the clap easier to catch then a piece of shrapnel...screwing over people...kissing ass...what it was all about...screwing over people was the order of the day...but payback was a motherfucker...especially for that dude in Charley Company...he thought it was cool ripping off his whore...not paying for all the joints she gave him...laughing in her face...bad ass Marine doing a number on a Vietnamese chick...he didn't give a shit...to him she was just a dink whore...a slant-eyed gook bitch...too bad he was too stupid to know she'd tell her VC buddies to put the zap on him...next day the Cong sent his ass home early.

Within a few hours, we would be landing in Hawaii. We still had a thousand miles worth of powder-blue ocean carpet between us. Seascape and skyscape, nothing more. I was still drowsy after three hours of restless sleep. The Nam was still holding my mind for ransom.

numbers...everything in the Nam had a number...Hill 502... Hill 10...Hill 881...casualty count...86 wounded...14 killed...grid coordinates...935526...time left in the Nam...108 days short...weapons...81mm mortar...60mm mortar...M60 machine gun...M16...AK-47...105s...B-52s...fire adjustment...right 100 meters...left 50 meters...GI numba one...GI numba ten-thow...we're numba one...the Seventh Marines...rank...E-4...MOS...0341...paycheck...$180 a month...25 cents an hour...numbers' game...the whole thing a big game.

After only spending an hour or two in Hawaii, we began the final leg of our odyssey back to sanity. Simon and Garfunkel knew what they were talking about. "Homeward Bound" was what the past thirteen months had been all about. The Pacific was still down there, reminding us how small we really were.

things the Marine Corps manual forgot to tell me...when you bleed it hurts...when you kill you die a little...not seeing the people I killed makes it easier...maybe I can forget about it...when you get killed it's forever...out on Operation Mameluke Thrust...shitty operation...Ho Chi Minh's birthday...great day to make some news for Walter Cronkite...folks back in the World sitting down to 5:30 family dinner...tripping out watching TV...saying grace...chowing down...checking out the news from the war zone...excuse me...police action...don't think so...mommy's little girl can't wait until she's in high school with the big kids...very politely...please pass the butter...on the boob tube some unlucky son of a bitch has his guts rolling out for the folks back home...it's show time and he gargles his red ooze...thank you the salt please...and he gags his last breath...and some perfect Donna-Reed-mother-type is thrilled...how nice only fifty dead this week...and some grunt is no more...his birthday party canceled...one year...ten years...twenty years later...the grunt who just wanted to be lucky is still nineteen...the king of Fathers' Day replying to his wife...yes how nice...but not so for that dude wasted on Ho Chi Minh's birthday...thrown on the side of a dead tank...no room for the KIAs on the medevac choppers...too many wounded...sorry about that shit...you have to wait in one more line...your final Marine Corps line...damn it dead dude...wish you'd go away...that bullet hole in your side...your clammy cream-colored flesh staring at me...one color my fifth-grade art teacher forgot to tell us about...what will your wife and the baby you never met say...it's not fair...you only had a few weeks left in the Nam...getting short was a bummer for you...why did LBJ let the NVA blow out all your birthday candles...forever is too damn long when you're only nineteen...why did that dude from Up North have to fire his message at you...your tired eyes knowing...one minute a short-timer...the next his target...finally becoming a bullet catcher...tomorrow with its good times and its bummers rolling off your shaking hands slipping away through your desperate fingers...silent red hands...no more pain for you...but your old lady and your kid have to live in Bummer City...and your wife will be lonely on your birthday made useless...she will ache for her man...but he was stolen from a wife...and his son will never discover that Santa Claus is really dad...I wanted to hate the motherfucker who blew you away...it's so easy to hate when you're beat on your ass...and if it makes you feel better...we had integration of the races on your death day...it finally worked...a white boy a black boy a brown boy a yellow boy all got together...equality day...the boys all lay on the battlefield drained of their red blood...free at last...rainbow armies spilling red blood under blue skies...heroes fertilizing green fields for the next army the next flag the next blood...but always...the clouds looking down laughing at us...and when they sent your dead ass back to the World they called you hero and said thanks...draping your casket with the red white and blue...all your neighbors paying their respects at your funeral...you were the main attraction...magic Latin words bouncing around that sacred place...zombies surrounding you...their ebony costumes proof of their grief...stares of the sorrowful shrouding you...bouquets of their guilt drowning you...twenty years from now your baby son will see graveyards with flowers dotting the green blanket pulled over loved ones...bouquets that show we care or flowers of our guilt...do these cut flowers really matter...maybe so...why not a flower when it mattered...when love could be shared...and forever is too damn long for a babysan who never knew his dad.

A voice on the intercom announced that we would be landing shortly. I had finally become the ultimate short-timer. Oakland. California. USA. The World.

down there...the ape still dashing through the maze of four-letter-word engraved walls...down the litter strewn handiwork of the WPA...sidewalks so convenient for us...but we spit and drop our gum on you...people say thanks in the strangest ways...the ape still rushing across the black arteries choked with Henry Ford's metal monsters...running away from hell...toward the garden... getting closer to civilization...dittoed houses...painted green blankets...regiments of daisies...but nowhere a weed.

"Far Out! The World. The Jello Kid actually made it." The travelers from Chicago, New York, Atlanta, the Nam: we all had deplaned. They walked on concrete runways to get to the terminal. We walked on gold. The World was ours.

the magic of Jello came through for me and got my ass home alive...damn...I lucked out.

The two Marines who sat next to me during the flight suggested that we get a cup of coffee at the airport restaurant. Real coffee, not that crude oil the Marine Corps had pawned off as coffee. Sitting at the counter, we smiled triumphantly. We had won the big game. Although we sat there unnoticed for five minutes, it did not bother us. We had waited more than a year and had grown accustomed to waiting. Hurry up and wait was what the Marine Corps and the Nam had been all about.

The waitress, twice our age and looking trapped by her

nowhere job, was consumed in a conversation with a businessman who smoked a raunchy smelling cigar. After twenty minutes the two other Marines and I stared at each other, wondering if maybe we were invisible. Maybe we had been killed that last night in the Nam, and our ghosts were sitting at the counter.

Having waited there for thirty minutes, we left our seats at the counter and returned to the boarding area. The plane, now refueled, was ready to fly us to El Toro Marine Air Station. The plane took off on its final leg of the journey. The Marine next to me shared his sarcastic hope that all the women back in the World would not be as *friendly* as the waitress had been.

"No shit! With people like this, who needs enemies?"

Chuckling at my response, he replied, "The goddamn NVA were friendlier than that bitch. At least you knew where they were coming from. They were supposed to kill us."

"I hope this is not what the World is going to be all about. I just don't need it. Thirteen months of bullshit is enough to last me for a long damn time."

Down below, the giant freeways were becoming skinny lines, and the clouds were just cotton candy.

I didn't really expect a welcome home parade...God Bless America and all that shit...but I sure would have appreciated a cup of coffee.

Chapter 4
Spring 1968

JELL-O's Magic

Addicts have their dope. Alcoholics have their liquor, and I, a fanatical JELL-O worshiper, had my JELL-O. To the ignorant infidels, the powers of the sacred JELL-O were a mystery. How strange that someone would indulge in eating these fine sugary grains; not a drop of water added, not even an opportunity for the transformation to its traditional jelled state. Odd, yes, but such a peculiarity became an asset, especially at mail call.

Packages from home were well appreciated by one and all. Unfortunately, these packages from the World would attract a horde of admirers frantically seeking the recipient's friendship. They neglected to arrive bearing gifts, yet these part-time *friends* seemed to exit bearing gifts, ours.

The solution to this problem was simple; I acquired a reputation for receiving packages containing only JELL-O. Since very few Marines had acquired a taste for the sweet grains, my packages laden with boxes of JELL-O failed to generate interest. Candy bars, sausage, and other forms of pogey bait—aka junk food—were neatly camouflaged by a top layer of JELL-O boxes. On one glorious occasion, my sagging morale was bolstered when I received a package containing thirty-two boxes of the magical substance. The eight-thousand-mile journey had taken its toll; two of the boxes had become casualties.

"You get another JELL-O shipment?"

"Yeah, this far out dude back in the World whipped up a big-ass CARE package."

"Damn, there must be at least..." Cossack, who joined my squad back in January just before the Tet Offensive, was the proud owner of an impish grin and a Fu Manchu mustache; he stopped counting at twenty. "*Boo coo* JELL-O. Must be over thirty boxes of that crap there."

"Thirty-two to be exact, but two took gas," I replied with a hint of sadness in my voice.

Boksa, a tall and gangly Marine from New Jersey, pulled back the canvas flap that pretended to be the door to our sixteen-man tent. With his eyes bulging with visions of junk food, his drool glands were churning on overdrive as he strolled into the tent. With the feast only a few delicious feet away, he lurched toward my cot, a banquet table of goodies.

GREAT...here come the maggots...too bad they'll be disappointed when they find out I've received another JELL-O shipment...blows them away...must think I'm strange or un-American or somethin'...guess they're right...who in the hell would eat JELL-O straight out of the box...weird...but delicious...beats the hell out of dog shit from the mess hall.

"Somethin' for me, Jello?"

I snarled back, "What's your problem, Boksa?"

Undeterred by the tone in my voice, Boksa replied, "No problem, man. What you got for your ol' friend?"

"Suck out, maggot! You're one hell of a friend...always doin' jive ass shit that gets the lifers pissed off at me."

"Well, that's what a squad leader's for."

"Bullshit. Besides...didn't get any pogey bait, just JELL-O...all JELL-O."

Boksa left disappointed but not defeated. Another Marine had made the costly mistake of opening a package from home, and Boksa honed in on that package and became his instant friend.

Upon returning from evening chow, we were informed that an officer would inspect our footlockers in the hope of finding several cameras, which had disappeared in the past several days. It was not that some of the men could not be trusted; the crux of the problem was that some of the men *could* be trusted to rip off anything that was not bolted down; in some cases, even the bolts might disappear.

After all, because the NVA [North Vietnamese Army] were doing their best to deplete the ranks of the line companies in the field, the Corps was not very discrete in its choice of volunteers;

some recruits had opted for service in the Marine Corps rather than doing prison time when given that choice by a judge. Most normal types stayed away from such an outfit with a renowned reputation for seeking and finding trouble. The way most Marines saw it, doggies, aka the Army, and Marines were most definitely two distinctly different breeds.

Sitting on his cot, Cossack, who was tired of wondering, looked over at me and asked, "So what's the story?"

"Got me, Cossack. Guess some officer is going to try to catch himself a thief."

"By checkin' footlockers? No way, Jello. He's got to catch the dude in the act...just like with the gooks and their mortars." Sporting what seemed to be a permanent grin on his tanned face, Cossack snickered. His mother, a good Catholic Michigan woman who had named him Walter, probably would not have approved of his new name or his expression, but she wasn't in the Nam, so it didn't matter.

"Well, at any rate, I hear the lifers just outside the tent. Get ready for the atten-hut-sir-blah-blah routine."

"Atten..."

"At ease, men. I'll be here for just a few minutes. Stand by your racks...have your footlockers open."

probably a cool dude on the outside back in the World...didn't even go in for that 'ATTEN-HUT' crap...we're freaking him out...JELL-O boxes nailed over everyone's rack...Christians have their crucifixes...we have our sacred JELL-O boxes...keeps evil spirits away....Jello Squad we're messing up his brain housing group...flipped out...what a hard ass...it's cool...green berets have their A-Team...we have our Jello Squad...right on...JELL-O power.

The captain walked up to me and said, "Lance corporal."

"Yes, sir?"

"What's under your footlocker tray?"

"Nothin' much...just some chow from back in the World and some..."

"JELL-O," he replied with a hint of bewilderment at the odd sight.

"Yeah...I mean...yes, Sir. It's JELL-O. It's pretty good. Kinda boosts my morale."

"I'm sure, but the entire bottom of your footlocker is packed with boxes of JELL-O."

"Can't afford to run out. Want to try some?"

"No. I'll pass," he said as he smiled an ounce more than a captain is permitted.

It was sad that he failed to embrace the opportunity I had afforded him; as the Jello Kid, I did not make such an offering frequently: his loss, my gain. As officers go, the JELL-O inspector was tolerable, especially when compared to some of the other lifer types that infested our battalion. One such junior Napoleon was our mortar platoon commander. Spit-shined combat boots, freshly-starched utilities [work clothes], unsoiled web belt, clean shaven Boy Scout face, and starched cover [hat] with its bill resting squarely two regulation-fingers above his regulation nose: this was our wooden Toy Soldier who liked to play lieutenant.

Without his inspections and lectures to the troops, our fearless leader would have been an average earthling like the rest of us. Our by-the-book platoon commander failed, however, to embrace such an egalitarian perspective of humanity. Could one blame him? After all, he had endured the *rigors* of OCS training, had acquired vast experience during his ten or so months as a Marine, and had participated in two or three patrols while he had been attached to Bravo Company.

We could have used his thunderbolts and his spit-shined boots during Tet. Because the Communists had been deceptive, he would have disapproved of their Tet Offensive, even with all its potential medals. He would not have had ample opportunity to get his utilities starched on a daily basis.

While we were awaiting an inspection, all the procrastinators back in the World were rushing to meet the April 15 income tax filing deadline. All my mortar rounds, each one costing about fifty dollars, weren't cheap, and someone had to pay for them. Because I was in a combat zone, I didn't have to pay any taxes on my below-minimum-wage paycheck; I got to keep all 180 dollars each month. Because I didn't have to worry about filing my income tax return, I began writing a letter home.

Hi Family,

It's me again. Sorry that I haven't written in a while, but I just can't find any peace and quiet. It looks like I'll be studying in the hallowed halls of the Great Desert University this September. It seems that Boston College wants me to take those required entrance tests, but my being in the Nam just doesn't make it too easy for me to take them. I wrote and asked if they could take this into consideration; however, they seemed to have never been in a war zone, so they don't sympathize with my predicament. What can I say!

Things around my area are pretty quiet at this time, and I hope they remain so. I've got more to talk about, but we have a fun Mickey-Mouse inspection in a few minutes, so I'll close for now.

Jello

I looked over at Cossack and noticed that he was sprawled out on his cot. His face owned a blank stare.

"Cossack, get off your ass! Got an inspection coming up...compliments of super lifer."

"Shit."

"What can I say, dude? War's hell. At any rate, better get out there and give the Toy Soldier his cheap thrills."

Cossack got up from his cot with the enthusiasm of a Marine who has just learned that he has been volunteered to be point man on a patrol into Charlie Ridge. "Yeah, sure...but I'd rather give him a swift kick in the ass...that son of a bitch. God, he pisses me off!"

"I thought you dug this spit and polish crap, Cossack," I said sarcastically.

"Cut me some slack. You're the lifer...not me."

"I'm no lifer. And there's no slack due for you, maggot...it's all been issued this month."

In the midst of our bantering, our own personal version of Ichabod Crane walked into our tent. In our eyes, he was a lifer—a by-the-book Marine without a sense of humor—and in his sergeant's eyes, we were considered to be shitbirds. Back in the World, he would never ask either of us to double date with him and his honey. He relished the role of a Marine sergeant. He seemed to take pleasure in yelling at the troops, which he believed was the essence of an effective NCO [non-commissioned officer]. When he yelled, it started out that way, but it always came out as a shriek.

Cossack and I would never volunteer to throw ourselves on a hand-grenade for our sergeant; we counted the days until he would leave the Nam.

"Okay, you two ... hurry it up!"

"Sure thing, sarge, be right out...in just a minute."

"Jello...Cossack...move it...now!"

suck out lifer...rotate it sideways...all you do is sweat...so lucky to have your skinny ugly bod around here for so damn long...why did you have to extend for six more months...those first months with you were shitty enough but six more...God...you got your precious sergeant stripes...wow a genuine Marine Corps sergeant.

We casually strolled out of the tent and walked toward the sergeant's glaring face.

"About time, you two. Jello, is all of your squad present?"

"Think so. Yeah, we're all here...at least our bods are. Can't vouch for our minds."

Although agitated by my commentary, he ignored my comments and asked, "Everyone squared away?" He paused and then continued, "The lieutenant will be here in just a minute! Rifles, covers, belts, magazines, boots...yeah, boots! Jello, are your boots shined this time?"

"Yeah, sarg...nice and shiny."

"Okay, men... ATTENTION!"

how 'bout a little slack...you've already made sergeant...no medals for playin' drill instructor...atten-hut...who are you kidding...lifer-and-a-half...you love all this bullshit.

"Thank you, sergeant."

"Yes, sir."

"Sergeant, stand by and take notes as I inspect each man."

"Aye, aye, sir."

"Lance corporal, I see you've shined your boots since the last inspection. Rifle's spotless, utilities clean, cover squared away, no dust in your magazines, good shave... excellent. Just keep it up." Unimpressed by his compliment, I rolled my eyes when he moved on to inspect the next man.

The inspection continued with the lieutenant carefully scrutinizing each man. We passed the inspection, but barely. The lieutenant chose to perceive us as rogues bent on avoiding as much work as possible. This characterization failed to bother most of us, except for our few lifers. Although our wooden Toy Soldier saw some essential military value in these inspections, most of us felt they belonged to garrison duty back in the World.

"Okay, men, overall you showed poorly. Some of you were squared away the way a Marine should be, but the rest of you...well there's just no excuse for a dirty rifle, and when there's an inspection, that means HAIRCUTS! Some of you men are beginning to look like hippies."

jive city...who are you shitting...get off the soap box...at least the hippies aren't in this cesspool getting shot at and listening to idiots like you harass the troopies...lieutenant go out on a one man search and destroy op and take on uncle ho's boys...they wouldn't exactly groove on your commands or be impressed with your second lieutenant's bars...you're too much...hippies...too damn much.

Unimpressed by the lieutenant's feeble attempt at being a 1968 version of General George Patton, we stood there waiting for either the end of his tirade or for the end of war; eventually both would happen. By yelling, belittling and glaring, he seemed to believe that we would become motivated Marines. He, however, failed to realize that this wasn't boot camp, and he wasn't a drill instructor.

In the Nam, the genuine leaders earned the respect of their men by being doers and not talkers. Telling an eighteen-year-old to take a hill was not as effective as leading the assault up that hill. Sadly, our lieutenant was typical of many of the officers on our hill.

Unaware that he was only playing leader, he continued to spew forth his sanctimonious speech, telling us that he expected us to have haircuts by the next inspection, *real ones*, as he put it. He continued his rant in black and white about how our lives were simple; moreover, we were slackers because we *only* had to fire a few mortar rounds and clean our mortar each day.

"You should be out in the field like the grunts in Bravo Company. When I was attached to them for two weeks, I saw more of the bush than all you men put together. You should be out there where it's at...that's where the war is...not back here on the hill with your mortar tubes. You sure have it rough!"

asshole...want your ass kicked...slimy wimp...bet you were in one of those ROTC programs back in college...getting kind of high and mighty since you've been in the bush for two whole weeks...a regular hardcore combat veteran...shit...you're too much...so full of shit that it's rolling out your ears...where the hell were you during Tet...so we're skaters and we don't do shit around here...who's standing up dropping the rounds down that tube when we get incoming mortars and 122s...for sure it's not you lieutenant...just us bums in 81s...everyone else is hiding their asses in a bunker or a fighting hole when the shit hits the fan...good old 81s on the job knocking out NVA mortars and rockets...you think you're a salty veteran...what a crock of shit.

"Okay, sergeant, dismiss your men."

"ATTEN-HUT...fall out."

Back in the tent, the lieutenant was passing my rack when he noticed that I was changing my special-occasions jungle boots. The lieutenant, feeling duped, glared at me as I laced up my shoddy boots, the pair with my toes hanging out. Time and the tropics had inflicted wounds on my torn and leather-cracked jungle boots. A pitiful sight indeed, but they afforded me comfort, and that was what jungle boots were all about. The lieutenant saw things in a different light though, probably because an enlisted man, a *peon*, had fooled him. I would not even shine those fine treads for the super lifers, the generals, when they would inspect our hill to evaluate the war effort.

Now standing at attention so the lieutenant could yell at me officially, I filed his words in the 'oh-that's-fascinating' file. "Lance corporal, what's the meaning of this?"

"Well, sir, those shiny boots just aren't comfortable, but these other boots...I know they don't look too military-like, but they sure feel..."

The lieutenant's boyish face was becoming an instant portrait of anger as he bellowed in his best I-am-in-charge voice, "Enough of this! Shined boots from now on, lance corporal. Do you understand?"

"Yes."

"What, lance corporal?"

An unenthusiastic, "Yes, sir," rolled from my lips.

suck out maggot...take my shiny boots and cram them up your rosy red ass...I'm sure they issued you one...they put it on your shoulders instead lieutenant...SIR hope you get your bod transferred up to the DMZ...you'd love it up there...brave gung ho lifer that you are.

The lieutenant and our section leader turned away and left the tent; standing several yards in front of the entrance, they discussed their mutual headaches. The lieutenant peered up toward the entrance and began gawking, forgetting for a moment that his expression was unbecoming of an officer.

"Sergeant, what's going on in there? What ..."

"Oh. It's that lance corporal..."

Having forgotten to bring his sense of humor with him, he impatiently replied, "Yes, I know...but what's he doing hanging upside down from the tent rafters?"

"Well, sir, he's been here for almost..."

"What's that noise, sergeant? It sounds like a...giant bird or something."

Wishing he could divorce us, our sergeant said, "Oh...sir, let me explain."

His irritation was three shades less than subtle. "Please do. I'm waiting, sergeant."

"As I was saying, sir, the lance corporal...they call him Jello...the Jello Kid..."

"The what!" The lieutenant, wondering what had happened to the Marine Corps, shook his head. This was a war, and he was a lieutenant, not an orderly in charge of a mental ward.

"The Jello Kid...on account of all the JELL-0 he eats...right out of the box. Anyway the noise you heard...well, that no doubt was his sidekick PFC...well, they call him the Mad Cossack, and he likes to let out these giant eagle calls...Strange pair."

"To say the least, but why is that Jello nut hanging there like a bat? Doesn't he care that an officer is watching all of this...I mean, doesn't he care?"

"Don't think so, sir. He's been here for over ten months and no R&R."

"That's no excuse. He should act like the professional he's supposed to be. Disgusting!"

The bewildered lieutenant shook his head and sighed. He walked off, certain the war effort was being impeded by the likes of us. Hanging from tent rafters in a war zone; was that any way for a pair of Marine mortar men to act? Cossack and I were positive it was the only way to act, especially if we were to escape from the Nam compliments of a Section 8, which was the military's synonym for insanity. Cossack and I had both joined the Marines and had volunteered for duty in Vietnam, ample proof of our mental derailment.

We decided that we both must be suffering from paranoia and schizophrenia. After all, we believed there were people trying to cause us harm; the Communists kept trying to blow up our hill with their mortars and rockets. Anyone who acted like a giant eagle and called himself the Mad Russian Cossack had to be a little kooky. The Marine Corps had given him a mortar, but he felt robbed. He would continue to be a second-rate Cossack warrior until he had a white stallion. Only then would he truly become a big-time Cossack warrior. Until then, he would have to content himself with the likes of the Jello Kid who was first known as the Candy Man.

I was dubbed with this name during my first month in the Nam because someone felt I had an excessively optimistic view of life. That name and I did not get along, so we got divorced. I met up with my new name. We fell in love and lived happily ever after in spite of the lifers and the North Vietnamese Army. Some people thought I was crazy when I would sprinkle grains of JELL-0 around our mortar gun pit. Although my behavior was somewhere between crazy and odd, not one member of my Jello Squad was ever wounded or killed while I was in the Nam. Maybe God just wanted to be able to laugh a little when he would look at Vietnam, or maybe the North Vietnamese liked to laugh also.

The lifers had become immune to our giant eagle calls and our hanging like bats from the tent rafters. Even the lieutenant was no longer shocked when we would swing around the tent acting like juvenile delinquent chimpanzees. With this realization, we knew we would never escape the Nam because of our madness. We would have to either survive the thirteen-month tour or go home early in a green plastic bag. With less than a hundred days remaining in my tour, I opted for the first method of removal from the war zone.

Within a week, our lieutenant left us just as all the others had done. Job opening: second lieutenant. No experience necessary. Be in charge until you find something more exciting to do.

According to the latest rumor, our wooden Toy Soldier was off to Da Nang and the Big Time, or at least his version of it. He walked into the lifer's dream; he became the general's aide. All sides were happy; he was mortar platoonless, and we were second lieutenantless. Things always seemed to work out for the Jello Squad.

Chapter 5
May 1965

Class Of '65

High school was a month away from becoming memories. Spring was overrun with the hot Arizona air. I would rather have been chugging malt liquor in Sabino Canyon on the outskirts of Tucson, but I was sitting at my appointed desk in my Latin Class. The nun, who usually smiled, was angry at the class, but her anger glided by me. I had translated the ten lines of Caesar. In her class, I always did, but I had not always been a serious Latin student.

When I was a freshman, I was not a Latin scholar. My freshman Latin teacher was a drill instructor disguised as a priest. Half the class usually was standing as punishment for not translating the fifteen lines of Latin homework. Those being punished were not permitted to smile, but I was a fourteen-year-old—not caring about dead languages—so I grinned while my Latin teacher's back was turned. The classroom was a forest of failures. Someone must have amputated my Latin teacher's sense of humor when he was a child. The smile on my face evaporated when the Latin teacher caught me smiling and demonstrated Carmelite discipline by drumming the top of my head with his priestly knuckles.

Each morning my Latin class was an instant replay of the previous one, and unfortunately, each afternoon the Latin teacher became my religion teacher. I was beginning to question whether God really loved me. Being a good Catholic, I knew that suffering was part of life. As a five-foot-tall freshman boy, I experienced suffering. Why then did God torment me with the monster-priest, not once, but twice each day? I had ample time to ponder the reason for God's wrath each day in my Latin class, but I never fully discovered a satisfactory answer. I decided that God must have not been a morning person because the demon-priest seemed more human after lunch. Maybe his morning coffee finally kicked in. Eventually, I grew to accept that God looked out for me and did love me: my proof being that I never stood in religion class. Failing religion class was difficult to do, even for an unmotivated freshman boy.

One afternoon when I was in an adventurous mood, I asked my religion teacher about a hypothetical situation about committing a mortal sin, such as having an impure thought, and then getting killed on my way to church, and thus being unable to make a confession.

"So, Father, what would happen to me?" The priest informed me that my soul would go to hell since I had not been able to make a confession.

I politely responded, "Oh, really." It was safer to end the conversation here.

The priest continued to explain to the class the difference between a venial sin and a mortal sin, but I was not listening. I was wondering why I would go to hell because of a thought, and yet not be allowed to go to Heaven simply because I had been unfortunate enough to be killed before I could confess to a priest. This seemed ridiculous to me. I was certain that a thought would get my soul into Heaven as easily as a thought would send my soul to hell.

The idea of spending eternity in Lucifer's barbecue pit, with such notables as Hitler and Attila the Hun, seemed outrageous, especially for having an impure thought. If I were to spend forever burning with such spiritual felons, I might as well translate my impure fantasies into sexual realities. At least I would enjoy myself before doing time in the eternal prison; however, shyness keep me pure, but I had jumped off the Catholic dogma train. My God was a merciful God whom had better things to do than to punish teenagers for being normal. My religion teacher had cured me of my need to ask religious questions of mere mortals: I was a one-man Protestant Reformation.

My Latin teacher during my senior year was a nun whom was the antithesis of my freshman Latin teacher. She was sitting at her desk as she looked through a stack of homework. Graduation was a few days away, and the birds outside the windows were chattering, not worrying about Caesar or mortal sins. I was certain that the girls in my class were skags, a thousand miles past homely. They made it easy for me to not have impure thoughts. No mortal sins for me on this hot afternoon in May of 1965.

It was my last class of the day; I had finished my work, so I wrote a poem. I called it "World Where?"

> *Yankee no—Cuba yes*
> *Burnt library in Cairo*
> *Japan yes—Yankee no*
> *All the world's a mess*
>
> *Southern Democrats*
> *Right Republicans*
> *Negroes are Americans*
> *Selma clubs and bats*
>
> *White lady killed*
> *Burning cross*
> *Freedom's loss*
> *Hate fulfilled*
>
> *Santo Domingo*
> *Another Cuba*
> *Not for America*
> *Left stay—Yankee go*
>
> *Strike North*
> *Very hard*
> *Death's on the card*
> *We must go forth*
>
> *Attack and kill*
> *Bomb and fight*
> *Day and night*
> *They must be still*

Send more troops
Not just machines
But U.S. Marines
Additional scoops

Why Vietnam?
Won't they quit
It doesn't fit
War is a sham

Life at home
Easy and free
Insanity
We're like Rome

Many poor
Here and afar
Mankind's scar
Where's the cure?

We're not all bad
There's the Peace Corps
And much more
It makes you glad

A war is here
Against poverty
It's not free
Removes the fear

Johnson became sick
Ten to a house
Food for a mouse
Legislation came quick

*It's Medicare
Care for the old
It's very bold
Is it really fair?*

*With the AMA
There is a clash
Not enough cash
But that was yesterday*

*Without finesse
We fight for freedom
We're Yankee scum
The world's a mess*

*Tell me why?
Give a reason
Mankind's treason
Makes you cry*

*War is a must
Hatred and fear
Religion they jeer
Lack of trust*

*Love your neighbor
Where is salvation?
Life's on the run
Where is the Savior?*

Chapter 6
May 1966

Thank You For Your Interest, But...

PEACE CORPS
Washington, D. C. 20525
May 5, 1966

Pete M. Bourret
5320 E. Linden Place
Tucson, Arizona

Dear Mr. Bourret:
We appreciate your willingness to serve your country as a Peace Corps Volunteer. The response of dedicated persons like yourself to the call of the United States Government for citizens to work in nations requesting our help is most heartening.
Your application has been brought to the attention of our Medical Consultants because of the statements you made regarding your health. On the basis of these statements, they feel that you cannot be medically qualified for overseas service. We realize that this condition may offer no real problem to you here at home. However, on the basis of our experience with Peace Corps Volunteers overseas, we feel it unwise to encourage your application. We suggest that you discuss this matter with your personal physician. If you still wish to pursue your application, please have him submit a complete summary of your health history to the Director of our Medical Program Division, attention Medical Liaison.

PETER M. BOURRET

We do thank you for your interest in Peace Corps and look forward to your continued support.

Sincerely yours,
A. Carp
Director
Division of Selection
Questionnaire No. 165862

Chapter 7
Autumn 1966

Sir, The Private's Name Is Pronounced Boo-ray

I was a maggot one minute and a slimy scumbag the next. It would be a two-month odyssey through madness in search of manhood. Our three guides on this journey were called DIs. Staff Sergeant Jones, our senior drill instructor, was a no-nonsense, nails-for-lunch Marine, who was everything that John Wayne wanted to be. The Korean War veteran was a strict but fair papa bear to his eighty-four recruits. Our two junior drill instructors were both in their early twenties. An expert in the art of glaring, Staff Sergeant Bengen looked like he wanted to drink when he got off duty. Unlike Bengen, Sergeant Smith did not call cadence; he sang it, making words into music. He was the perfect DI, strutting with an air of confidence yet never needing to prove his toughness. Intelligent people never called him *'nigger'*

I was in the hero factory, and I loved it.

My twelve years in Catholic school had made me a salty veteran of discipline. Father Neal, my freshman Latin and religion teacher and Sister Luella, my second grade teacher who was really the Wicked Witch of the West, most certainly had taught the Marine Corps every trick they knew. They had been Marine drill instructors in disguised as a Carmelite priest and a Holy Cross nun.

With this kind of background, I knew that I would survive the rigors of Marine boot camp. I was also the beneficiary of an extensive briefing on the bizarre activities of recruit training by a friend from my days at Salpointe High School. I tested the water at the University of Arizona whereas my friend Richard dove headlong into being a Marine right after graduation from high school and ended up with the 9th Marine Regiment in Vietnam. He had advised me to memorize the Marine Corps eleven General Orders; this advice proved to be most beneficial.

Richard, who at the age of seventeen, had perfected the art of blowing people's minds. If an after-the-game dance were boring, and they usually were, he livened things up with a bellowing Tarzan call. With his calling card out of the way, he would sprint across the dance floor, throw a hook slide, and finally crash into a chair that was usually occupied by a flat-chested, fourteen-year-old girl. Always with a strawberry face and a gaping mouth, his prey would remain frozen in her metal, folding chair. Grinning up at her victoriously, he would ask, "Want a dance, sweetie?" The smart victims ran away.

He had also gained a reputation for shaving in restaurants. Even stranger was his choice of shaving cream. He usually ordered a banana split, requested a knife, and proceeded to lather up his face with the whipped cream. Having completed the first part of this ritual, he would karate chop the banana, which sometimes would end up landing on the floor. Strangely enough, we were never thrown out or arrested. It was much easier to not hassle their eccentric customer. A year later he gave up his civilian antics for a life with the 9th Marine Regiment in Vietnam.

It had been almost a week since the recruit in front of me had puked up his civilian guts. Our senior drill instructor was not happy, and he remembered the boy's face. It was our first Sunday in boot camp, and I would ask God to use His influence with my mom. I was certain she was still breathing fire and had remained furious with me for joining the Marines.

Having asthma, hay fever and high blood pressure were excellent reasons for remaining a civilian; however, in my gung ho, nineteen-year-old eyes, these were but mere obstacles that would not prevent me from achieving my goal of being a United States Marine, so I neglected to inform the Marine Corps about them. It was a fraudulent enlistment with a twist: I had lied to join so I could go to Vietnam. Having been rejected by the Marine reserves, I left honesty back at my house and decided not to provide the Marine recruiter at the downtown office with the note from my doctor about my asthma.

My tenacity was rewarded because I fearlessly lied about my previous attempt at enlisting, and of course, I knew that the lying had to continue so as not to reveal the truth concerning my health issues. The posters on the walls at the recruiter's office detailed the penalties for a fraudulent enlistment; however, the threat of a fine and several years in prison failed to deter me. On the religious side of things, a few lies to achieve my goal would be quickly washed away, forgiven by a priest for the price of a few *Hail Marys* for my penance. I had learned how to play the Catholic confession game quite well.

My mother's anger, seething and silent, was understandable but less than enjoyable to be around. I was joining the Marines at a time when the Vietnam War was acting more like a war and less like a police action. Telling her that I had signed up for only two years offered her some consolation. Because the Marine Corps had not yet had a chance to train me in the art of being brave, I wisely neglected to inform her that a two-year enlistment would guarantee me a tour of duty in Vietnam as a grunt, an infantry rifleman. Of course, I also neglected to tell her that I intended be a Recon Marine so I could experience the adventure of sneaking around behind enemy lines. My mom had not raised her number-two son to be cannon fodder in a war that she did not support.

As I finished my Sunday morning coffee, I told my mom what she did not want to hear. She assumed that I would be going off to boot camp in a few months. I mustered all my courage, attempting to be casual when I told her that I was leaving for the Marines the next day. My mom was not smiling. I could not wait to leave for boot camp. The glare from a DI would pale in comparison to the look that shot out of my mother's angry Irish eyes.

Staff Sergeant Jones called the platoon to attention. With only six days of the Marine Corps under our web belts, we resembled Snow White's Dwarfs. Our white tennis shoes, baggy green utility trousers, yellow sweatshirts, and unstarched utility caps made us look ridiculous, but since everyone looked alike, our uncool appearance did not bother us.

"You maggots know it's Sunday, and it is time for church services."

"SIR, YES, SIR!," roared forth.

"Is there anyone here who would like to remain here and not go to church services?"

Unaware that the correct answer to Staff Sergeant Jones' question was an unequivocal NO, a dozen naive hands rose up into the San Diego sky. The DI stood there, grinning in amazement at the gullibility of these recruits; they failed to realize that Marine boot camp was not a democracy. As he shook his head back and forth, his Smokey-the-Bear hat sliced through the cool September air. The owners of the dozen hands were becoming apprehensive, realizing that they had made an unwise decision. The DI continued shaking his head as most of the raised hands evaporated; then, only two or three hands still remained conspicuously raised.

"Well, for you scum bags who intend on being atheists, I want you slimy pukes to remain here with your goddamn civilian-type heads in a bucket of water. That's a two-count exercise, maggots. When the rest of us God-fearing Christians return from church services in about an hour, all you atheists can take your goddamned heathen heads out of the buckets of water."

Inspired by his unorthodox, evangelical message, the entire platoon saw the light. This religious experience was democratic Christianity at its best. He asked his question one final time, "Do I have any volunteers? Any atheistic fucking Marines?" His steely eyes scanned the platoon, and then he bellowed, "No. I didn't think so. Outfuckingstanding!"

After our third week of boot camp, I was very proud of myself. I had only messed up once, which in combat is one time too many, but fortunately, this was not combat. We had been marching on the grinder, which resembled a giant asphalt parking lot. The platoon had come to a halt so that the DIs could explain why we were slimy maggots. We stood there at rigid attention, staring straight ahead at the 707s on the runway of the San Diego Airport.

"See that fence over there? Any of you pukes who can't goddamn hack it here, why don't you try to leave. All you got to do is hop over that ten-fucking-foot-high fence and run like hell across that runway. If you slimy maggots don't get your asses run over by one of those goddamn jets, you might be able to run home to mommy and your little girlfriend, who's getting fucked by

Jodie. But the MPs'll get your sorry ass, and if they don't, ladies, the FBI will for sure. And they'll drag your slimy civilian ass back to us. And after some goddamn time in the brig, they'll put your slimy civilian ass in Motivation Platoon. And let me tell you, that is one place you pukes do not want to fucking be. We treat you assholes nice compared to what they'll do to you there...so, if any of you ladies can't hack it, you know what to do. We'll take good fucking care of you because you belong to me."

The DI continued with his speech, but I unwisely decided to daydream.

four years ago...the last time at this airport...flying here compliments of the Navy for winning first place at the University of Arizona Science Fair...a week's stay with the Navy...what a joke it was...and they were hoping I'd join the Navy...if they could only see me now...just a dumb little sophomore...jive biology teacher only moving my grade up from a 'C' to a 'B' for winning First Place plus Best Boys' Project for all of southern Arizona...what the hell did that nun want...probably wouldn't have been much impressed if she had Isaac Newton in her class...would have given him a 'B'...what a bummer...same damn nun who got me thrown out of school just before graduation...Anderson, Murray and me out...what a hard ass...expelled for being real criminals...accused of leaving campus at lunchtime...having the intention of leaving...goddamn school never heard of the constitution...trying to get us to admit that we were in the process of leaving... amazing...too stubborn for them so out we went...what a bunch of shit...funnier than shit when their star witness fell through...and that damn dean of men wouldn't even apologize for expelling us...should have sued his holy Carmelite ass.

"Private!"

oh shit.

"Yes, sir." My face turned red, and I gulped my guilt. Staff Sergeant Bengen was staring at me with eyes exploding out of his head as he bellowed. Because he was only about a foot away from my face, I knew he wasn't screaming so I could hear him better. My mistake had provided him with an opportunity to make an example of me, something DIs relished. I would be the sacrificial lamb at the altar of Marine Corps discipline. This would be a bonus exercise; not only would I learn to daydream on my own time, of which there was none, but the rest of the platoon would learn that tomorrow any of them could be me. In the World of Marine Corps grammar, question marks really didn't exist. Our opinion was not something that a DI was ever interested in. If the Marine Corps wanted us to have an opinion, the Marine Corps would have issued us one; they hadn't, so I knew the importance of telling the DI what he wanted to hear.

"Do you want to be part of this platoon or do you want to form up your own platoon, maggot?!"

I had sinned against the Corps by standing at attention and continuing to face the west while the rest of the platoon had made a right-face movement and was pointed to the north. I thought I knew the correct answer to his question, so I bellowed, "No!"

"No! What the fuck did you say, maggot?" The DI continued his tirade, snarling angrily, "Did I hear you say, no?"

I was speechless, wondering what I should say. Silence seemed the best route to take at that moment. The DI's face was racing through all the shades of red until it settled on bright red, and it was not from embarrassment. His angry eyes bulged like a bullfrog as his screaming rant continued. Fortunately for me, I maintained my regulation-straight-ahead stare.

"Private, the first and last fucking word out of your slimy civilian mouth is sir. Boy, do you understand?!"

"Sir, yes, sir."

"I didn't hear you!"

"Sir, yes, sir!"

"Now that's more like it, puke."

Just as I had begun to relax, the DI rested his left forearm on my right shoulder. He looked cautiously from left to right, scanning the area. It was safe for him. There were no officers within sight. When he hit me, I had instinctively tightened my abdominal muscles. The thousands of sit-ups from my high school years finally paid their dividend. Although the blow to my midsection forced my rigid body to bend briefly, I sprang immediately back to attention. I wanted to grab my stomach, but I wisely chose to ignore that instinct. The DI smiled at the strain on my face.

"Think you can stay with the program, private?"

"Sir, yes, sir!"

I was proud. I was gung ho. I was a Marine.

A few days later, I found a way to anger my other junior drill instructor. Two DIs down and one to go.

It was that time in our boot camp career for us to take the X-1 Test, which was the type of exam that a person with an IQ a bit higher than a hand grenade should be able to pass. Sixty percent of our eighty-man platoon was from Texas. If some of our Lone Star Marines had been given a few bonus points for sheer patriotism, our platoon would have had a chance. This, however, was not the case on that fateful September morning in 1966.

Luckily for our DIs, there were a few college people in the platoon. We had one recruit who had a Master of Science in Biology. What he was doing in the Marine Corps was any one's guess. My guess was that he had to have been jilted by his sorority sweetie. A Marine private with a master's degree just did not make much sense.

Having spent less than a year in college, my being a Marine made a little more sense. I had good reasons, or at least good rationalizations, for joining the Marine Corps. First, I was nineteen, and nineteen-year-olds have the right to enter into irrational and hazardous enterprises. Second, I wanted to go to Vietnam so I could find out what was really going on over there. Third, I was tired of the games my girlfriend continued to play on my defenseless and naive mind. I let her walk all over my personal integrity and hated that I had allowed this to happen. I had not been courageous enough to tell her where she could stick it, so I took the coward's way out. Facing the North Vietnamese seemed like an easier alternative. Fourth, by joining the Marines, I could not only escape the clutches of my siren, but I would also be able to learn how to be assertive and be a leader. If I were killed in the process, that would not bother me since I was not exactly in love with myself. Life for me at this time could be described in one succinct word: shit. Fifth, I was running away from home, and by doing so, I was telling my controlling and emotionally absent mother to go to hell. My final reason for being a hero was that I was completely broke, and my parents, far from being Rockefellers, could not help finance my college education.

So, with my bank account and my personal life in a state of

bankruptcy, I decided to follow the patriotic example of my Uncle Kirk, who had been a lieutenant colonel in the Marines for over twenty years. The Marines were Number One in my nineteen-year-old eyes. I knew that a two-year enlistment would not be long enough for me to be as good as my uncle, but I still could attempt to be a hero with a small *h*. I might not ever be on the first string, but at least I was on the team.

The X-1 Test was over, and I was certain that I had done well.

cyclic rate of fire for the M14 rifle is 700-750 rounds per minute...first ten amendments are called the Bill of Rights...Chesty Puller was the winner of five Navy Crosses...Article 15 of the UCMJ deals with non-judicial punishment...for belly wounds don't touch intestines but use dry sterile dressing and must not have food or water...I think I got them all right...hope so...sure a lot easier than good old Geology 1a at the U of A.

Sergeant Smith interrupted my brief moment of daydreaming happiness. He motioned for me to leave the formation. I hoped he only wanted to talk, but if he felt like having me do fifty push-ups just because, I'd be fine with that; push-ups were like breathing for me. He was a demanding DI, but a reasonable human being, at least, so far.

"Yes, sir."

"Does the private realize that he got a score of one hundred percent on the X-1 Test? In fact, the private was the only one in this goddamn platoon who had enough G-2 [intelligence] to get a perfect score. Congratulations, Private Bourret."

Although I was shocked that I was the only boot to receive a perfect score, I was more amazed that a drill instructor had not only complimented me but had also not addressed me as *maggot, scum bag,* or *puke.* Although, as was typical, he had mispronounced my French last name, but for one moment, I was Private Bourret, a recruit without a pejorative but an actual civilian, family name.

"Sir, the private thanks the drill instructor, sir." I paused long enough to forget that Sergeant Smith was my drill instructor and not some civilian I was chatting with. Then, without being asked a question, I violated a cardinal rule of boot camp communication: never initiate the dialog. Foolishly deluding myself that I was being tactful, I said, "Sir, the private's last name is pronounced

Boo-ray. It's French, sir."

Although he was not impressed by my need to give him a French lesson, he resisted screaming obscenities at his singular academic star. Showing great patience, he calmly explained, as only a DI could, that my name was not pronounced *Boo-ray*. It would be pronounced the Anglicized way he had pronounced it, and if I had a problem with that, he thought that I could join the French Foreign Legion.

"Sir, yes, sir."

The DI had forgiven me for my French lesson. Now it was time to reward me for my success on the X-1 Test. "Private, the smoking lamp is lit for you and only you."

"Sir, the private thanks the drill instructor, but the private doesn't smoke."

Less than pleased by my response, Sergeant Smith sarcastically blurted out one of his favorite phases, "Now that's outfuckingstanding!" He continued yelling, "I give you a break and what the hell do you do? Turn my goddamn offer down. Get the hell out of here, maggot!"

I did an about face movement and began walking back toward the platoon. He bellowed, "Goddamn it, private...move, move, move!" My walk quickly became a sprint. Shaking his head, Sergeant Smith turned and walked away.

In Marine boot camp everything was done in the fast gear. *Putt-putt*, *meander*, *stroll* and *leisurely* were words absent from the lexicon of Marine Corps life. If the Army could do an activity quickly, we were expected to do it one step faster and better. We were United States Marines, or at least we wanted to be, and the Marines were the best.

Several days after I wished I had been the Marlboro Man, I injured my right knee. After morning formation, we were given five minutes to shit, shower, and shave. It was a formidable task, but amazingly, the eighty-four Marines in our platoon always accomplished it. Masters at the art of dancing on eggshells, we liked keeping our DIs content. It was safer that way.

As we were running to the showers, I tripped and banged my knee on the asphalt pavement. Washing the blood away in the shower did not make the intense pain disappear. I had re-injured the same knee, which I had hurt in a car accident the previous year. Informing my drill instructors that my knee hurt was the last thing on my mind. I would receive an Oscar for my performance at appearing normal; at least that was my intention.

Had I informed them, they would have screamed and yelled, of course, and accused me of being a malingerer, or even worse, they would have sent me to the base sickbay. This would have meant that I would have been dropped from the platoon. Upon recuperating from my injury, I would have been placed in a new platoon. My status as a second-class human being in my current platoon would have felt good compared to the treatment that I would have received as a member of a new platoon.

A truly wise Marine boot would always remain inconspicuous. Being a pimple on the face of the platoon would only bring suffering and humiliation; blending in to the unit meant success. The classic example of why blending was critical occurred when I was on mess duty for several days. My job as a smedley, the Marine Corps' version of a waiter for the drill instructors, provided me with the opportunity to observe the DIs as they harassed their recruits during chow time. Under normal circumstance a boot only stares straight ahead, regardless of the events that might surround him. If Christ's Second Coming had occurred in the mess hall, none of the boots would have noticed.

Having secured a tray full of the Marine Corps best epicurean delights, the recruits left-right-left their way to their designated table, which was typically long enough to seat about fifteen people on each side. Once all the recruits, holding their food trays at chest-level, had shuffled sideways to their places at the table, the DI would yell, "Ready, seats!" In unison, every tray would slam into the table. Obeying the laws of physics, green beans, corned beef hash or whatever was on the day's menu would bounce up and usually land on the table. If all trays met the table simultaneously, the drill instructor would command the recruits, aka boots, to eat: *a three-count exercise* he would call it.

Unfortunately, not all trays always landed on the table simultaneously; for the uncoordinated, the DI would have them repeat the exercise until they perfected it. A table of slow learners would spring up and slam themselves down until they got it right or until chow time was over. Appearing like a food-fight war zone during their learning process, their tabletop would eventually be clean before they finished chow.

The drill instructors' job was to teach the recruits to work as a cohesive unit and to do everything the Marine way: perfectly and quickly, anything else would get people killed in combat. During noon chow I noticed one Marine boot who seemed to be moping, which has never been authorized by the Marine Corps, and was not shoveling his food into his mouth very quickly.

Such behavior had probably been tolerated at home, but this was a Marine Corps mess hall and not home. Unfortunately for this recruit, his drill instructor had no desire to play the role of his mommy and baby him. Without warning, the DI sprang to the top of the table and began walking towards his unsuspecting target. Because his victim was more than halfway down the table, the DI needed to step between and over at least a dozen, half-finished food trays to arrive at his objective. None of the hungry recruits looked up. The DI owned them and the table; he could stroll wherever he wanted.

When he reached the unmotivated boot, the drill instructor turned and squatted, offering the recruit a free motivational course, as only a DI could. As he began yelling, he reached down and grabbed a handful of unwanted lunch and began shoving the mashed potatoes into the recruit's face. He continued helping him finish lunch, and then the DI nonchalantly stood up, made a left-face movement, and gingerly stepped through the maze of now empty trays until he reached the end of the table. Jumping off, he landed with the grace of a gymnast on the deck and strutted off. It was time for this DI to eat, and I would be his waiter.

On the way to morning chow, the DIs decided that we were maggots, one of their favorite terms of endearment. They called the platoon to a halt. After shouting the usual insults and obscenities at us, they decided that we needed some calisthenics before breakfast. They wanted exhausted, sweaty bodies to walk into the mess hall for morning chow.

The yelling began. "On your faces, pukes. You wanna fuck up, do ya? You're gonna smell like shit when you march into that mess hall. Goddamn it, you slimy scum bag pukes will learn to do things right...the Marine Corps way...not the fuckin' civilian way.

Understand, ladies? Goddamn it, on your backs. On your faces. On your backs. Get up. Too fucking slow, ladies. On your faces!"

Our chests were heaving and our faces were becoming caked with dust and sweat. Finally, after five minutes of rolling around in the sand, they ordered the platoon to stand at attention. Silent relief roamed the platoon. Before we could dust ourselves off, one of the drill instructors yelled that he wanted us to begin doing side-straddle-hop exercises.

As we did the exercise, the pain in my knee shot through me like a knife. After more than a dozen side-straddle-hops, I was struggling at even standing much less jumping. The pain was so intense that I could only grit my teeth and let the tears stream down my tanned face. I borrowed some stubbornness from an untapped reserve inside me. I would never stop. My name would be Tenacity. I was a Marine.

Sergeant Smith was zeroing in on me. His eyes knew. I was being noticed, and that was the one thing a Marine in boot camp did not need or want. Blending-in was the secret of success, and I wanted to succeed. His eyes kept honing in on me. I was doomed. Then my fears became reality; the sergeant motioned for me to come to him.

oh shit...I'm dead...don't let him know...fake it...I can do it...hang in there...my knee really doesn't hurt that much...I'm okay...get rid of those chicken shit tears...they'll give me away...I'm not hurt...I'm okay.

"Sir, yes, sir. The drill instructor wants to see the private?"

"No shit, private! Something wrong? The private looks like he isn't up for calisthenics today."

Breathing hard, but pretending to be relaxed, I offered a labored reply, "Sir, the private is fine, sir."

"Maggot, tryin' to skate out of a little work today? Does the private wanna be a malingerer or a Marine? Well, boy?"

Carefully avoiding eye contact with the DI, not wanting to anger him, I said, "Sir, the private wants to be a Marine. The private wants to do calisthenics, sir."

"So what's wrong with that knee, private? Looks like it's causing some problems."

Lying to a drill instructor was like trying to lie to my mother; it didn't work.

"Sir, the private is fine, sir."

"Bullshit, private. I want the private to escort himself back to my Quonset hut. Understand?"

"Sir, yes, sir!"

I walked away limping, hoping I could find my way back to his quarters. I felt like a lost four-year-old boy wandering aimlessly in a big city; I would be fair game for any Marine that was not a boot. I was a mouse in a maze of Quonset huts. My previous weeks in boot camp had been follow-the-leader times. The Marine who was marching three feet in front of me was the only thing that mattered. Now I was on my own.

After ten minutes of wandering and being lucky, I finally arrived at the Quonset hut, which housed our DIs as well as those of several other platoons. I wanted to sit down and rest my knee, but Marines in boot camp only stood at attention when in doubt.

After ten minutes a drill instructor, the wrong one, walked up to me. He was lean, red-haired, and hate held a permanent mortgage on his eyes. His demeanor made me long for my DIs, even my angry mother. He was a hungry alley cat, and I was the mouse.

"What the fuck you standin' around for, puke?"

"Sir, the private is waiting for his drill instructor, sir."

A sadistic grin slid across his face. "Goddamn it, maggot, don't just fucking stand there. Get on your goddamn face and give me some fucking push-ups...Marine Corps push-ups. Understand, boy?"

With a 'Sir, yes, sir,' I was in the push-up position. "Sir, the private would like to know how many push-ups the drill instructor would like the private to do."

He snarled, "When I tell the maggot that he's finished...that's when the private is done. Got that?"

"Sir, yes, sir."

Once I had begun doing my push-ups, the DI turned away and walked inside the Quonset hut.

seven...eight...nine...ten...what an asshole...at least my DI realized I was hurting...who the hell does this dude think he is...he's not even my drill instructor...damn jerk...he'll get his push-ups... twenty-one...twenty-two.

A few moments later the DI reappeared and sneered, "Well, I

see you're still doing push-ups. Fun, isn't it?"

"Sir, yes, sir"

"In that case, keep doing them, scum bag. I'll be back, so don't try to skate out on me."

I was doing my sixty-third push-up when Sergeant Smith walked up; his spit-shined, black shoes staring up at me. Remaining in the push-up position, I looked up at him when he asked, "What the hell does the private think he's doing?"

"Sir, the private is doing push-ups, sir."

"No shit, private! My mother didn't raise no fool."

"Sir, the private was told to do push-ups by another drill instructor. He..."

"Goddamn it, maggot, get your ass up. Do push-ups for your drill instructors and for no one else. Understand!"

Even with a sore knee, standing at attention felt good. My DI turned away from me and briskly walked inside the Quonset hut.

that other DI is in for a ration of shit from Smith...that dude should have known better than to mess with another DI's troopies.

Sergeant Smith spent about a minute squaring away the situation with the other DI.

"Private, come in here."

A few seconds later, I was standing in front of the DI's desk. He was thumbing through a stack of papers. Upon finding the right one, he pulled it out. He spent a few moments scanning the contents. "According to your records, you spent a year in college. You were the only one in the platoon to get a hundred percent on the X-1 Test. The private was in the top ten percent in the Physical Fitness Test, and he seems to be highly motivated."

"Sir, the private wants to be the best Marine possible, sir."

Wearing a skeptical face, he was unimpressed by my gung-ho attitude; he replied, "That's nice...but what's the third General Order?"

Sergeant Smith was positive he had ambushed me. Only two hours earlier the platoon had been told to memorize the eleven General Orders, which anyone on guard duty must know.

"To report all violations of orders I am instructed to enforce."

Beaming a smile was not an option, so I let the I'm-feeling-proud movie play in the theater of my mind. I was proud, and Sergeant Smith was baffled, but DIs don't hand out gold stars.

Fortunately, my friend Richard had informed me that it would be advantageous for me know my General Orders before arriving in boot camp. It had been a million-dollar tip.

"Very good, private, but what's the seventh General Order?"

"To talk to no one except in the line of duty."

The DI's forehead was overrun with wrinkles, like so many black furrows etched with his bewilderment. No one could learn all the General Orders in less than two hours, especially since the platoon had not been allotted any time for studying.

Sergeant Smith probably assumed that the Marine standing in front of him had just been lucky and had learned only the General Orders that he had been asked. The recruit was acting squared away. Maybe in another month, but squared away now, no way could that be possible. The DI fired another question. The eleventh General Order was the last and the longest one. He was positive that the boot Marine [Marine recruit in boot camp] could not possibly know this one.

"To be especially watchful at night and during the time for challenging, to challenge all persons on or near my post, and to allow no one to pass without proper authority."

If I had been stupid, I would have smiled. Most certainly, Sergeant Smith was stunned, but he wore his stoic mask, pretending to be unimpressed.

"Does the private realize that he said all of his General Orders wrong?"

"Sir, yes, sir. The private forgot to say, *Sir, the private's eleventh General Order is.*"

His ambush was a total failure.

He then asked a completely unexpected question, and of course, I knew the right answer. "Would the private like to be the platoon secretary?"

His question was really an order, so decided I wanted the new position. He offered me a seat in his chair. "Why don't you rest your knee for a while?"

Although stunned, I sat. A moment later he began to move toward the door, so I started to get up to say, "Sir, yes, sir," but he motioned for me to remain seated. In an instant I was a human being and not a maggot. He turned and left the hut. During the next half-hour I browsed through a binder, which contained the daily lesson plans for our platoon. I was interested to know what we would be doing in the future, so I turned to the page that contained the next day's agenda.

interesting...feels like I'm in the CIA or something...sure hope they don't catch me...let's see...wow...what a hard ass...0900 hours...harass the recruits...damn...it's all planned out...even the bullshit...it doesn't matter if we're doing things right...they're still going to yell at us...they just want to mess with our minds...what a hard ass.

The next day at 0900 hours, we were marching the Marine way, the right way. A few seconds later, the platoon was on the deck, doing push-ups because we were slimy maggots. Undetected, I smiled at the ground, aka the deck.

Chapter 8
August 1968

The Problem Of Going From Level Four To Level One

The Draft Classification Game, where you can win an all-expenses-paid trip to the Orient. You'll stay in the luxurious Khe Sanh Hilton, which over looks the scenic DMZ. You'll enjoy the colorful nightlife. During the day you'll have a chance to make contact with the local people. Yes, everyday you'll dine out on imported delicacies. For the connoisseur of fine mineral water, there is rice paddy water a la heliozoan purification tablets. Truly an epicurean delight, and that's not all. All tourists will receive a generous spending allowance of six dollars a day. Yes, you can have all this and much more if we pick your lucky number! And for those of you who do not choose this fantastic Patriots' Package, you can go to jail or run off to Canada, but you may not pass go or collect two hundred dollars. Yes, folks, we are an equal-opportunity employer. And to show you that we are not prejudiced, we'll guarantee that if you're Black, Chicano, or poor White, your chances of winning this vacation of a lifetime will be excellent. Sorry, ladies and gentlemen, but we've run out of time for today. The prizes on the Draft Classification Game have been donated by the Pentagon and Hawk Industries. The Executive Producers: Presidents Kennedy, Johnson, Nixon, Diem, Thieu, and Ho Chi Minh. The Directors: Generals Westmoreland and Giap; Secretaries of State Rusk and Kissinger; and Secretary of the Defense McNamara. Starring: a cast of millions. Shot on location. And a special thanks to Dow Chemicals for special effects.

As the door to the Tucson branch of the Selective Service closes behind him, his month of pondering about requesting a change in his draft classification to conscientious objector, is over;

he is certain that Henry David Thoreau and Albert Camus would applaud him. Opposite the door, a white-haired woman sits quietly behind a dark, oak desk. She is old enough to have kissed Buckey O'Neill, an Arizona hero who had charged up San Juan Hill in the Spanish-American War.

Smiling at him like a perfect grandmother, she looks up from her desk and politely asks, "May I help you?"

He nods. As she slowly stands up, she puts a file folder in its appointed pile at the rear of her desk. His Marine drill instructors would have been proud of her orderly desk.

"Ma'am, I am interested in having my draft classification changed." She interrupts him before he can explain that he has already served in combat in Vietnam, so he knows the horrors of war all too well. "Are you a college student, son?"

"Not at the moment, but I would like to have my current status changed to that of a conscientious objector."

"Well, if you are classified 1-A, I will see what I can do for you." She turns and shuffles slowly towards the file cabinet. She is searching for the forms he will need to fill out.

"But, Ma'am, I'm not 1-A. I've served with the Marines in Vietnam and..."

She interrupts his explanation with a classic burst of bureaucratic logic. He listens and his eyebrows are crumpled with confusion as she clarifies his particular situation. "Do you realize that your classification is on Level Four, and Conscientious Objector status is on Level One? It appears that we have a problem. If you would like to change your status from Level One, you are allowed to move to Level Two or to any of the higher levels." She sighs, and he wants to laugh.

"But, Ma'am, I've been in a war, and I know from personal experience that I want to be classified as a conscientious objector because killing in war is wrong." He remembers his high school Latin class: *Experientia docet*, experience is the best teacher. Ironically, his Latin teacher had been right; Latin would come in handy someday. He stands there like a statue, stunned, not believing what she has said.

Sensing a need for a more comprehensive explanation of the geography of the draft classification game, she continues, "If you would like to, you can take these forms with you, but I'm sure it would be fruitless. I'm sure the Draft Board would turn your request down to be reclassified as a conscientious objector. Remember that you are at Level Four because you have served as a Marine, and you are not allowed to move to Level Three or Level Two, much less be reclassified at Level One. We have our rules."

She smiles, and he grabs the forms from her. Turning abruptly, he strides quickly toward the door and yells, "Granny, you're a real trip. AMAZING! You must have overdosed on Geritol."

He is shaking his head in disbelief; the door slamming behind him as he shouts, "INSANE!" The people on the bus bench stare at him and are wondering, but he does not care. Crumpling up the forms, he tosses them into a trashcan next to the bus bench.

Chapter 9
June 1967

Cruising Sunset Strip In A Shopping Cart

We had just successfully finished our training in Staging Battalion, and we were ready to be sent to the War. Bring on Victor Charlie! [the Viet Cong]. Two hundred Marines stood in formation, awaiting our company commander. I was certain that he was going to do a Dale Carnegie number on us and immerse us in a pep talk, a go-get-'em speech about us being the best-trained fighting men in the world. He would remind us that we were Leathernecks, and we were responsible for maintaining our proud heritage. Instead, a staff sergeant with a potbelly and a clipboard tucked under his arm began bellowing six names.

"Any of you Marines whose names have been called out, step forward. It seems there ain't enough room on the plane to send all you men over to Vietnam right now. The Marine Corps is doing you a favor. One week's worth. Remember this when it's reenlistment time."

sarge, you can stick it...a three count exercise...rotate it sideways...first I got to make it through Vietnam...and if I do...don't hold your breath about me reenlisting...I'll be headed back to college.

My name had been called and, of course, mispronounced as usual, so I stood there with five other Marines. They were smiling, yet I was not. It was early June of 1967, and I had waited impatiently for almost ten months. The Marine Corps had already disappointed me by excluding me from being in Recon [Reconnaissance] because they had given me, a two-year enlistee, orders to North Carolina and 81mm mortar school rather than orders for WesPac, which was synonymous with a tour of duty in

Vietnam.

My incurable desire to volunteer was being thwarted at every turn. I was about seventeen million miles away from enthusiastic with the 0341 numbers they added to my MOS [military occupational specialty]. The only numbers that mattered were 0311: rifleman, ground-pounder, grunt. Once in Vietnam, I was certain that the Marine Corps would finally step out of my way and acquiesce, allowing me to indulge in my fantasy of being a grunt in the thick of combat.

damn...what do I have to do to get my ass over to Vietnam...a two-year enlistment should be a guaranteed ticket to the war zone...but not for me...wouldn't even allow me to volunteer for Recon so I could roam around deep in enemy territory keeping track of NVA movement...five months in this Green Machine and they send everyone else to Vietnam...but not me...giving me orders to Camp Lejeune...opposite direction of the war...three months of going crazy in North Carolina...didn't join the Crotch to be an 0341 and learn how to fire a mortar...just what I don't need...if I can't be in Recon then this kid wants to be a grunt...but no way...we just played war games...bang bang you're dead...best of all...cold weather training in Virginia...that's when I knew they'd send us to Vietnam...typical Marine Corps logic...train us to fight in the snow and then send us to the jungles of Vietnam...amazing...so here I wait one more damn week...what the hell do I have to do to get my ass into the war.

While I languished in the barracks as I waited for our eventual plane trip to the war zone, I occupied myself by reading while those who were more interested in gambling played cards. I read plays by George Bernard Shaw, Arthur Miller and Edward Albee. These books were short, and I liked that. I enjoyed acquiring a few ounces of culture before venturing into the world of war.

It was Friday night, and our plane was supposed to finally leave on Monday morning. The Marine Corps, feeling atypically generous, issued each of us a weekend liberty pass. They reminded us that Los Angeles was off limits. The Marine in the bunk above me asked me where I was going on liberty. "LA, of course."

"Great! Just where I'm goin'. I have relatives up there."

We decided to become traveling buddies. When he told me he was from Spain, I asked in amazement, "Why the hell did you join the Marines?"

He shrugged his shoulders, "Don't know...just thought it would be a good idea. Someone told me I could become a citizen faster that way."

Laughing, I raised my eyebrows. "Don't you realize...if you go to Vietnam, there's a real good chance you could get killed? Being dead won't help much with becoming a citizen. And I thought I was crazy."

We changed from our green utilities [work clothes] into our civilian clothes. We were going to the big city, and we did not want anyone to know that we were Marines. Unfortunately, our short hair made us stand out like nuns in a whorehouse.

We spent the next half-hour cursing the hundreds of cars that passed us by on the freeway entrance ramp. "Don't these assholes understand why we have our thumbs out? Maybe they'd understand the middle finger better."

Chico's temper was beginning to boil.

"Sure thing, Spaniard. We'd get all kinds of cars to stop. They'd all want to kick our asses."

"I am not afraid to fight," he said brashly, wearing a youthful smirk.

I started laughing. "You're smaller than me, and I'm no giant. You can't be anymore 5'6". I know we've had eight hours of hand-to-hand combat, but..."

"You're not too brave, are you?"

"If I'm going to get killed, the VC'll do it...not some slimy civilian."

Having decided that we had not been creative enough in our attempt to catch a ride, I shimmied up a yield-right-of-way sign. Once on top I stuck out my thumb. From bellow, Chico shouted the obvious, "You're crazy."

The third car, which passed us, slowed down and pulled over. "I'm crazy, but it worked." I slid down the sign, and we ran for our free transportation: the jackpot, a Lincoln Continental. Going off-limits in style.

An hour later, we were pulling into LA. "What'll you boys be doing in LA...partying?" The driver smiled in a way that we did not like. We knew he had something on his mind.

"How 'bout Sunset Strip?"

Pretending as though he had not heard me, he asked, "You boys need a place to stay?"

boys...what's the story with this dude...we're bad ass Marines...jarheads...leathernecks and we're on the way to Vietnam...boys...he's probably a faggot...just what we don't need...yuck...get hustled by a fag...bummer.

He insisted that we come over to his apartment, but I shook my head. As I slid closer to the door, I impatiently blurted out, "Right here's just fine!"

"Are you sure, boys?"

Chico had stopped relaxing in the back seat. He wanted out. "My friend said, "OUT", and now, motherfucker!"

As the car was rolling to a stop, we jumped out. As the Lincoln Continental drove off, Chico fired a volley of Spanish obscenities at the driver.

Wearing a triumphant grin, I blurted, "Goddamn, we made it!"

Chico, shifting from Spanish to English, muttered, "Damn faggot."

It took us another half-hour to reach our destination, Sunset Strip. It was eight o'clock on a summer Friday night, and LA was getting ready to party. We were in paradise.

The Strip was clogged with cars going somewhere, going nowhere. Friday night fantasies: getting drunk, getting stoned, getting laid. The Strip was a caravan of people experiencing the hazards of going from point A to point B. A '57 Chevy revving its engine, the light turning green, the squeal of tires, the high school girls behind the monster car were impressed, but the old lady with the shopping bag and the prune face did not care. She was looking for the southbound bus, squinting at a sunset, which was not there. Smiling at the bus bench, she talked to the warm June wind. She wondered why no one looked when the wind blew her dress up. It was Friday, but she was waiting for the Sunday express.

As we were passing the bus bench, a hippie—probably in his early twenties—shoved a newspaper in my face. From his sandals to his shoulder-length hair, he played the part well. He asked us to buy a copy of an underground newspaper. Although I had a rebellious gene, I told him that I was not interested. Chico, in his typical fashion, told him where he could stick it.

"At least read it. Find out what's really goin' on in Vietnam."

Chico walked away, but I was in the mood to argue. "In a couple of days, we'll know...first hand."

"Chico joined the conversation. "Listen, hippie...me and my friend are Marines, and we're gonna to kill us some Cong."

He shook his head back and forth in disdain as a response to Chico's statement of bravado. Then, he looked away from us and peered up into the LA night. Pausing, he sighed, and then spoke in a tone of voice that parents use to let their child know they aren't fooling around. "You're just a couple of dumb ass kids who don't know what the fuck you're getting into. My head was in the same damn place almost two years ago. I was in the Nam...the Airborne...thought I was a bad ass motherfucker also."

wow...a doggy...a kick ass doggy at that...almost as tough as a Marine...not quite...so why do you give a shit if I go and get myself killed...I sure don't care...it's up to fate.

"How do we know you were really over there?"

Chico, not wanting to be left out, added, "Yeah, hippie."

"You don't...but I know what the fuck I'm talkin' about. That war in the Nam is a motherfucker, and you guys are too fuckin' stupid to listen to some good advice. If I were you, I'd desert."

Chico blurted, "What the fuck!"

I was more restrained with my reply. "I'm only doin' a two-year hitch...I want to find out what Vietnam is all about...up close and personal."

The debate was at a standstill, so the Airborne hippie tried one last time to get us to buy his antiwar newspaper. It was only a quarter.

twenty-five cents...that's half the money we brought with us...going to be rough enough partying on fifty cents...damn hard with only a quarter...I'm creative but that's ridiculous.

"I'll tell you what, dude...since you've been such a fun guy, I'm gonna do you a favor." Grabbing a handful of his newspapers, I walked towards the cars that were waiting for the traffic light to turn green. "Extra, extra, read all about it! Only twenty-five cents, ladies and gentlemen. The truth about the war in Vietnam is inside these pages. Yes, only one thin quarter to learn about the horrors of war."

Chico, failing to pick up on my mocking tone, was certain that I was schizophrenic. He decided to charm a fifteen-year-old, barefoot girl who was sitting on the bus bench. After five minutes, I had sold two copies of the paper. Chico was too busy to notice my success. "Can you dig it, dude? Here's your money and your papers. Bet you never thought a gung-ho Marine would sell your antiwar rag. I figure the other side deserves some equal time also."

"Thanks, but I wish you'd reconsider. I know you're not gonna to like what's gonna to happen to you in the Nam."

"You might be right...but I have to find out for myself."

Convincing Chico that we should leave was difficult. He liked the scenery. "Come on...there'll be more chicks for us later. This is LA, not Camp Pendleton."

Armed with only fifty cents and our well-trained feet, we left the 1967 version of an Old Testament prophet and his admonitions and marched into the California night. To the disappointment of Chico, I had been wrong. The surfer girls, made famous by the Beach Boys, were not interested in us. They lusted for Jan and Dean, not two Marines with short hair.

The night had become a walking marathon. Without the money necessary to afford a motel room, we decided that our only option was to walk; fortunately, the Marine Corps had trained us to do this well. At about midnight we parked our tired bodies at the counter of an all-night, short-order restaurant. The booths were filled with teenagers who were acting as obnoxiously as my friends and I had just a year earlier.

cruising the parking lot of Johnnies' Restaurant...mooning people...coming back later to gross out the waitresses inside...unscrewing the top of the salt shaker...my friend asking for a knife for his cream pie...slapping the cream on his face...scraping it off with his knife...the manager giving us a nasty look...my friend taking a bite out of the meal ticket...the cashier looking at the manager...my friend slapping the money down...three of us running out...laughing.

The waitress was busy filling a drunk's coffee cup. With his head bobbing, he mumbled to himself. He stared at the cup as though it were interesting, and then he looked up and said something rude to the waitress. She had heard comments like that a thousand times before, but the scowling expression on her face was proof that she did not appreciate it. She came over and offered us menus. "Coffee, boys?" We pushed our cups forward. She filled them and told us that she would be back shortly for our order.

"You hungry, Chico?"

He nodded. "Yeah, but..."

"But...what? We're both hungry, and we both can run real fast, right? And if they catch us, they'll just make us wash some dishes. You know they're not gonna throw us in jail. They can't...in another two days we're leavin' for Vietnam."

Impressed with my analysis of the situation, I chuckled. Chico lit a cigarette and laughed. He liked my logic. I had been right; the night would be interesting. Two eggs over medium, hash browns, and bacon with a side order of French toast sounded deliciously inviting. "And throw in a couple a large orange juices."

Hoping for a good tip, the waitress decided to telegraph a smile. "Sure thing, boys. Your order 'll be right up."

Chico had been called a boy one too many times, so he tried to impress her with the fact that we were Marines on the way to Vietnam. Sitting two seats to our left was a young Marine. "What outfit are you men with?" I set my coffee cup down and told him that we were not part of any outfit yet. I explained how we had received a seven-day reprieve from going to Vietnam with the rest of our Staging Battalion unit. Although I was still gung ho about going to Vietnam, some down-time before going to war sounded like a good idea.

so what the hell is that dude wearing his uniform for...can't be a lifer...too young for that...must be a reservist.

I had been correct on both counts. He was a reservist and a college student.

After the waitress had brought our breakfast, I told him of our plan to make a fast exit when it came time to pay the bill. He chuckled and offered to pay the tab for our food. When we finished eating, we decided to accept his offer. The morning was still young, and there was plenty of time left for us to be adventurous.

As we left, he slipped two dollars into my shirt pocket. When I tried to return it, he refused. I smiled. "Thanks a lot, man."

"The least I could do for a couple of leathernecks going to Vietnam. You guys are okay."

"Later."

Being full felt good; being appreciated felt even better.

An hour later we were still walking. Only the faithful were

still cruising Sunset Strip, and Chico was beginning to complain about his tired feet. "We're tough Marines. We can hack it," I replied.

Chico was not convinced. "Maybe you can...but I'm tired of walking."

Before I was able to finish making fun of him, Chico grabbed a shopping cart, which lay wounded on its side. He tipped it upright and began grinning. "What do you intend to do, Spaniard...go shopping?"

"Fuck no! You're gonna give me a ride." He climbed inside the basket, and I pushed him for two blocks. "Hop out, dude...it's my turn."

As I was climbing into the shopping cart, an angry voice from a passing car bellowed at us. We ignored it, and Chico kept pushing the cart. The car, a Buick that coughed black smoke, screeched to an abrupt halt, and the driver slammed the car into reverse. Two black men in their twenties pulled along side us.

Not appreciating being ignored by us, one of them poked his head outside the window. "What the fuck you honkies think you doin'? It's muthafuckas like you that make prices go up. Stealin' shoppin' carts...just a bunch of fuckin' honkie jive shit!"

Chico was grinning, but I wanted to be in Vietnam, not in a shopping cart on Sunset Strip.

"Well, muthafuckas, I asked you goddamned assholes a fuckin' question!"

Chico was pushing the cart faster now, but the car full of anger would not evaporate in the June night. Chico, deciding to play the tough guy role to a tee, sarcastically replied, "Are you fuckin' blind or something? Looks like I'm pushin' my friend down the goddamn street in a fuckin' shopping cart, asshole."

I was not interested in getting involved in a fight. They looked as if they were strung out on drugs, and they appeared to be bigger than us, a combination that was less than appealing to me. I climbed out of the shopping cart in the hope of appeasing them, but most of all, I hoped that they would let me live to age twenty. "Be cool. We don't want any trouble...and besides, we didn't steal this damn thing."

The driver, having had enough fun with us, drove off. As I was expelling a sigh, one as big as California, Chico screamed at them, "FUCK YOU, NIGGERS. Up your fuckin' black asses!"

what the hell did you do that for...are you trying to get us killed...don't need a race war.

Chico was laughing hysterically, and I was gulping my fears and wishing I were as big as Dick Butkus or at least on another planet. Their car made a hasty U-turn. "Oh shit! I don't know you."

Chico was still laughing. "Try tellin' those niggers that."

The driver, not in the mood for Chico's racial slurs, slammed on his brakes a few feet from us. Chico was consumed with the idea of a physical altercation. Before our potential fight could hop out of their car, I dashed across the quiet street. Within seconds Chico sprinted across the street as the passenger swung open the car door and began getting out.

As I ran for my life, I was not laughing as I had during my high-school days when we had thrown water balloons at cars. The idea of my throat being slashed did not appeal to me. Although my mother, who was old-school when it came to enforcing our family's values, would have washed my mouth out with soap had I used the word 'nigger', this liberal credential was useless in my current predicament. Unfortunately, Chico didn't help our cause much; he continued yelling obscenities at the two black men who seemed bent on having us visit a hospital emergency room or the morgue; they definitely were not acting like apostles of Martin Luther King's idea of nonviolence.

They jumped back into their car. Behind us, two men with blood in their silver dollar eyes and the angry sound of their tires squealing. The race was on, down an alley, then another; the roar of their engine only interrupted by the sound of garbage cans bouncing off their car. Two head lights still behind us but getting closer, closer. Chico continued laughing and yelling at them. Breathing hard, I had turned the corner into the wrong kind of an alley, the dead-end type. "OH SHIT!" When I stopped, Chico caught up with me. "What the fuck do we do now?"

We looked at each other, hoping the other had a magical solution; we would need it soon. Lacking a magic wand, a .45, or a radio to call in mortar fire, we just sprinted as fast as we could. Chico, gasping for air and still laughing, offered his impulsive reply to my question. "Fight the niggers...what else."

"You fight 'em!" There was a six-foot-high fence in front of us. A few seconds later, I was on the other side of it. The death car screeched to a halt as Chico jumped from the top of the fence. We felt safer being in someone's backyard, but we had been ambushed. A German shepherd was barking his neurosis at the intruders. He upped and downed his hungry jaws, white teeth in the black night. We were nothing more than breakfast in his angry eyes.

Chico had finally put laughing on the back burner. Two strung-out black men and a crazy German shepherd on a June night were too much for Chico. His brain was beginning to work. The dog was only a foot behind us as we escaped over another fence.

With three fences, two angry black men, and a growling German shepherd behind us, we finally reached a well-lit street. We did not stop running for a half-mile. Finally, when we realized that we were safe, Chico lit a well-deserved cigarette. We looked at each other, laughing uncontrollably like schoolboys who had gotten away with something. We relished the idea of being alive. Now we could go to Vietnam and discover if the Airborne hippie had been right.

Chapter 10
First Semester 1970

A Star-Spangled Thank-You

He is sitting outside of the principal's office. The calendar on the wall, a reminder that the 1970-71 school year is beginning. A frumpy-looking, middle-aged secretary informs him that the principal will see him shortly. The clock on the wall is spending thirty minutes of its life staring at a young man who is still waiting for *shortly* to happen, but this is nothing new. As a former Marine, he has ample experience in the art of waiting

With time to let his mind wander, he remembers why he had become so angry the previous week. He and his pregnant wife only wanted an apartment close to the high school where he would spend a semester doing his student-teaching. The apartment manager had informed him that the vacancies had been filled; however, he was certain she had lied. His long hair was the problem, but they would not allow this woman's fears to stop them.

Two days later his wife returned alone and inquired about renting an apartment. The manager, failing to recognize her, told her that she had a vacant apartment and accepted a deposit of fifty dollars. Later that night, the manager, realizing she had been duped, called them, scolding them for being deceptive. When they returned to the apartment complex an hour later, she flung their fifty-dollar check at them. His wife, feeling uncomfortable, wanted to leave the nightmare behind; however, her husband would leave only after first screaming obscenities at the woman. The Marine Corps had taught him the art of using a variety of choice obscenities.

Stunned by his colorful language, the apartment manager's mouth was agape as the former Marine rambled on about the injustice of her decision and about how he had fought for this country so others could be free. He hated the thought that he had wasted his time. He jumped in his car and flipped her the middle finger as he peeled out on her front lawn.

The principal motions for the young man to come into his office. "I have been looking through your records. Academically, you have done very well for yourself. You come highly recommended by your professors, but..." He hates that word. He wants to tell the principal that he is tired of hearing people tell him 'yes, but.' The only butt he cares about is the one he protected in Vietnam. He knows that the man on the other side of the desk has the power to accept or reject him as a student-teacher, but he does not care to listen.

"What seems to be the problem, sir?"

The principal clears his throat. "Young man, we have our standards at this high school. The people in our community feel that a teacher should be a model for their children. A teacher has certain responsibilities. One of these being the responsibility to look like a teacher and not like a bum. I am sorry, but your hair and beard are just not appropriate for the classroom of 1970."

Sitting silently, the young man wonders why people are so afraid of his hair. It is clean, his beard is well groomed, and his clothes are clean and ironed. He has served his country in the Marine Corps and has worked his way through the University of Arizona. The resumé of his life is impeccable, but none of that matters to the principal. Unlike the Nam, the rules are different back in the World.

The following day, the professor who is in charge of the student-teaching program encourages the young man to play the game. "Compromise and cut your hair if you truly want to teach." The former Marine wants the opportunity to become a teacher, but he also wants to be accepted for himself. He would like to tell the professor that Jesus wore long hair and a beard, but he is certain the professor will tell him that this is irrelevant. The student-teaching candidate has not survived Vietnam to be just one more player in someone else's game. He knows what the professor is unwilling to tell him: that he is involved on the wrong side of a power struggle with the status quo.

Several days later, the former-Marine, who hungers to teach, is telling his story to the American Civil Liberties Union; a dozen defenders of individual freedom listen intently. They tell him that they admire his principles but explain that if he wins his case, he, not the school, will be the loser. Confronting the discrimination of the high school will make him appear to be a troublemaker, and in the atmosphere of the early 1970s, gaining a teaching job would be virtually impossible. The difficult choice is his.

Two days later, he begins his student-teaching experience at Amphitheater High School. He has lost before, but he is a fighter. He understands what the principal has failed to realize: that he is much more than his hair. The young man is willing to sacrifice momentary trappings so that he can offer his talents and be the person he truly is with the students. Three years earlier, the Việt Cong had schooled him in two valuable lessons: going underground doesn't mean surrender and it is critical to choose one's battles carefully.

The student-teacher is reading the responses from the questionnaire. Many of the students in his senior American Problems class are worried—as they put it—about the hippies and the niggers. Life is so simple for these teenagers. Shaking his head in disgust, he knows the challenge is there.

Several weeks later, he is writing statistics about the Vietnam War on the board. "On both sides, hundreds of thousands of people have died. Millions have been left homeless." He scans the faces of the seventeen-year-old girls in the room. He pauses and then tells them that if they were Vietnamese, many of them would become whores, either to support their families or to gain information for the Việt Cong.

Ignoring their giggles and laughter, he continues, "Survival is the name of the game when armies decide to fight a war in your backyard, and if you were eight or nine years old, you'd probably be pimping or selling drugs or whatever to the soldiers. It's a hell of a way to spend your childhood."

Thirty faces honing in on his words. The humming of the fluorescent lights goes unnoticed. He turns to write *one hundred billion dollars* on the chalkboard. He turns back towards the class to elaborate on the significance of the figure, which he has just written. He is not Johnny Carson, so he is perplexed why they are laughing and pointing at him. He raises his voice, asking them what they find to be so humorous. An eighteen-year-old, who thinks he is Billy the Kid, decides to shift out of the slouching mode, finally stops snickering and tells the student-teacher what is so humorous. "You don't know how to spell, and you think you're a teacher. Thought teachers were supposed to be better than us. You ain't no better, sir." The student-teacher looks at the chalk board and realizes that he has written "bilion.". He wants to turn down the thermostat on his anger, but this time he does not.

"Damn it! I don't believe you! You're more concerned that a teacher can make a mistake than you care about the fact that so much blood has been spilled and so much money has been wasted in a war that is going nowhere. Perhaps you need to see what war is really like...I got news for some of you, you'll get your chance. It's too bad you'll have to learn the hard way. Maybe then you'll understand and appreciate life!"

There is a part of him that wants to use the f-word to make his point in a way that these teenagers would grasp, but Marine Corps discipline kicks in, and the f-word stays neatly tucked away in his mind. The laughter vanishes. It is safer and wiser to listen. Now, feeling less agitated, he sighs and continues, "I'm amazed you think that teachers can't make a mistake. Well, it's this way...teachers are human beings. The only bad mistake is the one from which you learn nothing. When I was just a year older than you, I made the mistake of goin' off to Vietnam, but I sure as hell learned somethin' important from it. I learned to appreciate life. It's too bad I had to go to a death factory to learn about growing up and caring. Maybe I wasted my time cutting my hair so I could teach you."

He is tired of being on his soapbox, so he sits at his desk and pretends to be looking over some test papers. Emotionally spent, he peers up long enough to halfheartedly say, "Spend the rest of the time in class doing the questions at the end of chapter four. I have nothing more to say."

The hands of the clock are moving in slow motion, each minute feeling like an hour. He is staring at the test papers on his desk, but he only sees the laughing face of the boy who thinks he is a cowboy. The student-teacher is certain that back in elementary school, a teacher told the cowboy that he was a slow learner and filed him under *S*. Judgment-rocks pelt the boys and girls. Through the noisy silence of lectures and put downs, rocks rape the boys and girls, ripping smiles from the freckled face of the third-grader, a slow learner who is slow to learn that Webster called rocks stones. His third-grade teacher tells him that he is just a dumb kid for not knowing that, but he tells the teacher that even a slow learner knows that a kid is a baby goat. Webster said so. And the kid who wants to be a cowboy tells the teacher that he does not even like tin cans. But the slow learner is fast to learn that rocks hurt when they leave Webster's book to pelt the boys and the girls. He calls his teacher *Sir* and proudly announces that he did learn. Sir, let me throw rocks, rocks, rocks.

The bell finally rings, sucking the students out of the classroom and into the hall. One growing-up girl remains in the room. She cries tears of caring because others did not seem to care. This rain is good for the drought.

He offers her a Kleenex for her tears. "I feel very badly about the way we acted. We shouldn't have..."

He interrupts her unexpected apology. "Danetta, I guess I'm overestimating people. Maybe the older generation has been right all along when they tell us that change doesn't happen over night. My problem is that I'm still just too close to my war experience to accept that people just don't seem to care."

With insight beyond her years, she replies, "If you don't understand something, it's easier not to care." Another bell rings. She is late for her next class. Saying nothing, she smiles at him. Behind her, the door closes; her past-tense pain, vanishing.

Finally, the long semester is coming to a close. The third-period bell will ring in five minutes. It will be a special bell for him, the final one of his student-teaching career at the high school. His hair has spent the past four months growing. It would be too long for the principal, but he has not bothered to notice.

The chatter in the room surrenders to unanimous silence. With the prodding of several of his classmates, the student who wants to be Billy the Kid stands up slowly. Strolling to the front of the room, he wishes he was in the parking lot picking a fight; it would be easier for him. He arrives at the student-teacher's desk. Without a word, he hands a long narrow box to him. The student-teacher opens it. Smiling, he knows that it has all been worth it. He holds up their gift, an American-flag tie, their star-spangled thank-you. The class applauding and whistling as a gentle smile on the student-teacher's face whispers its thank-you. With a message in his eyes, the teenage cowboy looks at his teacher and finds the courage. "You know, sir, you're an okay hippie."

Chapter 11
November 1967

Too Busy To Write

Liz, now a sophomore, had not written in over four weeks. All I had were memories of the college girl whom I had met on my return trip from liberty in Washington, DC. She was definitely anti-war, but I figured I was cute enough for her to overlook my status as a Marine. When I watched *The Flies*, a play by Jean Paul Sartre, with her, she was probably amazed that a Marine would understand and appreciate Sartre's existential philosophy. Liz, Mary Washington College, and Fredericksburg, Virginia were just yesterday's images; for me, the Nam was the only thing that was real in early November of 1967. Virginia's chilly autumn evenings were an illusion and nothing more in Vietnam's November heat.

My first two weeks of mess duty had replaced working parties and guard duty. Each day, I was up before sunrise, so I could fill large cans with clean water and then light the immersion burners in them so there would be hot water available to clean the pots and pans of the Staff and Officers' mess. Likewise, the dishes were washed, compliments of the Magic Hot Water Man. My magic show usually lasted for twelve to sixteen hours each day.

Because I found time every night after mess duty to practice setting up the mortar, those hours of practice at gun drill eventually paid off. I finally became an assistant-gunner, better known as an A-gunner. I had finally joined the war. I would be the one dropping the rounds down the mortar tube.

The following day I was certain that I had caught the worms again. I was wrong, but I was given a twenty-four hour, no-duty chit, which made the pain worthwhile. The next morning, I was no longer considered sick, so I was back at work: sixteen hours worth.

At nine that evening, I was *volunteered* to guard the food storage refrigerators until midnight. With the door flaps of the food storage tent closed, I turned on my flashlight and seated myself on a comfortable crate of oranges. A Lazy-Boy recliner it was not, but it beat standing. My weary but officially healthy body was glad about that. I had not written to anyone in eighteen days. Feeling guilty, I took out my pen and paper. With a noisy yawn, I began thinking about what to write.

Halloween 1967...Hi WORLD, I'M TIRED...are you?...you probably aren't since you sleep at night...you get safe and restful sleep...well it's nine in the evening and it's the first chance I've had to write...I have to stay up until midnight to stand reefer watch and make sure no one steals any food from my favorite mess hall...boy do I love mess duty...I hope the goblins and ghosts cut me some slack and don't haunt the reefer tonight...oh that would be TERRIFYING wouldn't it...I have seven and a half months left in the NAM...in the next couple of weeks we should go up to the DMZ and get into some real war...boy this place really screws my mind up...sometimes I don't know what's happening...like now...I like to write but I just don't give a shit anymore but every once in awhile someone halfway intelligent asks to read one of my books and shows some GCT...brains...sometimes I even get into a decent conversation...I've written two new poems so far...this one dude read "World Where" and my two new poems and he liked them...little stuff like this and occasional letters from the World keep me going...sorry if I sound blah...seems I'm like this every time I get around to writing...I haven't heard from Liz in thirty days...what can I say...boy am I a lover or what...well I can't think of anything exciting to say...I forget stuff that happened yesterday...boy I'm in a hum so I'll say bye...write soon...Jello...SHIT ON THIS BUMMER LETTER...I'll save it and mail it to myself if I ever get back to the World...good for a laugh...might as well have an orange...probably a navel orange...can never get away from the military...juicy...I wonder if I'll be sick of them by midnight...probably.

Six hours later, I was lighting the two immersion burners again. My legs ached, and I had two more weeks of mess duty.

Seven weeks later, I received a letter from Liz. She apologized. She had been too busy to write.

Chapter 12
November 1967

I Kind Of Lied To The Recruiter

It was November 10, and I was celebrating. Everyone was celebrating. On this grand day, the lifers were jubilant because it was their Marine Corps' birthday. For most non-lifers, this was just a good excuse to get drunk. I was a card-carrying non-lifer, and this would be my last opportunity to drink to excess because I would be returning to my job as a mortarman the next day. Although a few of my peers in 81s put drinking and getting stoned first and their job as mortarmen second, I realized that being sober was my obligation to the grunts because they relied on us for accurate and fast fire support.

For me, being reminded of the Crotch's [pejorative name for U S Marine Corps] inception two centuries earlier was more of a time for mourning, a time for wondering why I had ever joined the Marines. The gung ho Marine I once was had begun checking out of the war several months earlier. When I had joined the Marines, I had high expectations, but I had become increasing disillusioned with my Corps. A few beers would help me drown my sorrows; however, in one area, there was some cause for jubilation; it was my final day of mess duty although tomorrow meant the return to the infamous sandbag details; these and other assorted working details were erroneously dubbed working parties. But for Dale, my partner in the pot shack who was taking a welcome break from hauling his 60mm mortar around on daily patrols, the new day would only mean moving up to my just vacated position of smedley, a Marine Corps term for busboy and waiter for the staff NCOs and officers; it also meant that he could fatten up his lanky frame. Even for those who didn't need to shed any flab, life in an infantry line company had made it easy to lose weight: the Nam-daily-patrol diet.

The November sun was sneaking away unnoticed, and Dale and I were halfheartedly washing the few remaining pots and pans. My friend from Charley Company, an infantry company better known as Suicide Charley, offered me another beer. I set an unwashed pot down, enthusiastically accepting the can of beer.

"But that'll be your third."

"Whoopee! Then I'd better get my ass in gear and guzzle this baby down."

"Better not get drunk. Wouldn't want to...the...the...yeah...the lifers...yeah Jello, better not..." Dale's ability to be lucid had gone AWOL a few beers earlier.

"Sober up, dude. What the hell you babbling about? You're sounding like a lifer."

"Fuck off! The lifers are inside their chow hall, not out here. They're drunk, and this farm boy is just enjoyin' himself."

"Let's drink to...yeah, sure...to Lifer Day."

"Hell yeah. I'm not proud. I'll drink to anything," Dale blurted out.

"Ah, that's deee...licious. Hamms is okay."

"I'll drink to that, Jello."

me too...get completely ripped...hallelujah...finally off this goddamn mess duty...a lot of bullshit but it sure beats the hell out of filling those jive ass sandbags...sandbags everywhere...who the hell invented those damn things...a lifer for sure...quit bitching and moaning...filling sandbags beats the hell out of going back to patrols in the bush...I got it made compared to Dale and the other grunts...especially Charley Company...mess duty's a genuine vacation for them...Dale's probably getting smashed because he's got ten days left on mess duty...then back to Charley Company and the bush and who knows what...damn...he's lucky...damn lucky...just about everyone in Charley Company got a Purp or two or three or the green plastic bag routine...those dudes run into more heavy shit than anyone...always getting their asses in the thick of it...most of them only eighteen...don't even get to vote...shit...who gives a damn anyway...but we can drink...two beers with a beer pass...don't want the troopies too ripped to fight off hordes of NVA...keep the lifers nice and safe...they're probably smashed on their no-limit hard stuff...yeah...they need the potent stuff more than us peons...they got to make all the decisions...where to send us to get our asses kicked...who gets killed...which hill is worth a Silver Star for them.

When we finished our beers, we threw the empty cans into the darkness. Dale grabbed two more, tossing one to me while chugging one more unnecessary beer. His utility shirt quickly soaked up the beer that missed his mouth. Dale's ability to think and speak was evaporating into the night, but the grunt from Charley Company needed to drown his sorrows, and he had more of them than he wished to remember; they would wait patiently, lurking below the surface, and have a reunion down the road. Before I could thank him for the beer, he had opened another and sarcastically offered a toast to the Marine Corps.

"Here's to this Green Machine. May it misplace my enlistment...my enlist...ah...that thing I signed way back when I was a damn fool."

"Contract, Dale. Your four-year enlistment contract."

"Don't remind...me...jus' because you're smart enough to join this green mother for only two years. Shit."

I began laughing sardonically. "Hell, I wasn't smart. I didn't even have to join up...Army, Navy, anything."

Dale closed one eye and jerked his head back in stunned disbelief. "What? You gotta be kidding! Did I hear you right? I must be gettin' smashed."

"You are, but your ears aren't drunk."

"Wow, you're too much. I need another swig. You mean you didn't have to join up at all?"

I chuckled as I explained the obstacle course that I had conquered to gain my status as a member of the Marine Corps. "Yeah, they didn't want me. Tried both the Navy and Marine reserve units...they're both together, same building back in Tucson...but my jive doctor screwed me over, so I couldn't get in."

"Fucked you over! Sounds more like a pal. Wish I had one like that."

"Shut up and drink your beer. I'm tryin' to tell you a fascinating story."

Dale squinted in my direction in an attempt at focusing his eyes, and his head was beginning to bob helplessly in the late night air as he slurred at me, "Yeah, yeah...go on, lifer."

Before I explained the details, I gulped more beer than I needed and belched proudly.

"Anyway...I always had asthma. Bein' in Arizona kind of helped." I continued with my explanation: my family doctor believed that my asthma and a stint in the Marine Corps would be a bad match. On the other hand, I, being nineteen, thought I knew better. Knowing that my asthma, as well as my high blood pressure, would be impediments to my enlisting in the Marine Corps, I asked my doctor for a letter that would clarify that my lungs were just fine at this point in my life. Assuming that his letter would resolve my enlistment problem, I handed my doctor's letter to the Naval doctor in charge; the path was cleared; my doctor's note would be my passport to glory as a United States Marine.

Dale shook his head, wondering what my problem was. "Wow, Jello, sounds like your bod was messed up. Now it's your fuckin' mind that's messed up."

I continued my saga. "At any rate, the head corpsman down there told my brother, who was a Navy corpsman, to take my blood pressure when I was asleep to see if he could get a low enough reading to make the Navy doctor who had checked me out earlier all happy. That didn't even work. I think the head corpsman was nipping a little juice on the side. Miraculously, my blood pressure dropped to just the right level, but then, this jive ass head doctor read the letter from my doctor, and that's when I found out that my family doctor had written that my asthma was very bad, but I hadn't had any issues in a few years. That fucked me. Boy, I was pissed off."

"Jello, you're weird. Strange."

"Now that I think about it...not strange...STUPID!"

"Don't know 'bout you, but I'm ready for another one."

I passed on his offer. Finishing my bizarre tale was more important, so I continued. "So there I was...turned down nice and official, but I was a hard charger, so I decided to join the regulars because their recruiting station was about five miles from the Reserve Center. So I diddy bopped down there. My neighborhood friend Dave and I wanted to go in on the buddy-plan and be in Recon together. I told the recruiter we wanted their two-year plan. Well, this shithead of a lifer..."

"Don't tell me...he told you they didn't have the two year plan anymore."

"Yeah. How did you know?"

Dale's face winced. "They whipped that line of shit on me, and here I sit with a four-year hitch."

"Well, as we were walkin' out the door, the dude tells me he thinks he can still get us in on that plan. Tricky bastard. So then, I fill out all these forms. They wanted to know if I've been in any commie organizations and if I have any relatives livin' in foreign countries. The usual cheap shit questions. Like the treasurer of the Karl Marx fan club is gonna admit it on the form. Government forms, aren't they great. Then they want to know if I've ever tried to join the military, and if I've been turned down, they also want to know why."

So wha'd you do, Jello?"

"I bullshitted 'em, of course. Then they whipped this form on me that had the name of four diseases on it: asthma, etcetera. I had asthma and two of the etceteras, I figured that at this point, I might as well lie like a son of a bitch. I started gettin' scared when I realized that they might check up and find out about the Reserves not acceptin' me. Then I read the fine print: "Fraudulent enlistment is punishable by fine or imprisonment."

the induction center in Phoenix...FINE...IMPRISONMENT...or both...FRAUDULENT ENLISTMENT...phony ass cough...thank God they fell for it...I did it...trickier than shit Jello...faked your way into this wonderful green nightmare...not too bright but only two years...I hope Dave is staying safe doin' his Recon thing...haven't gotten a letter from him in a bit...I need a drink.

Several beers later, Dale and I decided to finish up the day's dirty pots and pans. Once we had this task squared away, we could settle down to some serious drinking. We were unconcerned about the quality of our labor; the lifers never gave rank or medals for our usual good work, so we adopted a laissez faire approach. The next day our poor washing and rinsing techniques would reap consequences that the best laxative on the market would have trouble competing with.

It was my last night on mess duty, and I knew that Dale, a farm boy from a small town in western Iowa, was capable of handling the wrath of the staff NCOs and the officers. At that moment, we were two half-inebriated drinking buddies, and tomorrow's consequences were unimportant. As captives of a month's worth of mess duty, we were not an integral part of the war effort, so being drunk did not matter. The only negative consequences for our drinking would be our hangovers in the morning.

Dale grabbed a large metal cooking pot, which he had just scrubbed, and threw it at me. I discovered that I was not as inebriated as I thought I was; I caught the metal pot. The next item on the agenda was to rinse it, but a cupful of semi-clean water was all I was willing to use.

"Hope the lifers don't mind us conservin' on the water. I sure don't want to light up that damn immersion burner again to heat up a new batch of water. There must be at least a half gallon left."

Dale nodded, concurring with my sarcastic and inaccurate analysis of the clean water situation. "Plenty, Jello. We only got about...dozen more pots to clean."

Beginning to feel a twinge of deeply embedded Catholic guilt, I replied, "But if they get the shits...they'll be..."

"If they get 'em...hell, I'll guarantee they'll get the genuine certified shits. Those maggots are goin' to be in the hurt locker...and without a key."

I replied, "I feel kind a sorry for them. After all, there are a few okay officers. A few. Like that gook lieutenant...the one that gave us this beer."

"Yum, a whole case of Hamms." Dale grinned in my general direction.

"He's a pretty decent dude. All I did was give'm a few apples and oranges one day after chow..."

Dale staggered back, bursting into uncontrollable laughter. The beer that was splashing from his can went unnoticed. "A few apples and oranges!"

"Would you believe two crates?"

"That's more like it, Jello."

"Who cares...they would've just gone to feed some jive lifer's face."

Dale nodded. "Yeah, right. Now hurry up with that damn pot. Just heave the goddamn thing over here."

The muddy ground to the left of Dale made an easy target for the clean pot. "Good shot. Right in the mud."

"Two points for our side."

"Another beer, Dale, old buddy?"

"Yeah, sure...why not. Whoopie! Now that's tastin' better every time. Too bad you won't be gettin' the good chow anymore. Tomorrow you gotta eat that dog shit at the mess hall with the rest of the peons."

"Right, but I don't know which'll be worse...that garbage or the hangover I'll have tomorrow."

"Hey, Jello, you remember the time the colonel..." Dale belched and continued strolling down mess-duty memory lane. "The lifer got all freaked out when he found that thing...yeah, the lid from a can in his soup?"

The image of the colonel's baffled look made me chuckle. "Yeah! Let's drink to that. What a hard ass. That dude was too much when he asked me what the lid was doin' in his soup. Hell, I felt like tellin' him the VC put it there. What really got me was him first askin' me what it was. All I could say to the dude was, 'looks like the lid of a can, sir'. Don't know what he expected me to say. Yeah, how was I s'ppose to know what it was doin' in his soup? Dumb lifer."

Bursting into laughter, Dale staggered, lost his balance and fell down. Sitting in the mud, Dale stared at his beer can, now lying on its side, empty. Dale attempted to smash it with his fist, but he missed his target. In two weeks he would not have that luxury. In two weeks there would be zero margin for error. Patiently, Victor Charlie would wait for Dale. Tonight the Viêt Cong who roamed the rice paddies around our hill would seek other targets, and Dale and I would not be seeking our mothers' approval for our drinking behavior; home was ten thousand miles and a lifetime away. Mrs. Bourret and Mrs. Witzman were back in the World with its own set of rules, but we were in a place that, especially at night, had only one rule: *get out alive.*

Chapter 13
December 1967

Got Those Blindfolded Blues

The bunker had a late-1967 sandbag decor. Our sleeping facilities were done in natural hard-ground, with odd-sized pebbles thrown in as a bonus. The shoulder high sandbag walls afforded us two to three feet of protection. The wood plank roof, covered with three layers of rock-hard sandbags, overlapped the body of the bunker. The entrance in the rear made it possible for the extra wet brand of Vietnamese rain and shrapnel, of either friendly or enemy origin, to join us in our little palace of sand.

The recipe for guard duty Nam style on Hill 10 consisted of the sultry night air, three drowsy Marines, and an army of aimless and famished mosquitoes. Taunted by these Asian demons, we ritualistically smeared a stinking oil repellent on our arms and faces. The repellent seemed to ruin the sweet taste of our sticky, sweat-laden skin, but someone usually procrastinated.

"Son of a bitch...you little bastard!" The mosquito won this round.

guard duty...a real drag...hope I get a good bunker...don't need one with a listening post...bummer and a half...let's see...hope someone brought the Claymore mines and the trip flares although the trip flares are a waste...the NVA aren't bothered much by the flares...they just might turn the Claymores around...if they do we're in a world of shit if we set them off...700 pellets flyin' our way...don't need that...damn that scrawny mosquito...didn't even give me a chance to slime that repellent on my dumb bod.

When I arrived at the bunker, the other two men with whom

I'd be on bunker watch were already there, so I decided to find out if they had put out any trip flares and, more importantly, the two very deadly Claymore mines out by the barbed wire yet.

"Got the Claymore mines out?"

"Yeah."

"How 'bout the trip flares? Did either of you guys take care of them?"

"The hell with 'em."

I hoped that such a cavalier attitude would not mean that either of these Marines would sleep during their time on watch.

"Let's flip for first watch."

"Shit. I always lose at this jive coin flipping."

"That's cool. I don't mind if you have middle watch. I kind of appreciate you losing. First watch is great."

"Middle watch....what a dud."

I was stuck with middle, but I would survive. The Marine who hadn't bothered setting up the trip flares shifted the conversation away from complaining about bunker watch when he noticed a Marine squad approaching our hill's western perimeter.

"Hey, it looks like they're bringing in a fuckin' gook suspect."

"Wow, that fucker's still alive! Charley Company must be slippin'."

The squad of eighteen and nineteen-year-old Marines was almost back home on the battalion hill. This meant an hour of rest and an opportunity to indulge in what had originally been hot Marine Corps chow before they would be going back out to set up a night ambush. Had the squad not been detained by the events of war, which always seemed to get in the way, they would have had the opportunity to stand in typically long chow lines, receive their food, and methodically complain as they made attempts at digesting the hot morsels.

While the majority of us on our hill were indulging in the tragicomedy, better known as evening chow, this squad had been searching for the Cong or the VC, better known as Charlie. Members of the Viet Cong were South Vietnamese guerillas whereas the NVA were their North Vietnamese allies in their war against the Saigon regime. Anybody in South Vietnam could be considered a VC suspect, especially if he or she did not possess the right answers at the right time for the right person, notably a physically and emotionally drained Marine with a short temper and, sometimes, a racist attitude. The grunts had seen enough of the VC's and the NVA's gruesome handiwork to be hungry for some payback.

One such bamboo-legged papasan, who was only wearing black shorts, was probably a farmer from one of the nearby villes, and he unfortunately appeared to have come up with the wrong answers for the Marine squad. His young captors jeered and, not so gently, prodded him along. Only a few hundred more uncertain meters before he would meet the unbending interrogators and their difficult questions; they would be hungry for answers, and the Constitution would not be an obstacle.

With hands bound behind him, this blindfolded, toothpick of a senior citizen cautiously chose each new and uncertain step. He stopped abruptly. Blindfolded, his senses of smell and hearing told of the stream just in front of him. How deep? How wide? The suspect did not know. His shaky legs turned his wiry body away from the wet unknown. His caution was only to be met by a young rifleman's anger as he bellowed, "Get your ass going, gook. *Didi mau*! Into the fucking water. Now!"

The lanky Marine's order failed to advance the suspect in the direction of the stream. A shove from the Marine sent the confused papasan tumbling into the cold water. Once again he failed to advance through the stream. When the papasan did an about-face movement, the Marine, who had been prodding him, proceeded to do a John-the-Baptist routine on him. His submergence drew cheers and loud laughter from the squad of Marines. Ten-seconds: tense, struggling. Laughter. Fifteen-seconds: squirming, floundering. Cheers. Twenty-seconds: gasping, choking, alive. Booing. The Marine who had held the suspect under water was angry and astonished. "Damn! That fuckin' gook's got some lungs!"

"Shit. You should've kept the son of a bitch under water."

Another Marine in the squad replied, "Yeah. One less fuckin' gook to worry about."

Before he could regain his senses, the waterlogged papasan was abruptly dragged out of the stream, which had almost become his watery grave. Still blindfolded and quivering, he regained his footing, but a shove from the Marine quickly threw the suspect off balance again. With five or six more cautious steps, he escaped his watery nightmare but moved closer to the uncertainty of his upcoming interrogation.

With the help of a South Vietnamese interrogator, the Marines from S-2 [Intelligence] would decide if he was a patriot or a traitor. There would be no intermission during the search for right answers; ultimately, someone would win the battle of wills. For the papasan, that victory could be costly.

Again, the prisoner's sense of direction failed him. His forward movement halted as he stood trembling, his heaving chest was scraped up and smeared with mud. The grunt next to the suspect prodded him with the muzzle of his rifle and yelled, "I didn't say, *dung lai*, you fuckin idiot-gook-ass-motherfucker!"

Disoriented, his quivering body mistakenly veered to his left. Exasperated with the error, the grunt swung his rifle in a horizontal motion, slamming the butt of his M16 hard against the right side of the papasan's head. Smashing against the sightless papasan's jaw, the sudden impact of the Marine's rifle butt thrust his head to one side with a violent jolt. His defenseless body tumbled to the ground. The cheers of the frenzied Marines drowned out the papasan's anguished screams. This mad marriage of sounds infected our three-man bunker.

OH SHIT...that's fucked up...goddamn...chicken-shit assholes...shitty....he must be in his sixties...unreal...can't be happening...no...it can't...it is...shit...IT IS.

The instinct to nurse his bloody jaw was frustrated. The papasan's unsuccessful attempts to free his bound hands brought neither freedom nor relief, only rope burns to his lank wrists.

"Get up, you sorry ass fuckin' gook, or I'll really get pissed!" *amazing...sick...this place is fucking crazy...too much...no wonder they hate us...unreal...ungoddamn real...a crock of shit.*

Wearing a mask of red and brown on the left side of his face, the papasan struggled as an impatient Marine yanked him abruptly to his unsteady feet. His thin yet muscular legs quivered as he stumbled and almost fell. Fifty meters of occasional shoves from his captors brought him inside our perimeter. A minute later, the old man and the squad disappeared into the maze of bureaucratic hooches [slang for tents serving as living or work quarters]; the images seared in my mind, becoming forever memories, haunting my innocence.

The Marine, who was happy about not having middle watch, smirked as he proudly announced with callous disregard, "Guess they showed that damn gook?"

Unenthusiastically, I replied, "Yeah, guess so."

"These slant-eyed bastards only understand a good ass-kickin' like that. You can bet he'll remember us after that."

I nodded. "You're right about that."

"Hell, yeah. These goddamn fuckin' gooks'll take ya for everything. Money...that's all they want. And every damn one of them little fuckers is a VC or a fuckin' friend of one. These goddamn yella bastards can't be trusted one damn bit. Always smilin'. Always wantin' somethin' for free. Ya know...just like the niggers back home...always wantin' somethin' for nothin'."

Lacking a cheerleader's enthusiasm, I replied, "If you say so."

you racist asshole...'niggers'...up your racist ass...hope Martin Luther King integrates your shitty fuckin' neighborhood and you have to live next to some 'nigger' family and your ugly ass sister goes out and marries herself one of those 'niggers'...didn't your parents teach you anything...we're all human beings...when will this shit stop?

"Did a number on his jaw. Like, numba one [slang for the best]. Beautiful."

With an uncomfortable feeling gnawing at me like a hungry dog, I changed the subject. "I don't know about you two, but I'm gonna crash and catch a few zees before second watch. If you feel like taking my watch, you can. I won't complain."

"Don't worry, I'll wake your ass up."

The top of the bunker offered the best available sleeping accommodations. The sandbag mattress was rock hard, yet it lacked the irksome pebbles found on the ground. Best of all, being on top of the bunker meant an occasional breeze.

humid...hot...lousy ass night for bunker watch...skinny old papasan...Marine swinging the butt of his rifle at the old man's head...jaw probably broken...bullshit...I hate this shitty place...I want to quit this fucking war.

"Hey, you up there."

"Yeah, what?"

"Got the password?"

"Yeah. Now let me catch some damn zees."

The simmering air mellowed as the last remnants of a sunset that rivaled any I'd ever seen in Arizona surrendered to the charcoal night. Drained, I rolled over and was asleep.

from the halls of Montezuma to the shores of Tripoli we will fight our country's battles...Marine...rifle butt...thud...papasan on the ground rolling...ha...ha...four cheerleaders...whistles...cat calls...thunderous applause...Susie and Sally and Mary Lou and Betty Jo...yay...sis boom bah...the papasan on the fifty-yard line looking up and seeing the crowd of crescent grins and exploding eyes and ten thousand pairs of hands clapping faster... faster...louder...louder...the little old man's face wearing wrinkles of confusion...an announcement...ladies and gentlemen...let's all stand for the playing of our National Anthem...someone pick up that little old man so he can show some respect for our flag...thank you young man for getting that little old man up...oh say can you see by the dawn's early light what so proudly...proudly...would someone unstick that needle...thank you young man...proud to claim the title of United States Marine...a truly beautiful song...we're proud of our boys overseas fighting the red menace...thunderous applause...the little old man wondering why his hands are tied why he is blindfolded why he is not harvesting his rice in his country why the sea of white faces is grinning and yelling and wondering if he would be here if he were a little old man with a white face or would he be playing shuffle board or waiting for the never-to-come little white faces of his grinning children...but he is quivering...his hands are bound...the crowd becoming noisier...he cannot see the quartet of thirty-eight-inch busts disguised as Susie and Sally and Mary Lou and Betty Jo grinning at the ten thousand pairs of lusting eyes...all wanting to get into these girls' all-American pants...four coy grins teasing the mob of white faces...the red white and blue hanging limp from a pole...the crowd bobbing and swaying...the papasan on the fifty-yard line wanting to harvest his rice...the four cheerleaders chanting...the crowd joining in...two bits four bits six bits a dollar...all for the right side stand up and holler...the young man in a green uniform lifting the little old man to his feet and raising his rifle into the air...clubbing the papasan's jaw with the butt of his rifle...blood covering his jaw...an announcement for the audience...forget about the little old man with the red jaw...folks...look at the fine demonstration at the other end of the field...three hundred boot Marines standing in formation clutching bayoneted rifles...a drill instructor telling the young warriors how to do the job right...three hundred bayonets lunging forward...three hundred voices in unison roaring...KILL VC KILL...KILL VC KILL...the four cheerleaders bouncing up and down...grinning and cheering...hit him again...hit him again...hit him again harder...the young man in the green uniform hitting the little old man harder and harder...Susie and her three friends cheering...the ocean of white faces grinning...their eyes bulging...the little old man lying on the fifty-yard line in a puddle of crimson pain...Susie leading a cheer...fight team fight...do your best...remember that you're fighting for America...the land of the free and the home of the brave...God bless America...what are we going to do tonight...beat the gooks...beat the gooks...hit him again harder...the little old man lying on the fifty-yard line wanting to harvest his rice...the frenzied mob clapping and stomping...Susie and her three friends smiling...the hungry crowd veering from the quartet of thirty-eight-inch busts...ten-thousand pairs of wild eyes focusing on the young man in the green uniform with the bloodied rifle...Susie smiling at him...knowing she will let him get into her all-American pants if he proves his manhood...the young man bashing the little old man's skull to pieces...the throng of white faces loving it...the cheerleaders cheesing their pearlies...the young man in the green uniform receiving the most valuable player award and the game rifle and the new title of United States Marine...Susie grinning and whispering in the Marine's ear...you were first to fight for right and freedom and to keep our honor clean...the three hundred boot Marines at the opposite end of the field singing...we are proud to claim the title of United States Marine...the little old man lying on the fifty-yard line drained lifeless...Susie smiling...the young Marine smiling...the crowd chanting...more...more...more.

"Damn. I hate this fucking place."

Suddenly, wide-awake, the nightmare was over. Images of the papasan raced through my mind. In the black night, the cicada chatter was drowned out by the sound of my heart pounding double-time, and the papasan's blindfolded and wrinkled face stared back at me.

Chapter 14
January 1968

Dying In The Darkness Of The New Year

It was the first week of January 1968, and in spite of myself, I had survived the first half of my thirteen-month tour of duty in the Nam.

For Marines in Vietnam, only two places existed: the Nam and the World. The Nam was our immediate predicament, and the World was tomorrow's fantasies. Vietnam only existed in the geography books: the Mekong Delta, the Central Highlands, the thousand-mile coastline, the Buddhist temples, the water buffaloes, the banana trees, the monsoon rains, the rice paddies, and the bamboo vipers were all there; so were our hatreds and our hang ups.

We were in the Nam, and it was a Cowboys-and-Indians war. Being Vietnamese and dead meant the unfortunate person instantly became a Communist. Even a dead water buffalo that might have been counted as a Communist casualty. No matter how heavy the casualties were for us, we always won. It sounded better that way for the people who liked to believe that we were Ohio State in the game of war. A large enemy body count became more important than taking and holding a hill, but the only counting that mattered for us was the number of days that remained in our tours of duty in the Nam. Getting short was what the Nam was all about.

We fought gooks since we did not know what Communists looked like. We quickly learned that a noncommissioned officer's ass was for kissing if we were interested in promotions in rank; I remained a lance corporal for eleven months although I had become eligible for promotion to corporal after four months. We forged beer passes so we could buy more than the imposed two-beer limit. Rather than gag on the food that the mess hall offered, sometimes we stole C-rations although these canned delights were barely a notch up from the mess hall's offerings. We hoped for night radio watch in our tent to escape the monsoon rains and the mosquitoes of guard duty. We volunteered for day patrols to elude the monotony of sandbag-filling details. We found time to build gun pits and bunkers, to string barbed wire, to pick up someone else's cigarette butts, to have weekly rifle and personnel inspections, and to hope for a cool breeze.

Some found time to die.

Sergeant O'Connor ended his tour of duty on January 3, 1968, and eight men from Bravo Company had been wounded seriously enough to be medevaced to the Naval Hospital in Da Nang. A pair of bullet-riddled NVA bodies were found tangled in the barbed wire perimeter of our hill. A dozen more North Vietnamese bodies littered the area inside the South Vietnamese compound, located several hundred meters east of our hill. On the dirt road half way to this CAP unit [Combined Action Platoon], two more victims of the highly successful Communist ambush lay useless: two abandoned Marine tanks had been knocked out by the devastatingly effective B40 anti-tank rockets. As the sun was waking up to begin its day, a patrol from Bravo Company returned to our hill with the jackpot: forty 122mm rockets which they had found at an NVA rocket launching site nearly four thousand meters east of us. On our hill, the plywood walls of the mess hall wore a new look, compliments of the Communist mortarmen. Trying to catch up on lost sleep, four squads of Marine mortarmen slept hard. The five-hour attack had become history, something for Nam diaries and the evening news back in the World.

On the day before Sergeant O'Connor had been killed, two good things happened: it did not rain and we received a unit citation. The letter of commendation from the Commanding General of the First Marine Division informed us that we had been aggressive, decisive and professional. He was thankful that our battalion had prevented the NVA from rocketing Da Nang from our TAOR [tactical area of responsibility]. For the previous five months 1/7's patrols had successfully kept the rocket belt, the area six miles southwest of the Da Nang airstrip, free of Communist

122mm and 140mm rocket launchings. Because of our experience and success, another unit took our place as a floating battalion when it was our turn; had we become the floating battalion, we would have been the reaction force that was sent to the DMZ [Demilitarized Zone that separate North and South Vietnam] and to Hue during the Tet Offensive. Fate favored us; another battalion did the bleeding and dying.

Being good subordinates, both our regimental and battalion commanding officers followed their superior's example and wrote us letters of thanks. We played along because we knew how brave and wonderful we were. We gladly accepted their kudos, but we were a bit suspicious of these rare gestures of appreciation from the men at the top. After all, we had learned that nothing in the Nam was as it seemed.

After morning chow, which was its usual bland self, my section leader informed me that I needed to send three men on a working party to fill sandbags. With only three squad members awake, including myself, I decided to let the others, who had been on guard duty, continue sleeping.

We went to the battalion's supply bunker where three Marines from artillery joined us. Three shovels and several hundred empty sandbags awaited us. Sugar Bear, a muscular black Marine of average height, worked with a short, chunky Marine from artillery, whose skin was peeling from his sunburn. He was obviously a new guy, a cherry; his weight and the condition of his skin were strong clues that he had not been here long enough for the Nam to work its magic on his young body, much less his psyche. Sugar Bear, who was grumpy when he did not get much sleep, did not bother to tell the new guy about his childhood in DC; he wasn't in the mood for conversation or shoveling, so he held the sandbags open for the man filling them.

Cossack and I, working as a team, decided to rotate tasks every two hours. We were both sweating heavily by the time Cossack took over the shoveling. The late morning clouds owned the powder blue sky, but no rain clouds floated above us. The time dragged by, and we had run out of things to complain about. It was almost time for noon chow, and we were glad for the break in the routine.

"Wonder what's on the menu at our favorite mess hall?"

I looked up from the partially full sand bag that I was holding and laughed. "What else but garbage a la garbage...and it's your favorite mess hall, not mine, Cossack."

Rather than talk about something we detested, we decided to end our attempt at a conversation.

rice paddies looking good today...peaceful and ready for the camera...nice day for a nature walk...ha ha...a fine little day patrol would sure beat the hell out of this suck ass work detail...nothing happening out there...almost as boring as sitting here...sure am getting enough exercise for my back and arms...dumb sandbags...a five-thousand meter diddy bop through the countryside sounds okay to me...might even run into the Cong and get a little action...GUNG HO...your drill instructors would love you Jello...better get out of the sun...it's affecting your brain-housing group...must be at least two weeks since the last patrol when we walked through a super booby trapped area out near Charlie Ridge...clumsy around the tent but no sweat going through booby-trap city...damn lucky...the patrol the week before ran into two real live booby traps...damn glad we found them before they found us...LUCKY.

"How 'bout quitting for lunch as soon as we get another dozen sandbags filled?"

Not responding to Cossack's suggestion, I only stared out towards the moss green foothills to the north. Cossack's second attempt drew me out of my daydream. "Sure. Sounds great."

the paddies sure dried up a lot in the last two weeks...a regular swamp out there three weeks ago...paddy water up to my neck in some places...a real gung ho recruiting poster scene if there ever was one...expected to see good old hard chargin' John Wayne out there...CHARGE...LET'S GET THEM COMMIES...get some big John...anyone want to buy any US Savings Bonds...remember to buy them where you work...LOVE IT...GUNG HO...still raining...finally out of the paddies...some high ground...jungle utilities and boots drenched...more rain...wet on wet...shivering all over...wrinkled white hand clenching the dangling steel cold rifle...our ten-man patrol bunching up...dumb...stretching for fifty meters then turning and snaking south...a tree line to the west...VC ambush site...maybe...too wet to care...then south...a few hundred meters away...near our hill a ville...must be Khuong My 2...the rain slowing down...a thatch hut with a porch...a hog pen twenty feet away...only the sound of raindrops dancing in the mud puddles...eighteen-year-old voices yelling...ANYBODY AROUND...GET THE FUCK OUT HERE...DI DI MAO...old lady clutching a crying baby...her wrinkled face staring down at the baby...SHUT YOUR GODDAMN BRAT UP MAMASAN...WHAT THE FUCK IS THIS...eighteen-year-old girl standing behind the trembling old mamasan...shoulder-length jet-black hair...penetrating dark eyes...gentle unwhored face...a squad of grins and lusting eyes...CHECK OUT THIS BITCH...FINE PIECE OF MEAT...BETTER SEARCH THE FUCKIN' SLUT IF YOU KNOW WHAT I MEAN...two Marines moving closer...pulling up the girl's black pajama top...FINE LOOKING TITS...Marines ooing...FEEL NICE TOO...old lady cursing rapid fire...flapping her skinny arms at the Marines. COOL IT YOU OLD BAG...WE AIN'T GONNA FUCK YOUR DAUGHTER...a Marine chasing a squealing pig...three others joining in...Marines laughing...old lady crying...baby screaming...pig dashing into the hut...two Marines following...a crashing noise...a table tumbling over...the pig escaping out the hut...two grunts huffing and cursing...Marines ripping thatch out of the wall...mamasan yelling and begging...grunts chuckling and pulling out a zippo lighter...lighting the thatch pile on the porch floor...ten Marines circling the fire...drying off and feeling warm...the baby still crying...Marines tearing out more thatch and dropping it into the fire...one Marine straying off and wandering inside the hut...finding a king-size handmade quilt...admiring it and taking it...mamasan protesting...begging...SHUT UP YOU SORRY ASS FUCKIN' GOOK BITCH...the quiet rain stopping...the fire smoldering...the old lady yelling her hate at the Marine squad moving out...laughing their asses off...leaving the mamasan...the girl...the baby...FUCKING BULLSHIT!

    The monotonous nature of filling sandbags made it too easy for my mind to wander. Being ambushed by the all too clear memory of the patrol was beginning to gnaw at my conscience. No one had been raped, killed, or even beaten up, yet the stench of this sad remembrance lingered, haunting me.

    My Catholic upbringing was intruding on my life in the war zone. Having recounted the events in the ville [rural village or hamlet], I began to wonder why I had failed to intercede when the other Marines treated the mamasan and the girl in such a shameful manner; I believed their behavior to be antithetical to the 'code of conduct' which I expected from Marines. These women were not even Viêt Cong suspects. Volunteering for that patrol helped me to escape the daily boredom on our hill, but my conscience paid a significant price.

Unmotivated and unsupervised, we left for noon chow about fifteen minutes early and returned to our sandbags a half-hour late. The men from artillery never returned. We were not sure if the mess hall food had done them in or if they were just smart. While one of us shoveled, the other two could have held sandbags. Because we had no loyalty to the people at battalion supply, the recipients of our work, we chose to be inefficient. They had never shown any concern for our needs, so we embraced their take-it-or-leave-it attitude.

Besides being unmotivated, we were a trio, so one person would rest while the other two worked: one shoveling and the other holding and tying the sandbag shut. When it was Sugar Bear's turn for a break, he hid in the bushes behind us and lit up a joint. Our productivity dropped off drastically, but we did not care. Sugar Bear sat there grinning.

It was soon time for another bout with the mess hall. Sugar Bear, still stoned enough to find humor staring at the food on his tray, gobbled up his dinner and ate Cossack's peas. Once back in our tent, I turned down an offer to play some gin rummy. I decided the folks back in the World deserved to know if I were still alive.

As I was getting out my pen and paper, a squad from Charley Company burst into our tent. They were laughing as they pulled down the flaps at the western entrance of our tent; the night air remaining outside. Someone pulled out a joint, lit it, and passed it around to a dozen eager lips. A few minutes later a second joint appeared.

A burly Marine, the size of a college fullback, moved away from the cluster of soon-to-be-stoned Marines and ambled towards my cot. It was Bullis: quiet, confident and powerful, yet the owner of a gentle face.

"So what's happenin', Jello? Fired at any water buffalo

recently?"

We both chuckled. As he pulled off his steel helmet, plopping it on the plywood floor, I peered up at him and said, "Take the rest of your shit off and stay awhile."

Next to it, four bandoleers, carrying more than two-dozen magazines of M16 ammo, landed with a thud. On top of these he piled his flak jacket, two canteens, three frag grenades, two illumination pop-ups, a bayonet, and a plastic poncho.

"As a matter of fact, we're kinda interested in stayin' up here with you dudes tonight. We just don't feel like being heroes tonight."

"So Bullis and the bad ass dudes of Charley Company want to bag a bush. Sounds like you like living. I can dig it."

Bullis nodded. "There it is. Night ambushes get to be a real drag...and I have a bad feelin' about tonight."

"Shit, nothing's going to happen. This place is too damn boring."

squad from Charley Company...guilty of conspiracy to pull a fast one on the lifers...far out...my kind of people...shitbirds of the world unite.

"Sure hope you're right, Jello."

"No sweat, GI."

We both laughed. Then, opening my footlocker, I pulled out a box of raspberry JELL-O. After I opened it, I offered Bullis some. Unaware of the significance of my offer, he smiled and turned it down. Only members of the Jello Squad were permitted to indulge in the all powerful, sacred sugary grains, but Bullis seemed like the type of person that deserved an extra advantage in the survival game. JELL-O would have provided that magical edge, but he would have to rely on his own survival instincts and fate for the grand prize: a non-body-bag flight back to the World.

Noticing my pen and writing tablet, he apologetically said, "It looks like you're tryin' to write a letter, so I'll leave you alone."

"No sweat, dude. I can write any time. I don't get to see you that often. Hang around and..."

"Thanks, but I think I'll go over and rap with Cossack and Sugar Bear."

"Later."

The smell of the marijuana roamed freely through our

overcrowded tent. The naked light bulb dangling in the center of our tent accented the smoky air. I set my JELL-O box on the floor between my leather-cracked jungle boots. I blocked out the nowhere conversations and the silly laughter. It was getting late, and it was time to write.

2 January 1968
Hi folks,
It's your illustrious son or brother. I'm glad everything is going fine at home. It seems that everything goes well when I take long trips. I guess I better join the Peace Corps down the road for twenty years and good fortune will reign on our house. Really it wouldn't be that long, maybe only two years, that is, if the Peace Corps will take me this time. It seems I picked a bad time to leave since everyone is making a big transition--Bette to a teenager, Mary to a college student, Paul to completion of college and maybe a commission in the Navy and then on to be a sixth grade teacher. You better become an officer so you don't stay a corpsman and get yourself sent over here. That is an order, swabbie. Oh, and then there is me. Wines have good years and families do too. 1967 was our family's good year, but I feel like a failure in the Marine Corps, but that doesn't bother me much since it's so phony and against a lot of what I believe in. But by challenging me, it is strengthening me and my ideals. It's made me want to be a teacher more than ever. Everyday I see ignorance at its worst. It's exasperating, especially when it is usually the idiots who are making the decisions over here. We're lucky there are a few smart eighteen-year-olds over here; otherwise, we'd be in big trouble. Believe it or not, being in the Nam has made me be a better person. I still have a long way to go, but I'm on the way at least. I've also gained a love for reading. I've been reading some inspiring books: one about the Peace Corps, one by Thomas Merton, one about Dr. Tom Dooley, and one about John Kennedy. When I go back to college, I'll be ready. Life has so much more to offer now. Some of the things that used to run my life are now part of the past.

Being in the Nam has definitely helped me to find myself.

Don't worry. It's not as bad as you think it is in the old war zone. Occasionally, I go out into the bush. That means into the field or the countryside, but I don't get to do this very often. About two weeks ago I volunteered to go on a patrol, just for a little excitement. Life on our hill gets real boring sometimes. At any rate, the patrol was kind of fun but not completely. It looked like a news special. Pouring rain and wading through rice paddies with water up to my shoulders in some places. Rifle over the head. The whole bit. I don't know if I would like doing that everyday though. Being a mortarman has its advantages sometimes. Our destination was a clump of trees where a Vietnamese family lived. All the men in the family were gone. They were in the South Vietnamese army. An old lady, her daughter and a baby were the only ones there. They seemed to be okay people. So many of the Vietnamese seem to have been changed for the worse and have become very bitter. Fighting for so long is definitely taking its toll in more than one way. Many of these people couldn't care less who rules them, just so long as the soldiers stop bugging them and they get a chance to grow their rice. For this reason many Americans over here hold little love for them and vice versa. That's what is so sad and frustrating about this war. It makes me wonder if it is worth all the misery and trouble. I just don't know what to think. I'm not for it or against it. One good thing—I can make an intelligent decision about the war, and it will mean something since I have experienced it. There I go philosophizing. Oh, well. I guess that's good sometimes. By the way, I made squad leader. Enough. Write soon.
Love,
Pete, alias Jello
P.S. Don't worry.

Upon completion of the letter, I lay back on my cot. I shifted my sore body, hoping that I'd find a more comfortable position. Going on working parties and standing gun-watch at two in the morning were the type of activities that I had grown to accept in my pre-squad-leader days. After three days at my new position of squad leader, I was beginning to wonder if the job's eagerly sought-after benefits were only figments of my imagination. My sore biceps and the knowledge that I would have gun watch in about five hours were uncomfortably real.

The party at the other end of the tent was still in session. Someone dropped a half-full fifth of Southern Comfort on the plywood floor, which, like an ink blotter, lapped up the precious brew. Most of the whiskey was saved, yet this did not pacify the dozen angry Marines. A rapid-fire volley of the choicest obscenities was hurled against the culprit who was in the process of passing out.

The nearly empty bottle continued its appointed rounds. Almost as high as they had been at their senior proms six months earlier, the glassy-eyed Marines rambled on about the patrol last week. Being stoned on marijuana had made it much easier for their squad to walk unflinchingly on-line into a withering hail of NVA automatic-weapons fire. They remembered how they shouted and laughed as they routed the NVA. Unfortunately for the Communists, they had chosen a bad time to ambush a squad from Suicide Charley, an infantry company with a reputation for kicking ass. Someone belched, and I finally dozed off.

Small-arms fire crackled in the midnight air. The first rapid burst came from a bunker at the western end of our hill. Following suit, several other bunkers opened up with their volleys. Slicing through the black night, fiery-orange tracer rounds streaked toward their targets, flashes of light coming from a tree line four hundred meters west of us.

Springing from my cot, I instinctively grabbed my jungle boots and threw on my flak jacket and helmet as I dashed out our tent's eastern doorway. A few seconds later, I was standing inside our gun pit, which was only about ten feet from our tent. Sugar Bear, who was still cursing the drunk Marine that he had tripped over on his way out, was kneeling to the left of the mortar legs, which we usually referred to as bipods. Pink Rat would have preferred being back in Detroit with his girl friend, but he was our A-gunner tonight. Having grabbed an illumination mortar round, he rubbed his eyes with his free hand. Standing to the right of Sugar Bear, Pink Rat prepared to quickly slide the round down the tube upon receiving a fire mission.

Sneering and grumbling about not getting enough sleep, Pink Rat waited for my order to fire. Waiting impatiently for the expected fire mission, we looked west and could see tracer rounds spraying the area just south of Khuong My 2. Then, Sugar Bear spotted the flashes of light.

"Shit! INCOMING! INCOMING!"

In a split second we were all making love with the ground. A few seconds later, the first NVA mortar round exploded approximately a hundred meters east of our mortar position. Five-seconds later there was another loud concussion. The 105mm howitzer battery was the recipient of these and a half-dozen additional NVA mortar rounds.

As the NVA mortar barrage pounded the boys from arty, my squad and two others were responding by firing illumination rounds to keep the area around our battalion perimeter lit up.

"Fire in the hole!"

As another illumination round raced into the night sky to make the western end of our 1,000-meter-long hill seem a bit safer, the squad from Charley Company was still hiding inside our tent. Most of the members of the truant squad had passed out and were unaware of the assault on our hill. When Bullis peered out of the tent, he realized that the enemy mortar rounds were exploding more than one hundred meters away. His squad was safe for now.

"Turn down the volume on your mortar."

"Sorry, Bullis, but we weren't issued any mufflers this month."

Bullis chuckled and left the tent, carrying his squad's radio with him. The radio check from Charley Company's command bunker was overdue. He knew the captain would be interested to know if they had sighted the enemy mortar positions, which were within fifty meters of the squad's proposed ambush site. Within a few seconds, Bullis was replying to questions, which seemed to be coming from his captain. He wanted to know if Bullis was close enough to see the enemy's mortars.

Bullis looked at us as we fired another illumination round. Squeezing his radio handset, he grinned as he informed the captain that he was so close he could see the men firing the rounds. He knew the captain would be pleased. More importantly, he knew what the captain would do if he realized that Bullis was not describing the scene to the west of the hill, but rather was describing the action going on in a US Marine Corps mortar gun pit on the very hill which was being mortared. Bullis keyed down on the radio handset again. He wanted to laugh, but he restrained himself. He did not want to be the point man on the next company-size operation. He wanted to go home alive. Bullis creatively confirmed his present position.

"Grid six-niner-two...niner-zero-five, over."

We had just fired another illumination round when an NVA mortar round exploded only fifty meters east of our gun pits. Then, a second and a third. The crashing sounds were getting closer as the NVA were walking the mortar rounds in our direction. They had toyed with the boys at artillery; now they wanted to silence the source of the illumination rounds, which robbed them of darkness, their ally.

Bullis, in search of cover, jumped into our gun pit. His fellow squad members, those who had not passed out, scampered for cover, which meant hugging the ground and hoping the NVA mortars did not have their number. Those that were still passed out in our tent would have to rely solely on the luck that had kept them alive during their firefight with the NVA the previous week.

Bullis did not want to take any casualties for the obvious reasons, but he had a secondary motive: if his squad were to take any casualties on the hill, his ruse would have been discovered. The captain would not be very understanding, and Bullis would become an ex-squad leader for his *crime* of bagging a bush [not showing up at his assigned ambush site]. With Bullis protected by the two-foot-high sandbag walls of our gun pit, his odds were improving.

OH SHIT...I don't think we're going to get away clean this time...getting closer...they've got us pegged...should have added those two extra rows of sandbags...DAMN IT...wouldn't do much good against damn mortars dropping out of the sky...twenty years old...too damn young for this bullshit...SHIT...another one exploding closer...twenty meters away...CLOSER...let me get out of here...please...come on God...I was an altar boy...twelve years of Catholic school...what do you want...SHIT...another one...TOO CLOSE...keep moving those damn rounds...walk 'em west...please don't decide to fire for effect...not here...I'm going to survive...got to...GODDAMN IT.

Only a direct hit would uncover Bullis' ploy; fortunately, tonight there would be no checkmate for the captain nor would there be a bull's-eye for the NVA mortarmen. Their mortar barrage continued, but the rounds were moving west, missing us, so we sprang to our feet.

Forgetting my new role as squad leader, I instinctively grabbed the bipods, swinging our mortar in the direction of NVA mortar flashes. I turned the elevating nob until I reached what seemed to be the correct elevation for firing at the NVA mortar site. Sugar Bear, too impatient to wait for the official clearance for this fire mission, was sliding an HE [high explosive] round into our mortar tube when our section leader finally yelled that we had a fire mission. Within a minute, our mortar rounds were returning the compliment to the NVA. Between our three mortar tubes, we dumped a sixty-round barrage on the Communists.

It was now time to restock the gun. The NVA very probably would be back, but we would be waiting. Bullis, being helpful, broke open several cases of mortar rounds as we chuckled about how his squad had duped his captain, who had transmitted his fictional account to the Battalion Command Center. In turn, they had sent that information to our mortar Fire Direction Center bunker where it was translated into a fire mission, which ultimately was relayed to us.

We had successfully conspired to keep the captain in the dark about the Bullis' bagged ambush, and the Jello Squad would not pop any illumination rounds of enlightenment for him. If he were to figure it out, he would have to accomplish this on his own; no help from the troops.

We spent the next half-hour stacking empty ammunition boxes and cleaning up the after-the-battle trash. Just as one o'clock was sneaking up on us, the NVA sent a dozen 122mm rockets on their way: their destination, the air base at Da Nang and its parked F-4 Phantom jets.

The 106mm recoilless rifle, strategically positioned on top of a thirty-foot tower, opened fire on the rocket site. With a gigantic blast, an angry round rushed east; then, more than four thousand meters away a fiery explosion in the far away night, but another dozen orderly red streaks rose up and glided casually through the eastern sky. With the first volley of rockets finally finishing their five-mile journey, they ended their lives in a symphony of angry, colorful explosions: bright yellow, fiery orange, then black clouds rolling up into what would soon become the early morning sky. This all too familiar sight was a photo opportunity for some, a dying time for others.

The 106 fired again, hurling Hill 10's emphatic response. Because the rocket site was just out our range, our services were not required, so we stood on top of an ammunition bunker and cheered as its red steak raced east toward the rocket site. The second volley of rockets was beginning to pound Da Nang when we turned to one another in disbelief, a classic oh-shit moment.

A reddish-orange ball was rushing towards us, the spectators instantly becoming participants. Leaping from the ammunition bunker, everyone scurried for the first available gun pit. We waited for the explosion. The NVA were having better luck with Da Nang. Aimed too high, the 57mm-recoilless-rifle round flew over us like a high fastball, over the plate but not a strike.

The NVA fired another half-dozen rockets into the Da Nang airstrip before they ended that part of their show. For the next four hours, they engaged several of our hill's patrols in firefights. This kept us busy because the Marine squad-size patrols that were under attack needed instant daylight, so we popped illumination rounds for them. When the NVA were careless and were spotted in the open, our deadly talents were called upon. We had no time to be bored. The NVA were on the move and eager for blood.

Less than a mile east of our position, an ARVN [Army of the Republic of Viet Nam] unit was being hit by a fierce NVA ground assault. They had already softened up the South Vietnamese position with an intense 82mm mortar attack. Our illumination rounds were not enough. We began firing HE [High Explosive] rounds to help push back the attackers. Our fire missions were calling for us to drop rounds inside the South Vietnamese perimeter.

A reaction force assembled at the eastern end our hill and moved quickly down the dark road to save the compound from being overrun by the NVA. Not out of character, Sergeant O'Connor, a Marine I admired and our platoon's best forward observer, volunteered to go. Having already served one tour of duty, he had just returned from a thirty-day vacation in London, his reward for signing up for a six-month extension of his tour of duty in Vietnam. The vacation was over; the war was in session. The compound that was under siege would need Sergeant O'Connor's talent at calling in accurate fire support, and both would need a friendly wink from above.

"Keep your head down, Sarge."

"Sure thing."

The NVA ambushed the reaction force just outside our perimeter. NVA mortar rounds and B40 rockets exploded everywhere. Sergeant O'Connor grabbed his guts, rolled over, and died in the darkness of the New Year.

Chapter 15
July 1968

No Longer Killing The Problem

He is working as a waiter at the country club, and he appreciates them for rehiring him when he returned from the war, but he is dissatisfied with their wage policy: one dollar and seventy-five cents per hour. He is an excellent waiter. The job would pay well if they permitted tipping. The extra money would help, but he's on the wrong end of a policy. The GI Bill will only provide ninety dollars per month, but at least the University of Arizona will not be as expensive as Boston College would have been.

He remembers that upon reading BC's letter, which his mother had forwarded to him in Vietnam, his face beamed because he was only one obstacle away from his dream. Although taking a college entrance test in a war zone seemed to be more fitting for a scene in a theater of the absurd drama, he was motivated: going to Boston College would prepare him for his goal, law school. There would be no job opportunities for an 81mm mortarman back in the World, so college would be the answer. Unfortunately, his opportunity to take the SAT test evaporated because the NVA took control of the road to Da Nang. There would be no extra points awarded on the SAT for fighting his way through the NVA force to get to the test site in Da Nang. It was not a test worth dying for. He has since become an archeologist-philosopher, having learned to find the good news, which always seemed to be buried, waiting to be unearthed: fortunately, he had learned about the road closure before leaving his hill.

Fate had determined that he would be an Arizona Wildcat and not a BC Eagle, but tonight he is a twenty-one year old cocktail waiter, who said his goodbyes to his Jello Squad three weeks earlier. The lounge is full of nowhere conversations. Chattering people, emperors of their own universes, are listening to their own stories.

He wishes ten o'clock would hurry up, but he must serve out his sentence: three more hours with pretentious people. He is aware that his boyish face makes him appear like he is still in high school, but he hates it when people call him *boy*. He realizes a little bit of what it must feel like to be black in 1968 America. Although he does not like how it feels, he needs the money.

"Yes, sir...two martinis straight up with a twist." He returns quickly with their drinks. He does not hold his tray steady, and waves of vodka splash over the rims of the cocktail glasses. "One martini straight up with a twist."

He sets the glass on the cocktail napkin in front of the woman. On the tray, the vodka in the remaining martini glass is sloshing around, and the man awaiting his drink is laughing and proudly wearing a smirk. "Why are you so nervous, boy? This job too much for you?"

Setting the remaining martini glass on the table, he wonders why his customer finds it necessary to mock him. He hungers for ten o'clock. He's anxious to walk away, but he answers the man who is still laughing. "It's like this, sir. I just got back from Vietnam, and my hands just shake a lot. War does strange things to you."

Speaking in a condescending tone, the woman tells him that he looks too young to have been over there. Her husband has stopped laughing, but his face is the proud owner of an arrogant grin. "You know what we need to do over there? Bomb those Communists into the Stone Age. I don't know what's wrong with you boys...your generation is just too soft. Back in World War II, we taught those Jap's a lesson."

He wants to tell the man that it is easy to be an armchair general. Knowing that the man is uninterested in his opinion, he remains silent, burying his anger.

"Well, that's all, boy. Don't just stand there shaking. Be nervous somewhere else."

Although his customers are affluent, they are Appalachia-poor in perception, and their hearts are bankrupt of compassion. They only see the expressionless face of a boy with trembling hands without realizing that those hands have fired thousands of mortar rounds and have carried to safety the wounded grunts whose faces he has purged from his memory.

He wants to use his hands to gain their attention, choking the bad manners out of them, but there is no one with rank to reward him with a medal or a gift of a case of beer for killing them. After all, they are customers and not the Việt Cong; it is neither June nor the Nam, where killing the problem is the solution. It is late July in 1968, and he is back in the World where everything is going to be *numba* one. Taking a deep breath, he turns to another table and takes their order. He is a perfect waiter, serving the needs of the players for the next three hours.

At 10:30 he is in a college bar near the University of Arizona. He likes being a customer, but most of all, he likes the idea of getting drunk every night. It makes him feel better, and his hands stop shaking for a while.

Chapter 16
January 1968

A Triangle-Flag Month

January was a killing month. Sergeant O'Connor was dead, and too many of the grunts on our hill were getting old fast. The NVA had just reminded the air base in Da Nang that six miles was not that far away for a visit from their 122mm rockets.

Whenever the rockets slipped through and hit airstrip at Da Nang, some of us felt guilty that we were glad the desk jockeys could finally write home and tell an honest war story. At the same time, we were aware that this was the same way the grunts Up North by the DMZ probably felt about us.

On our hill southwest of Da Nang, rifle-and-personnel inspections and the art of picking up cigarette butts were in full bloom. Up North, the Marines only picked up the wounded, the dead, and Purple Hearts. Khe Sanh, Con Thien and the Rock Pile were all places that provided both sides with *boo coo* death, too much death for the grunt who might have wondered what he was doing here. *Is this a county fair-shooting gallery, ready-made with rifles and plastic ducks? If I am a duck, would someone please wake me up?* YOU'RE IN A COUNTY-FAIR SHOOTING GALLERY, SON. YOU'RE A PLASTIC DUCK AND THE GRAND PRIZE IS A THIRTEEN-MONTH SUPPLY OF HAM AND MOTHERFUCKERS. THE DOOR PRIZE IS AGE NINETEEN.

It was rough being a plastic duck at someone else's county-fair shooting gallery. It was a number ten [slang for very bad] experience. Had I made it up to Khe Sanh, I probably would never have written a single word about it. I would have been a prisoner of the night, with ten thousand Technicolor nightmares haunting me. The forever memories, like NVA sappers, infiltrating the barbed-wire defenses of my mind.

A few weeks earlier, we received the best Christmas present ever: someone wearing stars and a chest full of medals let another battalion go Up North in our place. We would have become a floating battalion, serving as a reaction force to be utilized in the northern part of I Corps. Having known friends who had served near the DMZ, I had a good idea that it was a place that I would willingly skip. I saw no reason for giving the NVA the opportunity to increase our battalion's fifty-percent casualty rate, which was light compared to other Marine battalions. Let someone else have the high casualty rate and the medals. I had been in the Nam for almost seven months, and although I was still interested in becoming a hero, the idea of getting back to the World alive was beginning to edge out my earlier gung ho ideas. For Marines who were interested in the live hero category, Up North was definitely not the place to be. For those Marines who did not mind death, loud noises, and fear, the Up North places like the Rockpile, Con Thien, and Khe Sanh were perfect grubstakes. Such places, however, were not my idea of a good real estate investment, much less a good *anything*.

That lucky December was gone, and we were glad that we could talk about Up North from our hill six miles southwest of Da Nang. January was still a babysan, and we continued to pick up cigarette butts, fill sandbags, and wait.

All my Saturdays in the Nam had been boring so far; January 6, 1968 was no exception. The anticipation of a Saturday night date, hot or otherwise, was eight thousand miles and six months away. The present moment, something that the Buddha cuddled up to, was all we had; however, it would be years before I would recognize the significance of this Buddhist concept.

Having recently ascended to the position of squad leader, I was no longer able to volunteer for patrols with the grunts. My leadership qualities were required on Hill 10. I had morphed into a decision-maker, the person who would decide who in my mortar squad would go on working parties.

Back in the World, Mike MacIntire had been a gymnast and had studied architecture at the University of Southern California, but in the Nam he was the Hippie Kid; he was living my dream because he had recently become an FO, a forward observer for

81mm mortars, which meant he'd be going on daily patrols with the grunts; January 6 was no exception.

The dozen grunts on patrol with MacIntire had spotted two VC in a village near our hill, and there was a brief firefight with the Cong. One was captured, and one, as was typical, evaded capture. Maybe this Houdini was the same sniper who had cranked off three rounds at the mess hall back on Thanksgiving Day. Someone had picked up an easy Purple Heart and a good war story. The sniper had done a Dr-Jekyll-Mr-Hyde routine on us, quickly becoming an instant farmer. He would have an I-LOVE-YOU-LBJ grin plastered on his leathery face the next time he and a Marine squad would meet.

On Sunday we held a gunner's test because I had vacated the position of gunner when I became a squad leader. The results from the gunner's test were less than spectacular. That Sunday would have been a bad day to have been a grunt in need of accurate mortar fire. Even going to Mass earlier that day did not help. A prayer of intercession to the patron saint of mortars was a definite necessity. Unfortunately, the Catholic Church had not seen fit to dub any of its saints with such a dubious title. Hopefully, the next day my squad would make a respectable showing, but we would have to succeed without Heaven's help.

Later in the evening the Viêt Cong initiated an hour long attack on a CAP unit [Combined Action Platoon], which was a few miles north of our hill. For the defenders, a squad of Marines and perhaps thirty South Vietnamese militiamen, the war was actually happening. Up North was meandering south. Later that night the Viêt Cong, who were exceptionally deceptive masters of stealth, made a mistake. A night patrol spotted a force of about one hundred VC carrying mortars; they were heading toward our battalion hill. A forward observer called in an artillery fire mission on this force, but most of the Viêt Cong escaped the unfriendly greetings sent by the battery of 105mm howitzers on Hill 10.

Inspired by these events and realizing that our killing talents would soon be needed, my squad made the gunner's test on Monday something to write home about. Sugar Bear made the best showing, so he officially became the new gunner for the Jello Squad.

During the first half of January something peculiar began

happening. The area around our hill was becoming safer to a certain degree; the booby traps were disappearing. The Marines who went on daily patrols did not understand why, but they appreciated this. The Viêt Cong, however, were not vanishing; instead, it seemed that they were becoming more brazen.

On the day before the Marine Corps Commandant's inspection of our hill, Bravo Company suffered 14 KIAs in a place called the Bo Bans, an area only three thousand meters east of Hill 10, our battalion hill. The operation only lasted two days, but the tears of fourteen mothers would stain their years, and grief would hold a forever-mortgage on their aching hearts. The official letter with its words of consolation would bring no solace; they desperately wanted to believe that the nation was grateful, but they watched the news. And even if the official words were true, a thank-you for the ultimate sacrifice paid by their sons somehow fell short. Mothers want sons and grandchildren, not flag-draped caskets and taps for their babies who died along with their dream of being Marines.

Standing inspection for the head lifer of the Marine Corps was not that appealing of an idea for the average pissed off grunt, but it was much more appealing than sleeping in the cold rain and being shot at by the Cong. I saw myself as a civilian who was only passing through the Marine Corps. My brief journey would be over in six months, so I was not at all interested in or impressed by the Commandant. The inspection would have to go on without me. When I saw his chopper approaching our hill, I made my exit from our tent. I took up residence in a fighting hole about thirty meters away. I liked that tall grass obscured the view of my hiding place from the tent. Then, I heard voices which were calling my name. I crouched lower. Boksa and MacIntire, two members of my mortar section, strolled up to the fighting hole. Looking up at my fellow ditchers, I said, "You dudes scared the shit out of me!"

"Don't be greedy. Move over."

"Sure. Hop in."

Shortly after Boksa and MacIntire joined me, it began raining, not hard, but steadily. Directly below our hiding place on the northern side of the hill was the LZ [landing zone] where the Commandant's helicopter was landing. In an irreverent voice, I jokingly suggested that we fire our M16s on full-automatic in the direction of his helicopter.

"Jello, you're crazy, but it sure would be funny."

"They'd probably even call in for a fire mission for us at 81s."

"Okay, we won't do that, but let's sing our favorite song...the Marine Corps Hymn."

Laughing and singing off key, "From the halls of Montezuma to the shores of Tripoli, we will fight or hide from the Marine Corps Commandant, dah dah, etcetera...okay, enough gung ho crap."

MacIntire was grinning, and his eyes were advertising a scheme. "Hold on, you two. What we should do is run down the hill...go up to the lifer and make all sorts of crazy monkey noises, and when he's about ready to have someone arrest our asses, I'll tickle him under his chin."

"Now that should do the trick. They'll have to give us a Section 8 after that stunt."

Boksa, unimpressed with our logic, replied, "Bullshit, Jello. We ain't never gonna get out of this shithole that easy. I tell you what, I'd like to forget about tickling that fucker's chin. A good swift kick in his Marine Corps regulation ass sounds like a better idea to me."

With both of us laughing, I turned toward MacIntire. "Bitter, bitter, bitter. Boksa, you have to admit you're pissed off because you were a dummy for signing up for a four-year hitch in this Green Machine. Well?"

A sullen Boksa knew we that were right, so he pouted while the Commandant of the Marine Corps inspected our hill, never missing us—three insignificant cogs in the war machine. A happy Commandant left our hill; after all, there weren't any discarded cigarette butts to be found during his inspection. If only our battalion could only clean up the countryside of the guerrillas as effectively as we had de-butted Hill 10.

Although we had yet to eliminated the Communist threat from our TAOR [tactical area of responsibility], a proud Commandant left a clean hill in a dirty war, where even our piss-tubes stood respectfully at attention. Main Street in the Nam shrank as his chopper crawled across the afternoon sky. There would be more ceremonies and inspections somewhere else.

The following day, promotions came out. My disappointment was becoming routine. Seven months as a lance corporal in a war zone was like being in the third grade for two years. I was not interested in the power that came with the rank of corporal; it was the extra fifty dollars each month that interested me. I was not greedy, just tired of making one hundred and eighty-six dollars a month.

I was aware that President Johnson was fighting a war on poverty back in the World, but I was beginning to wonder when he would attack my poverty. Luckily for us, our two-beer limit only cost us twenty cents: almost one hour's wages. Picking cantaloupes in Yuma, Arizona the summer before I joined the Marine Corps ran a close second. Although the *benefits* were similar, the only difference was that no one shot at me in Yuma.

January 14, 1968 was a Sunday: a praying day, a mail-from-home day. And typically, there was time for guard duty and work details for my squad. For nine men in Charley Company, it was a Purple-Heart day; for two others, it was their going-home-forever day; for the rest of us, one way or another, we would have to wait for our day.

We spent the following two days laying extra concertina [coiled] barbed wire around our battalion perimeter. We knew that the Communist sappers [elite forces who use stealth to infiltrate defensive perimeter to demolish key objectives] could easily sneak through our defenses or blast a path through them with Bangalore torpedoes or other explosive devices, but the lifers wanted to think that the hill would be safer with additional strands of barbed wire. They gave the orders, so we humored them and strung the wire.

Sometime in the middle of the day, a squad on patrol captured a North Vietnamese officer and brought him back to Hill 10. According to the rumor, upon giving up, he had talked like a machine gun. Supposedly, a force of twelve hundred NVA were planning to assault our hill that night, so we slept by our mortar.

In all directions and a thousand nervous meters away from our hill, squads of grunts set up their ambushes. Smoking dope would make it easier, especially for the grunts at their ambush sites south of Hill 10. The NVA force would come their way from Charlie Ridge, which was only about four thousand meters south of our battalion hill. The ridge was not named after the boys in Charley Company, but for the Communists who swarmed over it like the Lakota, the Arapaho, and the Northern Cheyenne at the Little Big

Horn. Charley Company would be ready and waiting but secretly hoping that the shadowless night would remain black and reticent with a dash of quiet.

No shadows. No battle. Only rumors that disappeared with the winking of the morning sun. Everyone was one day shorter in the Nam, but there would be other nights for the NVA to come out from the shadows.

Several days later I wrote only five words in my diary: *Saturday--the war drags on.* The following nights were cold, not teeth-chattering-Iowa-winter cold, but cold just the same. The days were warmer while we were filling sandbags. We were certain of one thing: our squad would set the world's record for filling sandbags. We had become connoisseurs at this art.

As far as we were concerned, the new synthetic sandbags were worthless, but someone far away had decided the synthetic bags were superior to the cloth type because they were guaranteed not to rot. The experts, however, failed to realize these sandbags were temperamental and did not like to stay in place well. On the bright side, they would last for years unlike the cloth bags, which tended to succumb to the harsh weather of Southeast Asia. I began to wonder why the Pentagon would want us to have such durable sandbags if the war effort were going so well.

It had been raining all day: gentle rain on a no-mail-Friday. Now our ammunition bunker was three layers of sandbags safer. It was nice to believe that. The Pueblo Incident was under discussion at the United Nations, and we were pleasantly surprised that the mess hall had given us strawberries for evening chow. This rare event predictably happened on a Sunday. It was Friday, and the Marine Corps was keeping us guessing.

After reading Dr. Tom Dooley's *The Night They Burned the Mountain* for about an hour, I decided to ease my guilty feelings about having not written home during the previous two weeks.

26 Jan 68
Hi folks,

It's the tardy letter writer again. I'm sorry, but I just haven't been in the mood to write. I should write more, but I can't find enough quiet to write. About five days ago I gave my Jello Squad the national citizenship test. They did pretty well on it; however, we got into this heated argument that night. A couple of the guys were really hurting when it comes to thinking logically. One John Birch type and one dude who just follows orders without questioning them. As you can probably imagine, I was standing on top of a table built out of ammunition boxes, screaming and yelling and trying to sober them up. The Birch type was out in right field playing catch with Mussolini, so I won't bore you with his problem. The other guy is an okay person, a farm boy from Pine Bluff, Arkansas who would do anything for you. Very unselfish but very unquestioning. I asked him why he was in Vietnam, and his answer was like every other answer I've heard. BECAUSE I WAS SENT HERE. So I probed a bit further and asked exactly why he was here. BECAUSE I HAVE TO BE SINCE I GOT ORDERS TO COME OVER HERE. He didn't know what to say when I asked him what he would do if someone gave him orders to walk across the LA freeway blindfolded. He thought this would be dumb since he could get killed. Then I came up with a hypothetical situation: what would you do if you were given orders to shoot someone who was an enemy of our country. Remember that the orders are being given by a general who is very important. GUESS I'D HAVE TO FOLLOW THE ORDERS. I double checked to make sure he really would follow these orders. He agreed once again. Then I hit him with a real whammy. I wrote out his orders from the general on a piece of paper. I folded it over, and as I handed the orders to him, I asked him one last time if he would follow the orders even if he didn't like them. He nodded his agreement. The stage was set. He read the orders and looked up with a drained look on his boyish face. He was stunned. The orders read: you will kill President John F. Kennedy. We have absolute proof that he is a Communist agent. I wasn't very nice, but at least now he will think about his reasons for doing things.

Every time I run into such a situation, I get inspired and realize that if I ever get out of this place, I must join the Peace Corps or become a teacher. Oh yes, I received

the pictures, and Paul just doesn't look like the Navy-officer-lifer type, but if it will keep him from being a corpsman in the Nam, then let him be an officer. Everyone thought Mary looks good, but they didn't like her boyfriend's long hair too much. Thanks for the package, and please send some more Saturday Review, Time and Newsweek magazines. Tell father to stay well. If I can stay out of the hospital in Vietnam, then he should be able to do the same back in the World. My mustache is looking good. Nice and bushy. They're finally legal now. 140 to 154 days left. Write soon.
LOVE,
Jello

Never tiring of His routine, God rolled up the pastel tapestry of His sunset and began sprinkling the velvet night with millions of stars: grains of salt casually spilled on God's evening table cloth. There were no traffic sounds. No engines being revved up as public proof of the drivers' manhood, just the noisy gossip of the night bugs with their tinnitus soundtrack. Being a good son, I had conveniently neglected to inform my family about the large North Vietnamese Army force of at least twelve hundred men that were attempting to encircle our battalion's hill; however, the night bugs knew.

If the entire NVA force decided to attack us, our typically under-strength battalion would become an ex-Marine battalion. I was not an apostle of reincarnation, so the idea of becoming permanently dead at the age of twenty was very unpopular with me. Going home in a green plastic bag with the letters KIA seared into my heart was not exactly part of my current plan. I was determined that the ending in my script would be much different and much healthier for me. A mundane death in my sleep in my golden years sounded much better.

The day before I had written my letter home, I had planned on going into Da Nang with a radio operator named Andy. When I checked my finances, I decided to remain on Hill 10. I was usually broke because I sent home most of my money. Each month fifteen dollars went to *Save the Children Foundation* to aid a Vietnamese family which I was sponsoring, and about one hundred and fifty dollars was deposited in my savings account for a new sports car. Once back in the World, I would drive in style; I had walked enough in the Nam.

Andy left for Da Nang without me. He and another corporal from our mortar platoon hitched a ride on a six-by truck. About a half mile down the road, the truck hit a land mine. Amazingly, no one was killed, but Purple Hearts were the order of the day. It had started out as a too-close-for-comfort day, and the rumors about the impending Communist assault were making January 25 a very unpopular day with me. I told my diary of our predicament: *We are supposed to get overrun tonight or tomorrow, and Da Nang is supposed to get wiped off the map. Our hill is low on men, and Bravo Company is still out on an operation.*

If the North Vietnamese were out there, my family would have to find this out from the newspapers and Walter Cronkite. I was not going to worry them with the truth about our predicament. They, moreover, did not realize that it would take more than twelve hundred NVA to stop me from doing what I wanted. I would be a survivor.

If I died as a Marine, I would wander through eternity like the Ancient Mariner, my dress green uniform as my albatross. This macabre scenario was so terribly frightening that I was determined to make it back to the World and die as a civilian in any decade other than the sixties. KIA would not be the last entry in the resumé of my life.

A day later, we had a relatively small fire mission. We fired our deadly message, ten mortar rounds. For our target, it was a bad day, a final day bathed in that light at the end of his tunnel. For us January 26, 1968 was a good day because my squad had excellent coverage of target, but the target, like all targets, had a name but no longer any use for his dreams.

In the morning I went to Sunday Mass with two friends. Having drunk crankcase oil that pretended to be coffee for chow, I hoped for strawberries at evening chow. No strawberries. Instead, the hill went on a one hundred-percent alert. The official rumor was that a patrol from Charley Company had captured a North Vietnamese battalion commander, and he was carrying a detailed map of our hill's defenses. We were up most of the night, but the NVA had enough sense to stay away.

The following night, however, the Communists were on the move. We fired a series of illumination rounds for the grunts who were out on night ambushes. There were even some night air strikes by jets from the airbase at Da Nang. Several Huey Cobra helicopter gunships prowled the night sky near our hill, pouring their rockets and machine-gun fire into the enemy troops on the ground. A large concentration of NVA were massed about five thousand meters southwest of Hill 10, so the 105mm howitzer battery on our hill pounded them relentlessly. It was an exhausting night but a successful one for artillery, who were responsible for forty NVA kills.

The NVA were out there waiting. If they wanted our hill, they were going to pay an expensive price for their real estate investment.

Chapter 17
January 1968

Some Orders Beg To Be Disobeyed

The JELL-O box was empty. A thousand grains of raspberry JELL-O wondered why their namesake had sprinkled them haphazardly around a gun pit in a place called the Nam. This man was not only crazy, he was cruel. Raspberry JELL-O did not belong on the ground in Southeast Asia, but in a refrigerator back in the World.

The Polish Pink Rat poked his too-young-to-be-in-the-war face out the rear entrance of our tent. His squinting was not from the sun, which was sneaking off in the west. Certain of my insanity, he shook his head. If only he had been the mythical officer who sent the crazies home, but unfortunately for me, he was only a Polish-American private first class wanting his two-year enlistment in the Green Machine to hurry up and become history so he could return to Detroit and his woman.

Pink Rat's fiancée loved letter writing as much as she loved him. Passionate love poured in faithfully from Detroit everyday. At the current rate, another three hundred and fifty epistles from his Mo Town love were due before Pink Rat would escape the Nam; however, if he were to leave the war zone early in a body bag, there would be no more letters, just a monsoon of sorrow in Motor City. They were high school sweethearts from the heartland; love would conquer all, and her undying love would protect him.

We envied his volume of mail, yet we were also thankful that we were not reminded daily about what we were missing back in the World. It was much easier to plug in Monologue Number One every morning. The bad thing was that everyone plugged in bitch-

and-moan-about-the-Crotch-and-the-Nam: Monologue Number One. What was worse, there was not even a Monologue Number Two. We heard one another, but no one listened. It was not worth the investment. We could not afford to get too close; it was safer that way.

"You do realize you're being strange again?" Pink Rat, chuckling and scratching his blond porcupine hair, sat down on the two-foot high sandbag wall of our gun pit.

"I know you're dying to know why I was sprinkling a box of JELL-O around the gun pit. Right?" Pink Rat nodded in agreement.

Grinning, I knew I had a captive audience. Pretending to be serious, I lowered my voice. "Well, my Polish friend from the car capital of the world, it's like this...Word is that we're supposed to have a division or two of NVA all around us...ten to one odds and all that...and I'm just taking some life saving precautions. When the red tide from the North decides to do a General Custer on us, well...this kid will skate out of that bummer. As I was saying, young lad, when the NVA swarm over our beloved Hill 10, they will slam on their brakes at the Jello Squad's gun pit...just like nasty old Attila the Hun was stopped at the gates of Rome back in the olden days by Pope Mung the Third."

"Pope Mung the Third?" Pink Rat winced, positive that I deserved a Section Eight discharge from the Marine Corps.

Opting for a little digression, I feigned sincerity and said, "You mean you never heard of that dude? He was a tall, short, fat, skinny dude. A far out pope. I think he was from Fresno."

I looked at Pink Rat whom I had only met a month earlier. His forehead was wrinkled up in disbelief. Only a single word dared to escape his mouth. "Fresno?"

"Well, I guess it could have been Topeka, That's in Kansas, isn't it? Who cares where Topeka is? I don't. On second thought, I do. In fact, I'm pissed off at Topeka. It's back in the World, and I'm stuck in this shithole for another five months. As matter of fact, I'm pissed at Dorothy and Toto. They survived a tornado, the wicked witch from wherever, and all sorts of weird crap. And all she had to do is click her magical shoes together and make a wish."

The tone in my voice became caustic as I continued. "But I'm in the Nam, and all I have are my beat-to-hell jungle boots, and clicking 'em together wouldn't do shit."

In an unsympathetic voice, Pink Rat fired back at me. "Twelve months left for this lovesick Pink Rat. That's one year, by the way. Damn, I should have been in the Army and had a twelve-month tour. But no, the Marine Corps had to out do the doggies. Thirteen months. Fun!"

There was nothing better to do, so Pink Rat, the helpless victim of my story-telling antics, politely let me continue my fantasy. "I'm sure you have realized by now that JELL-O is a magical substance. Now that I've sprinkled JELL-O around our gun pit, there's an invisible, protective shield around it. No commie bullets or shrapnel can penetrate it. Can you dig it? We're one hundred percent safe."

"Crazy. Demented!"

I responded sarcastically, "Thank you, but don't waste your time kissing your squad leader's ass. You still have guard duty tonight. But before you go, why don't you help me write a hard ass letter to that chick back in Ohio. See if your bizarre friend, the one with the Fu Manchu, wants to help out."

"Cossack?"

Smiling, I replied, "Yeah, that's the dude. He seems as crazy as me. Somehow I'm going to have to get him into the Jello Squad. The insane must stick together. Right?"

Once inside our tent, which was about twenty feet from our gun pit, Pink Rat made an excuse for leaving early for guard. I pretended to believe him, but I sensed that he wanted to avoid being part of our cruelty. Had he remained, he probably would have said something mature and sobering like, "You shouldn't mislead that poor girl." We liked him, but we were glad he would be on guard and unavailable for sermons, but he did ask me a completely unexpected question about the reason why I chose to be the kind of squad leader I was. He was on the mark; my leadership style was definitely atypical for the Marine Corps. Pink Rat continued, "I was wonderin' why you do the nasty job of cleaning the mortar base plate when you're officially suppose to just dust off the sight. A cake job. You're a squad leader, so why would you choose to do the job of a lowly ammo humper?"

I was in a goofy mood, so his serious question threw me off for a moment. "Hmm. Interesting question. I guess I figure I'm no better than the newest ammo humper without any power. Our squad is a team, and we all work for the same goal. Give the fastest and most accurate fire support to the grunts who need someone to take care of them. Save their asses. I guess I want everyone in the Jello Squad to give a hundred percent and do whatever's necessary to get the job done. I like to lead by example, and that's Jello power." I nodded my head and said, "Yeah, that's it." Pink Rat smiled and gave a thumbs up as he walked away.

With our mature conversation out of the way, it took Cossack and me about an hour to write the letter, but it would be a week before a gullible Ohio girl would read our John Wayne letter. As I read it aloud, Cossack and I laughed uncontrollably. It took almost five minutes for me to read our literary masterpiece. I had not realized what a hero I was. It was fun pretending.

I looked at Stan who was sitting on his cot, listening intently to our verbal antics. Although he was typically gregarious, he had shifted into a pensive gear. I sensed that he was beginning to regret giving us the girl's name and address. I asked, "Well, how'd the letter sound?"

Stan scratched his sandy-brown, Ohio head and sighed. "If that chick ever finds out that you've been feeding her the biggest line of shit since the recruiter talked me into joining this Green Machine, well..."

"No sweat, GI, a truly great bullshit artist never gets caught," I said confidently.

Unimpressed, he blurted, "Thanks a hell of a lot, Jello! That'll do me a lot of good if she decides to claw my eyes out."

Before I could reassure Stan that his eyes would remain unmarred, my A-gunner Legget, agitated by the ruckus, interrupted, "Think you crazies could hold it down. I'm trying to read." His eyes, glaring at us, peered over the top edge of his comic book, which covered the rest of his face. Because we were grinning and snickering, he quickly sat up, his comic book no longer masking his angry, eighteen-year-old face. "Stop interrupting my reading!"

Aaron C. Legget was from Chicago, and proud of it. He had never been caught in the simple act of walking. He was a strutter. He belonged in the '50s, riding shotgun in a cherry-red '32 coupe with James Dean at the steering wheel. Sadly for him, life had been cruel: it was 1968; he was resting on a cot in the Nam; and I was only the Jello Kid, not James Dean. His script had been poorly written, so Aaron C. Legget's face was a neon sign of cocky disgust.

Stan's worries had taken a backseat to an opportunity for Cossack and me to harass Legget, so Cossack fired his first zinger. "Read? But how can you *try* to read your comic book if you can't read in the first place?"

"Shove it, asshole!"

"Jello, I think he likes me. Maybe if I treat Aaron C. Maggot nice he'll let me read one of his comic books."

Not appreciating Cossack's sarcasm, he blurted, "Legget's the name!"

It was my turn to mock him. "Sure, Maggot, anything you say, but please put on your shirt. Your sexy chest is turning on Stan and Cossack."

A chorus of "BULLSHIT!" thundered back at me. Everyone but Legget was laughing. Shaking his head in disgust and realizing that the battle was lost, he retreated behind his half-finished comic book.

My A-gunner had quickly faded into ancient history. Returning to the letter, we chuckled about the absurd statements that it contained. I wondered aloud, "Do you really think that chick will believe the line about me holding off the NVA battalion single-handedly?"

Grinning as he looked directly at Stan, Cossack mocked him. "Since she's from Ohio, I guess she would buy all this bullshit. Dumb chicks there. Not like Michigan chicks."

Ohio womanhood had been slandered, so Stan let Cossack know that Michigan men were the only creatures dumber than Michigan women. The feud continued, with neither Cossack nor Stan giving in. Because I was from Arizona, I knew they were both wrong. I was feeling bored, so I lay back and pretended that I was sleeping in a bed and not on a sagging Marine Corps cot. January 30, 1968 was preparing to die, and I was beginning to doze off, wondering why the rice fields around our hill had become deserted.

where are the farmers...even the birds are quiet...must be that Buddhist holiday...Tet...their New Year...there's supposed to be cease fire for a couple of days...definitely could use some peace and quiet around here...about time...we're supposed to be winning...at least that's what Westmoreland and LBJ think...sure would be nice to win the damn thing and get the hell out of here early...five more months in this suck hole...bummmmer.

The quiet night was my friend. I was asleep.

Through the deserted village, they crouched, and with each silent step, moving closer. First, the barbed wire. Then, the bunkers. The ghost enemy coming, magically slicing through the coal black night. The stillness, undisturbed. The rancid odor of the dead chicken, which had been placed at a weak point in the concertina wire in the battalion's perimeter, drew them on like a magnet. Closer now. Sappers snaking and crawling in secret silence, closer. But the crickets, spectators for tomorrow's headlines, knew.

A nervous Marine on bunker watch at the eastern end of the hill thought he heard something in the village. He calmed himself by firing his rifle, eighteen quick rounds into the barbed wire that separated the village from his bunker.

Muzzle flashes from the ville. Unfriendly shadows firing back. The bunker riddled with NVA bullets. A dozen Purple Hearts for those sandbags. Pink Rat slammed another magazine into his rifle. This time the other two Marines joined him, cranking off their M16s on full- automatic as a siren began its wailing, signaling that Hill 10 was under attack.

"Fire mission! Fire mission!"

Springing up from my cot, I instinctively and methodically grabbed my jungle boots, helmet, M16 and a bandoleer of M16 ammo. Within a few seconds, I was slipping on my flak jacket, which was waiting for me at the gun pit, yet Sugar Bear, my gunner, was not. The obnoxiously loud sound of our hill's newly installed siren failed to break into Sugar Bear's dream world; he was a firm believer that sleep was what 1:00 a.m. was all about, war or no war.

Because my gunner was unavailable, I grabbed the mortar, swinging it to the northwest. About five hundred meters in that direction, tracer rounds were cutting through the night. Red and green slicing black. The quiet, gobbled up by a steady burst of machine-gun fire from a Marine squad at their ambush site. Ten M16s and an M14 rifle pouring out their ammo on full-automatic.

Then, a red star cluster popped overhead, Fourth-of-July fireworks for the Marine squad set up in the tree line. We anxiously waited for a second red star cluster, but it did not appear. Fortunately, the squad was not being overrun, but they still needed our help to evade the NVA whom outnumbered them.

Sugar Bear, having finally persuaded his drowsy body to vacate the tent, grumbled as he strolled into the gun pit and sank to his knees to the left of the mortar bipods. Although groggy and unhappy, he was ready for a fire mission. It was now up to the FDC [Fire Direction Center] boys to provide us with our fire mission, so we waited.

I knew we would wait for three to five minute before there would be clearance from all the appropriate channels, but I was angry with Bear for his casual approach to the fire mission. "No shit, Bear! Where the hell you been?"

Ignoring my question, he replied, "I wish they'd turn that jive-ass siren off. How the fuck they expect me to catch some zees?"

There was no time to argue with my sleepy gunner. Our section leader began shouting the deflection, elevation, and charge needed for the fire mission. The grunts involved in the firefight northwest our hill would have to wait their turn for fire support from 81s. Someone with more rank thought they could hold their own for now; the situation at the eastern end of our hill took priority.

Sugar Bear, my gunner, grabbed the mortar bipods and swung the mortar tube due east. Within ten-seconds Legget, the A-gunner, was sliding the first of three illumination rounds down the mortar tube. Our instant light show lasted for another two minutes. Pink Rat and the other men on bunker watch at the eastern end of Hill 10 appreciated being able to see their North Vietnamese attackers.

Pink Rat is wondering what is going on out there. The village just south of the barbed wire is supposed to be deserted. Bunker watch is supposed to be for watching, not for fighting. The trip flares out by the wire probably won't work, and he wishes the Marine next to him had not forgotten to bring the box of hand grenades. He is glad that at least he set the Claymore mine out by the wire, but then he wonders if he will squeeze the electrical detonating device if they break through the barbed wire perimeter, or will he be a cherry and freeze. Then, an "OH SHIT!" Pink Rat is certain the NVA sappers have turned around his Claymore mine. His hamburger maker will be pointed his way. He sucks in a deep breath. His bunker is strong. He has filled enough sandbags to know this. It will survive the blast, but all that firepower will be wasted. He is beginning to wonder if he will survive the night. He is certain that getting killed on bunker watch is not what he had in mind for his eighteen-year-old body. He peers down. On the bunker floor he sees several pop-ups. Someone brought some of the right equipment. His grin disappears. They are all red pop-ups. Just what Pink Rat doesn't want. He wants his fiancée in a black January night, not red star clusters popping in a black January night. He is pissed off at God for allowing the NVA to sneak up on his bunker. He is a Catholic, and God is supposed to like Catholics the best.

The NVA machine gunner, who was spraying the bunker with a quick burst, was not interested in Pink Rat's feud with God. His only concern was that Pink Rat and the other two Marines in the bunker should go home, early and dead. It took a twenty round mortar barrage to convince the NVA that Pink Rat should be allowed to survive for at least one more night and one more letter.

As we were restocking our gun pit, we received another fire mission. The Marine squad that had sent up a red star cluster ten minutes earlier signaling that they were under attack was trying to break contact and make it back to our hill alive. They were low on ammunition, but the fifty NVA were not.

Within less than a minute, two of the four mortar tubes on the hill were dropping rounds on the NVA, who abruptly stopped chasing the retreating Marine squad, but a few minutes later the NVA reminded us that they used mortars also. The western end of our hill received their proof: twenty rounds worth. For about five minutes, bunkers on that end of Hill 10 became very popular.

During the mortar attack, we, however, remained standing in our gun pits and returned mortar fire. Because the NVA had concentrated their barrage on the western end of our thousand-meter-long hill, it was unnecessary to seek cover. As long as the enemy rounds were exploding more than thirty meters away, we could afford to not take cover. We were not particularly brave; we just understood what an exploding mortar round could do.

During the next hour, we fired at two other enemy troop concentrations that were within 1500 meters of our hill. It had become clear why the birds and the Buddhist farmers had made their exit earlier in the day. The NVA were moving almost at will in the rice paddies around our battalion hill.

At about 2:30 a.m. the NVA broke off contact with Hill 10 and the dozen or so Marine squads that had set up ambushes in the flatlands surrounding our hill. Finally, no more red star-clusters in the January night. The siren sounded again; this time telling us that the hill was no longer under attack. It was time to secure our mortars and catch four hours of sleep.

Sugar Bear was glad to hear the siren this time. He plopped his tired black body on a welcomed cot. "It's about time the gooks and the lifers let us shitbirds blow some zees. Those dudes ain't got no sense."

Sitting on my cot, I stared pensively across the tent.

dumb...the siren going off...might as well tell the NVA we're heading to our cots...dumb...wonder what they're doing right about now...no shit...of course.

Reaching over, I shook Sugar Bear.

"What the hell you want?"

"You got a watch?"

Rolling over, he leered at me. "A watch? Is this a fucking Timex commercial or somethin'?"

Before he could turn away from my unanswered question, I interrupted him again. "What time is it?"

"2:33. Civilian time. No, 2:34, Jello. Now let me catch some goddamn sleep!"

Sugar Bear's blood pressure surely rose ten points when I continued my unwanted conversation. As far as he was concerned, the dialog was now a monolog: mine. Undeterred, I continued, "Don't waste your time tryin' to go to sleep. The NVA are going to rocket the holy shit out of Da Nang. I'll give those sly bastards another minute, and they'll be pouring those 122s into the airstrip."

His impatience with me was growing as he shouted, "Shut your goddamn mouth, or I'll shut it for you!"

I ignored his threat. "Unfortunately, for the airstrip in Da Nang, they didn't sprinkle any JELLO around it like I had with our gun pit. Notice that he NVA didn't overrun our hill. It's the magic of JELLO. There's the proof, but Da Nang doesn't have Jello magic to protect it, so I figure in another forty-five seconds, the shit'll hit the fan. That stupid siren told those dudes we'd be sittin' in our tents feeling cocky as all shit. If they had wanted to overrun our hill, they would have tried that earlier and failed, of course, due to my sprinkling the Jello around the gun pit. There has to be a reason for so damn much enemy activity. Right?"

My mini-lecture on NVA strategy was boring Sugar Bear. A Sherlock Holmes on Hill 10, this he did not need. Sleep, the uninterrupted kind, was the only thing he needed, so he decided it was time for a compromise. He would agree with my theory if I would only let him sleep.

Hoping I was incorrect, yet fairly confident in my theory, I continued my countdown. "Fifteen seconds more..." I stopped abruptly. Bear shot up from his cot, and we stared at each other for a second. We both knew what the swooshing sounds meant. The air base six miles away in Da Nang would soon be a 1968 version of Fort McHenry, and the NVA would be the British. Francis Scott Keyes, we missed you. The killing journey of the first volley of 122mm rockets was on its way.

"ROCKETS! ROCKETS! ON THE GODDAMN GUNS!"

Within seconds, our tent was empty, and four gun pits were full of tired Marines, but the mortar crews were ready. Four tubes pointing north. Our target was a thousand meters away, tucked safely behind a low ridgeline to the north. The NVA had chosen their rocket site wisely. Because the ridgeline to the north of our hill shielded the NVA rocket launching site, our hill's artillery could not reach the NVA position as effectively as mortars could. Likewise, our hill's two tower-based 106mm recoilless rifles were rendered useless because they fired their rounds in a straight trajectory; the ridgeline got in the way.

Although the nature of an 81mm mortar's trajectory was best suited for such a situation, the NVA also were aware that it typically took several minutes for 81s to receive clearance for a fire mission. They could count on three to five minutes to accomplish their task without any interruptions from American mortar fire.

With their mission accomplished, they would scurry off to

their sampans, which were waiting at the Song Tuy Loan, a river several hundred meters north of the rocket site. At least eighty rockets would pour into the American air base at Da Nang. The NVA rocket battalion would escape north. The Marines would drop mortar rounds on an ex-rocket site. It was a beautiful plan; however, Sugar Bear was pissed off at the NVA for interrupting his sleep, and the Jello Kid was unimpressed with proper procedure and other Marine Corps hang-ups.

Under the circumstances, I decided to be the gunner because I possessed the expertise for effectively hitting the area of the rocket launchings. My many months as a gunner had taught me how to instinctively direct-lay the mortar [instinctively determining the direction of a target and the appropriate angle of the mortar tub which is needed to fire a round that will hit a target a certain distance away]. This ability to determine the necessary elevation and deflection to hit a target without following the usual procedures was akin to flying a plane without looking at the instruments. By not having to rely on information from the Fire Direction Center personnel, an experienced gunner could react quickly, thus achieving an effective outcome. Speed was the essential ingredient if we were to successfully thwart at least a portion of the NVA's 122mm rocket barrage on the air base at Da Nang.

Bear, ready to send the NVA a do-not-disturb message, grabbed an H E [high explosive] round and started sliding it down the mortar tube. Just then another six bold red streaks climbed casually into the no-moon night. A staff sergeant ran up to our gun pit. He screamed at Bear. "Hold your fire. The fire mission isn't cleared yet!"

Bear peered down at me. I was on my knees and was like an octopus around the bipods of the mortar. It was pointed in the right direction, and the elevation was set. Our mortar rounds would find their mark if the staff sergeant would leave us alone to do the unexpected, but he was a by-the-book Marine. Fortunately for the men at the air base at Da Nang the word *procedure* was not in the dictionary of my life at that moment. The urgent nature of the situation called for decisive and immediate action; some orders beg to be disobeyed.

what's this lifer's problem...no way are there any Marine

squads out where we'll be firing...no friendly-fire possibility...they're blowing the goddamn shit out of Da Nang and he wants us to wait for goddamn clearance from the C.O.C. guys... BULLSHIT...FUCK HIM!

The Fourth Commandment never mentioned anything about honoring and obeying my staff sergeant, so I screamed my anger at the ground. "GODDAMN IT...FIRE THE FUCKING ROUND!" The staff sergeant tried to interrupt, but Bear ignored him and dropped the round down the tube. Racing up into the early morning sky, the NVA's unwelcome surprise was only twenty-seconds away. Before Bear could fire another round, the NVA had launched another volley of rockets. Six miles to the northeast of us, NVA success. Their first rockets were beginning to land on the runway of the Da Nang Air Base: a peacock of fiery colors, exploding wild flashes of light singeing the early morning blackness. Then another half-dozen red streaks arched up from the NVA rocket site. Soon Da Nang's airstrip would be ablaze again.

There was no time for hesitation, so Bear slid another round down the tube. The other three mortars began firing also. Within less than a minute, fifty mortar rounds were peppering the NVA rocket site. Our killing shrapnel was real, and the several hundred meters to the river became an eternity. Their escape on the sampans, now only a wish, becoming a last wish.

A few more rockets painted their proof across the northern sky. Nearly forty succeeded in reaching the Marine airfield. It was a Technicolor war movie on a silent screen. Intermission was early, compliments of our unexpected mortar barrage. Our shrapnel owned the northern side of the ridgeline. Within minutes, at least hundred rounds had rained down on the fleeing NVA. We continued firing at a hectic pace. Flashing light began silhouetting the ridgeline, and the once-quiet night reverberated with a chain of explosions, too loud to be only our mortar rounds exploding.

The NVA had been caught with their hand in the proverbial cookie jar, and the cookies were exploding. Unfortunately for them, our intense mortar fire was causing dozens of secondary explosions in an area about half the size of a football field. In a festival of death, frustrated rockets exploded, helping an NVA rocket battalion find the light at the end of its tunnel. For them, 3:00 a.m. was a dying time. For us, it was a busy time, a killing time.

We kept firing more rounds. Too many and too fast: over six hundred rounds by the time the battle would end. The heavy volume of firing caused one mortar tube to catch on fire. Luckily, the flames were extinguished, but that tube was out of commission for the night.

Only three mortars were firing, and as we kept up the frenetic and dangerous pace, the smoke from the secondary explosions at the NVA rocket site rolled across the rice paddies. For the living, the battle smoke, thick as Robert Frost's fog, oozed like cloudy grey molasses across the valley and slowly blanketed our hill. For the dead, the cloudbank of battle smoke was their death shroud, the flag on their casket.

This eerie scene was punctuated with frenzied activity around our gun pit. Using E-tools [entrenching tools], a lieutenant and the staff sergeant hacked open ammo boxes. Both men realized the importance of keeping the mortar barrage going, so they even passed mortar rounds to the A-gunners. The four gun pits were like rafts in a sea of empty ammo boxes. Bear just kept yelling for more rounds because he intended on maintaining the frenzied pace of firing, but there weren't any rounds ready yet.

Waggoner, a Marine with an old-fashioned work ethic, had just brought two cases of mortar rounds toward our gun pit and set them down. These cases needed to be opened, so I stopped hugging the mortar bipods. Hopping out of the gun pit, I began opening one of the cases of mortar rounds with an entrenching tool. I had spent several months as an ammo man, so I was well-skilled in the art of opening an ammo box. Before I could pull the rounds out of the box, Sugar Bear was beginning to slide a round down the mortar tube.

what the shit's he doin'...no one's holding the bipods...the concussion will knock the whole damn gun over...WAIT.

"The bipods! Don't fire yet!"

He did not hear my screams as he began sliding the round smoothly down the mortar tube. Diving into the gun pit, I desperately hoped to reach the bipods in time. I was in midair and my head was only a foot away from the breach of the mortar tube when the round was detonated. The round raced off in search of its target. I landed on the bipods a second late, but fortunately, the concussion failed to knock over our mortar.

"GODDAMN...MY EAR, MY GODDAMN EAR!"

someone turn off the war...OH SHIT.

Bear was ready to fire another round, but when he looked down at me, his eyes were a Western Union telegram of concern. My arms were wrapped around those sacred bipods, and my hands were cupped over my ears. Blood trickled out of my right ear, and I wanted to trade my head in for a newer model, one that did not constantly ring at maximum volume. Bear still waited, probably wondering if I had been hit by small-arms fire. I was impatient, and the adrenaline was flowing like a raging river.

"GODDAMN IT! FIRE THE SON OF A BITCH!"

And he did. The John Paul Jones in me screamed for Sugar Bear to continue firing, but then someone tried to pull me away from the mortar. Swinging my elbow around, I hit him. I was grabbed again, this time with some help from another Marine. "Quick get a corpsman over here. I think he's been hit!"

I hugged those bipods as though they were a game-winning fumble recovery. I was screaming crazy things, and it took a third Marine, Pfc. Wagoner from Pine Bluff, Arkansas, to pry my arms loose from the bipods. They finally dragged me out of the gun pit. My tantrum was over, but my head had gone from ringing to clanging with pain. A corpsman examined me and told me what I already knew; I had not been shot, but the stampeding herd of buffalo inside my head made me wish I was dead or at least dead drunk.

The corpsman thought my eardrum should be examined for internal damage, so he sent me to the sickbay bunker because of the blood that was trickling out of my ear. When two Marines carried in a grunt on a stretcher, I looked at his genuine Purple-Heart wounds and left sickbay immediately. A trickle of blood and a headache from below Dante's Ninth Circle of Hell did not deserve the valuable time of a corpsman. I was the Jello Kid, and I had a squad to lead.

A light breeze blew south. The routine smell of battle smoke loitered in the cool early morning air. The black night finally surrendering to the grey of a battle morning in a place called the Nam.

The sun woke up on time. The early morning's casualties were called light to moderate. They did not wake up on time. Someone in Washington said that we had won the battle. Someone in Washington woke up on time.

The Tet Offensive of 1968 had begun.

Chapter 18
Summer 1970

Job Skills Blues

When he is hitching a ride, cowboys in Ford pickup trucks like to yell at him. "Fuck you, hippie!" He wants to flip them off, but he is tired of fighting. He only wants a teaching job.

The Arizona State Employment building is full of typewriters, lines of the soon-to-be-disappointed, and zombies posing as interviewers. It is finally his turn. The woman on the other side of the desk stares down at his application. She has finished reading the pertinent facts about the applicant, but she does not look up. The young man sitting on the other side of her desk is number nine, but she would rather that he be number thirty. Her voice is a monotone as she asks the same programmed questions that she must have dribbled from her lips since John Kennedy had inspired a generation with his call to serve. Obviously, she hasn't heard JFK's call. Her eyes are still avoiding the applicant.

Uncertain if she is even listening, he asks, "Excuse me, ma'am, but should I mention that I am a Vietnam vet?" He has heard public-service advertisements reminding employers to hire veterans. She looks up from her desk for a moment. "Oh yes. That could be helpful. Many employers find it very useful to hire veterans."

She is staring at him and wondering why he is smiling. He is certain his hair is too long for this woman. He remembers that look because he's been down this road before, but maybe this time it will be different. Now he only wants a teaching job, so he hopes that his shoulder-length hair doesn't matter to her.

With an expressionless face that would have made the famous Greek philosopher Stoic almost consider smiling from his grave, she asks, "Do you have any job skills that you learned in the Marines...ones which could help you in the position you're applying for?" Before he can answer, she drones on, "For example, a construction company would be most interested in you if you had learned something about carpentry while you were in the service. If you'd been trained in engine repair, these skills would help you greatly in acquiring a job as an auto mechanic. Employers prefer to hire people who already have experience. Yes. Experience is the name of the game. So...do you have any skills that I should put on your employment application?"

He hesitates before answering. He knows what the Marine Corps has taught him: to pick up cigarette butts, to fill sand bags, to fire a rifle, to fire a mortar, to kill the enemy. He is wondering who is really the enemy. This woman is supposed to be on our side. He wants to teach and help people. He does not want a handout; he only wants a chance, but she is telling him the way it really is: employers do not care if you are a vet. There is no patriotism, no thanks in their hearts. They just want to save money by hiring someone who already has training.

His heart begins pounding faster, drumming his anger. Clenching his fists, his arms beginning to quiver, he leans toward her desk. His jaw is locked in stone, and his eyes glare their message. His chest begins heaving as his breathing becomes faster and deeper. He is a booby trap, ready to explode. He wants to leap over the desk and choke the lady. He wants to scream his rage at her and tell her that the only skill the Marine Corps bothered to teach him was how to kill people. As he stares past her, his mind is saturated with feelings of betrayal, but he is silent, knowing that she would not understand. He knows he has lost. He just wants to go home, so he closes his eyes for a moment and sighs.

"Well, young man, are there any skills you have that I can write down?"

With defeat etched on his face, he shakes his head and mumbles, "No, I'm afraid not."

Chapter 19
February 1968

Crimson Claw Marks Comin' Our Way

In early 1968 Marvin Gaye was singing his number-one song "I Heard It Through the Grapevine." We had our rumors also, but the King of Soul was not there to spread the rumor that the NVA had destroyed the bridge on the road to Da Nang. Supplies were being flown to our hill by chopper. An ammunition resupply truck had been ambushed earlier in the day. The Second NVA Division and their assorted friends were everywhere. Our being low on mortar rounds made us nervous. Having the Tet Offensive spill over into extra innings was not what we had in mind. We wondered how much longer the tenacious Communists could survive American air power.

The jitters were as prevalent as the ever-changing rumors. We had heard that US Army tanks had fired on Hill 22, home of Alpha Company 1/7. The tanks had been traveling at night in an area unfamiliar to them. When they saw mortar muzzle flashes, the tanks opened fire. The Marines on the hill, which was only several miles northwest of us, had heard stories of NVA tank assaults near the DMZ. Both sides, the Army tanks and the Marines on Hill 22, spent several minutes pouring rounds into each other before the mistake was rectified. Oh, the joys of friendly fire. Fortunately, there were no casualties due to this mistake.

Two nights earlier a pair of Marine squads had mistakenly ambushed each other outside the western end of our hill near a ville called Khuong My (2). I had just finished taking a shower and was returning to our tent when the sound of the firefight sent me sprinting for our gun pit. Tracer rounds streaking haphazardly through the black night; half of them spraying our hill. The safety of the gun pit was several feet away.

As I dove into the gun pit, my towel flew off. The Geneva Convention had its set of rules about acceptable conduct during wartime. Because the rules of modern warfare did not provide for the calling of a time-out due to nakedness during a firefight, I followed my instincts as mortarman: I was a naked mortarman firing illumination rounds, which eventually helped the two Marine squads realize that they were ambushing each other. Walter Cronkite missed this X-rated scoop from the war zone: naked Marine fires mortar.

The next morning our platoon sergeant informed our mortar section that we were to move our gun positions to the western end of the hill. As several members of the other mortar section snickered, we cursed them. The move meant we would be without the luxury of a tent for at least a week; worst of all, we would spend our days filling those dreaded sandbags for two new gun pits and a new ammunition bunker.

After two days, we had constructed two new gun pits, but dozens of wooden cases of mortar rounds lay naked and homeless. Their bunker would be built the next day. For those of us fortunate enough not to be on guard duty, the night would hopefully be for sleeping and not for dreaming about sandbags.

At one o'clock in the morning, I awoke with an overwhelming feeling of anxiety, the heebie-jeebies. Then, beginning to feel nauseous, I wanted to vomit although I could not, so I sucked in the cool night air. Cossack and Sugar Bear were being more successful at their attempts at sleep. Although the ground of the gun pit was hard, they were too exhausted to notice. Sitting in the gun pit, I stared to the south at the silhouette of Charlie Ridge in the distance.

wish those NVA would cool it with all their war shit...I'm too tired to be a hero...if it's not the Cong or the NVA it's those goddamn lifers...why in the hell did they have to choose our section to move down here...politics...pure and simple...we didn't kiss their asses enough...I'm so sick of filling sandbags...my recruiter conveniently forgot to tell me that the Nam's one giant sandbag filling detail...it sure would have been nice to have stayed up at the top of the hill...moving is such a drag.

Swooshing sounds from the base of Charlie Ridge, the beginnings of a rocket attack. Streaks of red arching up like crimson claw marks on the wounded night. The first rockets racing closer. They were headed for us, not Da Nang. One round after another, the powerful 122mm rockets slammed into Hill 10. The NVA's 1st Battalion of the 386B Artillery Regiment was paying us back for the times we had ruined their attacks on the air base at Da Nang.

Cossack, Sugar Bear and I, like vulnerable new-born puppies, huddled together in our gun pit. My body was too busy hugging the ground and trembling to notice the trails of crimson poison that continued to paint a path across the black sky. The battery of 105mm howitzers near the center of our hill was conspicuously silent. The evil dragon from Charlie Ridge kept spitting its fire at us; St. George had deserted us, and Beowulf had gone AWOL. No epic hero to save us. No outgoing rounds, only the terrible and deafening sound of the concussion from each 122mm rocket. As loud as two sixteen-wheelers having a head-on-collision, the crashing noise was seared into my memory, never to be expunged, only to be remembered forever.

goddamn it arty...fire back...get off your ass and stop those rockets...they're out of our mortar range...blast 'em.

I was hugging the ground, but then I decided to scan the area directly north of us in case the NVA might be trying to break through our perimeter there. As I was looking toward the barbed wire, which was about thirty meters to our north, a single 122mm rocket exploded about twenty-five meters north of our gun pit. The ground trembled like an earthquake. An angry giant walking, stomping at will on our hill. I grabbed the side of my face, which was stinging sharply. "Oh shit...I'm hit."

Anxiously touching an unwanted Purple Heart, but there was no blood. I had only been sprayed with chunks of dirt when the rocket landed down by the perimeter barbed wire. Miraculously, all the deadly shrapnel flew by me. Helpless tears trickled down my face as I prayed desperately, hoping for some divine intervention.

God...why did you let me join up...you're paying me back for all the times I have acted like an asshole...forgive me...please God I want to live...I'll do anything...I'll go to Mass every day...be a priest...anything...just don't let me die...why won't You let arty fire back...what's wrong up there...I hate one-sided battles...please God...please.

Having heard combatants' hollow promises before, I'm certain that God didn't take me too seriously or hold me to my desperate words. Divine intervention wasn't in the playbook for the center of Hill 10. God sat this one out as the rockets kept coming, relentlessly pounding their primary target, the area occupied by the 105mm artillery battery at the center of our hill and a short distance from my previous stomping grounds.

they're blowin' the shit out of arty and our old position...thank you lifers...you didn't realize you'd be doing us a favor...the NVA don't know our mortars are down here...we lucked out big time.

More rockets making direct hits and others failing; the noisy night air was saturated with dust, smoke and chunks of flying shrapnel. A hundred meters west of arty, three Marines were tired of being sardines in a gun pit. If artillery would not fire at the rocket sites, mortars would. The noise that had enveloped the hill was so deafening that I had to scream on the phone as I tried to contact the FDC [Fire Direction Center] bunker to get the coordinates of the NVA rocket site. Unable to get a response, I cursed the phone. Cossack, grabbing it, began yelling into it but to no avail. The phone line to the FDC bunker was dead, so Cossack hurled the phone down in frustration. "Nothing works in this fucking Marine Corps!"

At that point I jumped up and sprinted away, yelling to Cossack that I would run to the center of the hill to obtain some firing coordinates directly from of FDC [Fire Direction Center] bunker. If the rocket sites were within range, it was critical that someone return fire. The noise from the rocket explosions was so loud that Cossack could not hear me. I had run only ten meters before I made a hasty U-turn, returning to the semi-safety of the eighteen-inch-high sandbag walls of our gun pit. Furious that I had been thwarted, I dove in and rolled to one side of the gun pit. Within seconds, several more rockets exploded in the area where I had been headed. There was too much shrapnel flying around for me to be a hero. Being dead would have interfered with my plan of returning to college in the fall of 1968.

I was still hugging the semi-safety of the ground when I looked up and saw one of my ammo men standing outside the gun pit, laughing like an insane man. Punctuated with a pair of bulging eyes, his face was painted with a permanent grin as he stared at the fiery explosions a hundred meters away. "Get down you dumb shit!"

His laughter stopped long enough for him to tell me to go to hell. "It looks neat up there. Like the Forth of July. Like a movie. Far out!" He wandered away laughing. Aaron C. Legget was the proud owner of a unique view of reality. He was on another planet, but we were on Hill 10.

"The guy's out of his fuckin' mind!"

"Forget him. Let's direct-lay on the rockets."

Arching up, three more rockets headed for our hill. The trio of red lines coming closer as they streaked across the blackness of the southern sky.

I looked over at Cossack and yelled, "Forget it...they're out of range."

"Goddamn those sons of bitches! Fuck it! They went and got smart on us."

Red streaks becoming bright orange explosions. War stories for the boys in artillery. One, two, three. Quiet. The bright flashing silhouette of Hill 10 disappeared as quickly as the rockets had come. Only the black, early morning sky remained to shroud the hill with a deceptive and deadly silence.

By the time a fried egg, sunny side up, crawled over the tree line, the NVA, like Dracula, had vanished. They were gone, at least until the mountains, the rice paddies, and the villes would again be covered with the black cloak of the evil sorcerer, the Communists' ally.

It was time to write to the people back in the World, time to let them know that I was safe. I neglected to inform them about the two dozen 122mm rockets that tore up our hill a few hours earlier; or that a piece of rocket shrapnel as big as my hand lay next to our gun pit; or that the tent next to my tent at my previous mortar position had taken a direct hit; or that the man who was lying in my cot at our previous location had the back of his head blown off; or that friendly artillery from our regimental hill had accidentally hit one of our hill's howitzer positions with support fire, thus destroying the artillery piece and killing several wrong-place Marines. Fiction was the order of the day.

The NVA, however, had become increasingly brash, so my letter writing was postponed. They roamed the countryside like members of a cocky street gang believing that nothing would stop their advances and that they ultimately would push the Americans into the South China Sea; however, the two things that they dreaded most would make them pay for their confident attitude: our air power and artillery.

Hundreds of NVA had overrun two CAP units in our area of responsibility. Jets from Da Nang, Cobra helicopter gunships from the Marble Mountain chopper base, naval gunfire, and a wide range of artillery and mortars blasted the 1,500 NVA that had been spotted on the move toward our hill.

Each squad that left Hill 10 for a day patrol was smaller than it had been a week earlier. Many squads, typically with twelve or thirteen men, had shrunk to only five and six men. Both sides were paying war's price for tomorrow's victory, tomorrow's glory, but the sixth day of February was not a day for either victory or for glory. It was only a day for contact with a stubborn enemy.

For the next several days, the jets from the airbase at Da Nang cruised the early February sky, frequently swooping down on the NVA epidemic, which was tenaciously holding on. Huey helicopter gunships spent hours flying in the area near our hill, pumping the NVA positions with their rockets and M79-grenade fire.

The NVA, who were moving boldly during the daytime, had made the mistake of being spotted by an FO [Forward Observer] who radioed in their location. All four 81mm mortar tubes opened up on the troop movement. A barrage of one hundred and fifty mortar rounds poured in on the Communists. In the late afternoon, our mortar attack ended with the gratifying sound of secondary explosions. A half-dozen enemy rockets had been denied the opportunity of killing Marines.

Three days later, our new tent was finally ready, and Mike Rae, who had volunteered to be a radio operator for an 81s FO, stopped by for a brief visit before going out on a night ambush. On the night the NVA had rocketed our hill, the squad he was assigned to was set up east of Hill 10. He told me that when the rockets we exploding on our hill, it looked like a barbecue and was amazed that our casualty figurers weren't even higher. Fortunately, the NVA had disappeared for the moment. After Mike left for his ambush, I took advantage of some rare down-time, which granted me a rare opportunity to renew my friendship with my diary: *Lifers don't know what they're doing. More air strikes to the west of the hill about two thousand meters out. Got first mail in about five days.*

Pretty quiet day. Pretty tired. Wrote first letter in about ten days. Shaved first time in a week.

I spent the next half-hour trying to remember the details that my diary wanted to know. The Tet Offensive had kept me too busy to keep my diary current for the previous week, but I was finally able to fill the pages. With my diary happy, it was time for the long overdue letter to my family:

Feb. 12, 1968
Hi Family!

It's me again. I received your letter last night. I would have written then, but I was busy writing Pam a letter full of inside scoop on the political, strategic and military situation in Vietnam at the present time. I'll wait to fill you in when I get home. OK? Before I go any further, I must say HAPPY BIRTHDAY, BETTE! Forgive me, but will you be 14 or 15, Bette? Wait, isn't it 15? I've been in Vietnam too long, I guess. As soon as you get the book about Kennedy, please send it. I should have a lot more free time now. Do you realize, I've been here for 8 months? What a place to be during my nobody year. Remember, 20 years old is the time when you're not a teenager and not an adult. Vietnam's a heck of a place to be during this year of transition. I guess I look older, but I'm sure it's just my dashing mustache. My squad calls me 'Mother' because Pam wrote in a letter that I'm mother and father for my men. Another girl called me 'Pepe,' so I'm stuck with two wiped out names, but my favorite and only true name is Jello. If I ever get around to it, I'll send two rolls of John Wayne flicks to you. I look real grubby. Don't worry, things aren't that bad. If you haven't gotten the Save the Children Foundation form yet, just send them the money without the form. I can't get a money order very easily now.
Write soon,
Jello

Chapter 20
February 1968

The Price Of Lunch

Little children with their hunger pains. Skinny junior magicians slipping through our barbed wire, heading for our garbage dump. It was a MacDonald's fast food joint for the kids around our hill.

God-the-Father clouds were tiptoeing on the mountaintops, caressing lavender breasts, spying, knowing that someone had set a booby trap down by the barbed wire. It was meant for us, but booby traps are not smart. It did not even apologize yesterday when it scattered two children everywhere, to places they did not want to go.

And back in the World, ten million people were playing the green-light-red-light game; too busy to notice the God-the-Father clouds that tiptoed on the mountain tops, caressing lavender breasts, spying, laughing at the players below. The car in someone's rear view mirror, winning the race to the next red light.

But in the Nam, by a hill called 10, two children visited Shakespeare's 'undiscovered country from whose bourn no traveler returns,' and their dreams ran off to limbo. The crowd was back. Our restaurant was full. And someone was setting a booby trap that was meant for us. But booby traps are not smart. And they don't even apologize.

Chapter 21
March 1968

They Promised God Anything

The NVA soldiers laughed, and the pinned-down Marines promised God anything. Dying people bled, and it did not matter.

The Marines of Charley Company were certain that the next artillery barrage would not explode, like the others, high in the trees above their position. Marine artillery would finally get it right and be on target; the next barrage would explode with death language for the NVA ambushers entrenched fifty meters up the steep slopes of Hill 502, but my friend Dale, whose intuition had kept him alive for over nine months, had a bad feeling.

Finally, the next howitzer barrage arrived. It was all wrong. It exploded directly above the Marines. The people back at the artillery positions were still firing based on the original target calculations, which had failed to take into account the high jungle canopy that covered the hill. Impersonal chunks of shrapnel rained down on the trapped Marines. Ignorant shrapnel falling, racing to the ground, killing the wrong people. The good guys were dying while the bad guys only laughed.

It was a gone wrong afternoon. Friendly fire exploding again. The pinned-down Marines trying to crawl up the steep incline of Hill 502. Shrapnel dropping, burning, cutting. A Marine from higher up the slope tumbled down, falling hard on a grunt, who would become permanently eighteen in another two months. The lucky-for-now grunt pushed up on the one-hundred-and-fifty-pound permanent casualty figure. Half of the dead Marine's mangled body rolled right, and what remained of the other half rolled left. Being drenched in the dead grunt's blood was not what he had in mind. Two seconds were a year. Flashes of a drill instructor screaming. The marching band at half-time. Saturday night in the back seat of the '57 Chevy. Cruising the strip. The aroma of mom's lasagna a thousand Sundays ago.

There's no way out. The young body-catcher vomited for all those times he wanted to but had not. He did not care that he was not vomiting down hill. He wanted so badly to be puking because he was drunk. No bird sounds. The too familiar, acrid smell of battle smoke loitering over the Marines like a street corner punk waiting for something to happen. Another booming crash in the trees above. Reckless shrapnel raining down, slicing through jungle leaves. More dead men. Someone's heroes finding the light at the end of their tunnel.

That was the day I volunteered to go to that hill, but someone with more rank told me that I was crazy. That was the day, my friend Dale survived the friendly fire and the laughing enemy; the day typewriter keys in a Saigon office pounded, and Hill 502 became a victory; the day someone four miles from 502 pulled the pin on a map, and somehow, everything was all right. That was the last day for the unlucky ones on the slopes of 502.

Chapter 22
Summer 1971

Only

In June of 1971, three very different people had three uniquely different experiences. I graduated from the University of Arizona with a degree in Secondary Education but would spend the following year looking for a teaching position. Tricia Nixon was married in the White House Rose Garden on June 12. Only one Marine was killed in Vietnam during June, but for the Marine's mother, *only* was a word that brought no comfort.

"young ones"

taken...
  vows
  hills
words...
  i do
  i die
child gone...
  daughter, matrimony
  son, mortuary
musiqued air...
  sweet strings sooth
  malicious mortars maim
ceremony...
  plastic, pompous politicos
    garbed in 1971's best 1945
  damned, dead dunkirkers
    dressed in costumes of yesterday's dead
a sigh...
  how nice
  how dead

Chapter 23
Summer 1962

From Antics To Enlightenment

When it came to setting a shining example for her number two son, she was typical of many parents. "Don't smoke. It's bad for you." Both the smoke from her Kents and her warnings floated by me.

As Kennedy was asking us to join him in the New Frontier, I was forging notes that gave me permission to buy those delicious Mississippi River Crooks cigars for my mom. During our first year in Camelot, corner drugstore clerks were either gullible, dense, or didn't care about the source of their sales. Cash trumped a blatantly phony note. I had gotten away with something and was proud of it.

Summertime meant camping out in our backyard with my older brother Paul and Mike Fitz, my friend from across the alley. Mike and I would laugh about our adolescent innocence, and we always found time to mock the noofy [nerds] guys and the skaggy [homely] looking girls we had met in our first year in the big time, also known as high school. In a feeble attempt at appearing mature and intelligent, we even talked about life, God, and politics. Having just turned fifteen, I believed there was more to life than being a junior Aristotle.

Hormones had recently made me aware that there was something more exciting than making a diving shoestring catch in a baseball game with my neighborhood friends. I was still swooning over the fresh memory of Pam, Mike's cousin from Indiana who had captured my teenage heart, teaching it to sprint. When we first met the previous summer, I knew that Bobby Helms was describing her in his popular song. She was my special angel, big chest and all, and I was a bumbling, stuttering fool. I was certain that she either felt sorry for me or wanted someone harmless to be her boyfriend for the summer. Unfortunately, Indiana was more powerful than our summer love, so I bid farewell to the special memories of the summer of 1961.

It was now time to enjoy some cigars; 1962 would be the summer of smoke, and we were certain that we would get away with our plan. It was safe. After my night-owl father finally turned off the last light in the house, we talked about *someday* and laughed cautiously, making sure no lights came back on. The rum flavored cigar smoke filled every delinquent inch of our pup tent. At about three in the morning, we decided it was time to call a halt to our party. Sleep, as boring as it sounded, seemed like a good idea.

As I began to doze off, my sleeping bag felt uncomfortably warm. It was smoldering. I squirmed out of my Neanderthal electric blanket and tried to awaken my brother, but that was useless. Laughing the entire time, Fitzie checked his own sleeping bag, but it wasn't on-fire. With anxiety surging through me, I persuaded Fitzie to help me in the gargantuan task of waking up my brother, who was determined to maintain his residency in dreamland. I had not been as afraid since second grade when Sister Mary Luella literally scared the shit out of me. Desperate tears poured down my face. Fitzie kept laughing, and my brother kept trying to sleep. "Why don't you guys shut up and let me sleep."

We finally dragged my groggy brother out of the pup-tent. I had stopped crying, but Fitzie was still laughing uncontrollably. The bathroom light went on. Fitzie blurted, "Oh shit!" and then resumed laughing.

"Quick get the hose. Hurry, before my old man gets out here!"

My sleeping bag was still smoldering a bit after the dowsing when my father appeared. His hands were on his hips, and we knew that was not good. Miraculously he believed my rather ridiculous story about the fire. "Boys, next time be more careful and don't use matches to read by. Now clean this mess up and come inside."

A few months later, I was not as lucky. With my mom gone for the afternoon, I invited Fitzie over for a cigar smoking session. Obviously, I had learned nothing from my backyard-camping experience because we foolishly believed that my mom could not smell the odor of the cigars since she was a cigarette addict. "What's that?"

"Shit, it's your old lady!" My mother had returned home unexpectedly early. I slipped a half-empty pack of Havatampa cigars under a sofa cushion in my living room. Fitzie made futile attempts at fanning the smoke away. The front door opened. My mom's eyes, which were really radars, rolled back and forth, scanning the living room, and then homing in on my amateurishly innocent face. She wore her signature glare, so I knew that I wouldn't be getting an Oscar for my performance. She decided to lay one of her famous, soul-searing guilt-trips on me. A champion at giving *the look*, she was unimpressed and not duped by my been-to-the-cookie-jar grin. "Mike, I think you'd better go home."

Fitzie backed away, nodding politely. "Yes, ma'am...better be going. See you around." My fellow conspirator was out the back door so quickly that he missed her reply. "Don't count on it!"

I stood, alone, confronted by the judge, jury, and executioner. During the Spanish Inquisition, my mom would have been hired in a heartbeat as an interrogator for Tomás de Torquemada. This was almost as bad as having to stand in front of the entire fifth grade class and sing solo for a lousy 'C' in music on my report card. I had sinned; her face was etched in certitude as she informed me that smoking was a mortal sin, which meant a one-way, all-expenses-paid trip to Hell.

Having listened intently in religion class for over nine years, I was certain that this was one place I did not want to go to, especially on a permanent basis. Eternity was a long time, especially for a soon-to-be high school sophomore anxiously awaiting a driver's permit. I did not want to embarrass my uncle, a Jesuit priest, and my three aunts, who were nuns, by being the only one in the family in Hell. With a healthy dosage of guilt firmly implanted, my mom escorted me to church so that I could have the opportunity of confessing my mortal sin so I could rejoin the flock.

Although she was a smoker, I realized the wisdom in not pointing out her hypocrisy. Just as my going to Hell was unacceptable to her, questioning her was not an option available for her children. More importantly, to me, she held the greatest power in the world: the power to let me get a driving permit.

Almost six years later, I was a staunch antismoker: this time for health reasons. The readily available C-ration cigarettes were uninviting even in the monotonous routine of the long Vietnam days. I still had asthma, and I did not want to confuse my lungs with all that nasty air pollution. The Surgeon General's warnings also made sense. I was already doing one activity that was hazardous to my health, so I did not wish to press my luck.

Although I had made it through the Tet Offensive, I knew my mom's faith in my survival ability was probably waning. It had been two weeks since my last letter, and another week without word from the war zone would mean that her one-pack-a-day habit would turn into a two-pack-a-day smoke-athon. With this in mind, I left our tent and sought sanctuary in the quiet of our Fire Direction Center bunker.

A red and bright orange sunset streaked across the western sky. The mosquitoes were biting. The farmers were leaving the surrounding rice fields. With twilight gobbled up by the night, the Viet Cong would be on the move, hopefully somewhere else. I pulled the bunker door flap down, and with a half-twist of the dangling bulb, I had the luxury of light.

April 22, 1968
Dear Mom,
I've got about two and a half months left. Today we...

I scratched out the words that I had just written. They seemed unimportant. I began again, this time writing to no one in particular. Thoughts that had been smoldering for months poured out of me.

Life's meaning is found in the sense it makes...yet this curious creature must learn from his mistakes...discovery for the hippie is psychedelic...'solve our problems and do it QUICK...halt this foolhardy war...stop and fight never more...the child of the flower she's love...our national bird the dove'...yet is this conflict so wrong...has it produced a patriotic song...NO and why...men live and die...what's so different from any other...the loss of a son still hurts each mother...we must delve into our souls...and parents ask...did we fulfill our roles...some can answer 'yes'...not all...there is still this mess...so many have absolutely failed...for their evil they should be jailed... but still no answer to the question...is it that our souls are filled with sin...only a MAN can answer...an honest one who knows no fear...and he will shout these sad tidings... 'the guilt rests on the pawns...not only on the kings...your moves may seem insignificant...but with each there's full intent'...if we'd make peace in our hearts and not just at the table...an outdated tale we'd say of Cain and Abel...yet we seem to enjoy our present path...woe to its traveler when God shows His wrath...pleas and requests...these sound nice at best...but one day we must take them for their worth...ONLY THEN WILL WE TRULY HAVE PEACE ON EARTH.

Chapter 24
April 1968

Levity

If the NVA had been observing us from the mountains, they'd have done a double take. MacIntire, alias Hippie Kid, was becoming drunk, and he knew it. Cossack was inebriated also, but he was too drunk to admit it as he crawled precariously along the zenith of our tent. He was certain he could finally catch up with MacIntire who was only five or six feet away. Cossack was laughing as he boldly stood up, holding a half-full can of green paint. MacIntire, who had been a gymnast at the University of Southern California, relaxed as he strolled across the center beam of our tent. Several Marines inside the tent were betting whether the canvas would rip when one or both of the acrobats fell.

Clutching a can of shaving cream, MacIntire turned gingerly toward his foe, reaching out and spraying Cossack's dark hair with another dose of shaving cream. Lurking behind his tan, mustached face, wild fantasies of revenge were begging for fruition. Splashing paint on MacIntire would be great, but the paint was green, Marine Green, and that made his vengeance so sweet. The sight of a Marine Green MacIntire would truly be a thing of beauty.

The duelers, both chuckling, were ready for their showdown at the top of the world. Both were staring at each other as though they needed glasses. Both were lucky the Viet Cong snipers had taken a siesta for the afternoon.

"Let's talk this here thing over," Cossack slurred.

Before MacIntire replied, he smiled and belched. "Is that your answer, you drunk Russian commie pinko?"

Cossack stopped laughing. He reached up, wiping shaving cream from his hair, and then wiped his hand on his pant leg. His other hand still grasped the half-gallon of green revenge.

"How dare you call this Cossack warrior a commie pinko! My parents are Democrats. So there! Nice clouds out today...and besides...I'm drunk. So...it's not fair...for you to spray me with your shavin' cream...'specially since I was tryin' to pass out."

It was MacIntire's turn to journey in a time machine back to the days of junior high one-upmanship. He got an *A* for his reply: "I got news for you, lifer, that shaving cream was yours...got it out of your footlocker. So there...to you!"

MacIntire started to laugh. He was so proud of himself. Cossack hurled his can of paint at MacIntire who was realizing that he had no place to go.

SPLASH. MacIntire became an instant leprechaun.

Chapter 25
7 May 1968

Mickey Mouse And The Art Of [sic] Writing

HEADQUARTERS AND SERVICE COMPANY
lst Battalion, 7th Marines
lst Marine Division (Rein) FMF
FPO San Francisco, California 96602

7 May 1968
MEMORANDUM
From: First Sergeant
To: ALL HANDS, H&S Company
SUBJ: PERSONAL APPEARANCE

1. HAIRCUTS. ALL Section Cheefs [sic], Staff NCO's and NCO's will keep themselves and their troops. Well groomed at all times, and shall meet the following MINIMUM standards:

a. The face shall be kept clean shaven, except a NON-ECCENITRIC [sic] mustache is permissible.

b. Hair shall be worn NEATLY and CLOSELY TRIMMED. It shall be CLIPPED AT THE SIDES and BACK so as to present an evenly graduated appearance. The HAIR on top will not be over 3 inches in length.

c. No articles, such as pencils, pens, watch chains, handkerchiefs, combs, cigars, cigarettes, pipes, pins, or similar items shall be worn or carried exposed upon the utility or jungle uniform.

d. Lightweight or standard utility uniforms. Lightweight utilities may be worn with the sleeves rolled neatly above the elbow, with trousers, bloused, and the coat worn outside at the trousers. Standard utilities may be worn with the sleeves rolled neatly above the elbow the coat tucked in the trousers, and trousers will be bloused.

e. Rank insignia will be worn on utility caps, centered immediately below the stenciled Marine Corps insignia. In so far as compatible with operational conditions footwear will be shined and brass will be polished.

f. Utility shirts will be worn at all times, on no occasion will the utility shirt be removed. EXCEPT by working parties or recreation and athletic parties when authorized by the OFFICER in charge. At the discretion of the OFFICER in charge of personnel engaged in heavy work, the removal of the undershirt is permissible. It is the RESPONSIBILITY of personnel to not suffer from over-exposure from the sun.

g. The above WILL be done, any questions to the course of action you NCO's are to take, will be spelled out to you by the friendly First Sergeant, 48 hours to comply.

DAVID E. WILLIAMS
1st sgt   usmc [sic]

Chapter 26
8 May 1968

Rockets!

Pink Rat was still complaining because he had not received any mail that day; the Phantom Shitter had not been caught yet; and Khuong My (2), a village several hundred meters west of our hill, was dead.

The night before, a squad from Charley Company had spotted the NVA entering the ville. Sometimes night ambushes worked out. Unfortunately for Khuong My (2), the Communists had decided to set up their mortars there. We dropped at least thirty mortar rounds into the village. Once we had ceased firing, two squads from Charley Company swept through the ville. They returned within a half-hour, their ammo magazines empty and Khuong My (2) burning behind them. Once back on the hill, the two victorious squads cheered and yelled like they had been members of a team that had won the national championship of something.

The events of the previous night were finished. They had become two sentences in my diary. The page marked May 8, still naked at one o'clock in the morning, waited patiently for the events that I would scribble down later. After another hour of radio watch, I would be able to nod off for four or five hours of sleep.

less than two months to go...getting short is the only way to fly...almost the middle of May...damn...better get my ass in gear...Paul's birthday is less than a week away...Mary's just two days later...if the NVA cut me some slack I'll drop Paul and Mary a line...just my luck the NVA will keep me too busy...and if they don't the lifers will...if you don't get a birthday letter you can blame it on the war...if I ever get around to writing you I'm going to tell you one more time...don't get your ass sent over here Paul...you'd never survive this place...why did you have to be a corpsman...the NVA blow them away all the time...please don't volunteer for this shithole...our family only needs one dumb shit in this dump...I may be your younger brother but I know what I am talking about...stay the hell away...that's an order swabby.

Two thousand meters southwest of our hill was a mountain range called Charlie Ridge. At the base of it, the North Vietnamese were setting up their rockets to fire at Hill 10 and the airstrip at Da Nang, their favorite targets. Several hundred meters west of what remained of Khuong My (2), another group of NVA were also setting up a their rockets, thus forcing us to respond to separate rocket sites. They were learning from their earlier mistakes. The crickets around our hill were gossiping. The Jello Kid was sitting in his gun pit, hoping for an uneventful night and wanting two o'clock to hurry up.

The swishing sounds of nightmare rockets rising up in the black night. Red streaks coming from the west; then, more from the southwest. Immediately, I bellowed, "INCOMING! ROCKETS! Get on the guns!" A hill full of light sleepers emptied their tents and scampered for cover. Firing back at the rocket sites was the last thought on my mind. The memory of the rocket attack during the Tet Offensive had become a permanent fixture in my mind. It had been like a demolition derby. The concussion of the massive explosion of each rocket resembled the impact that would be felt in a head-on collision between two 18-wheelers. Being brave took second place to being alive. Instinctively grabbing my flak jacket, I jumped into an extra deep fighting hole. If they wanted to kill me, they would have to work for it.

The rockets from the area north of Charlie Ridge glided past our hill and headed for the airstrip at Da Nang. My relief at not being their target was fleeting. The rockets from the west arched up, traveling east. The nightmare was back. Hill 10 shook with the concussion of each. The first rocket making a direct hit on the officers quarters for Bravo Company. The center of our hill, their target. Off target, the second rocket swished past a large ammo bunker, landing twenty meters away, hurling chunks of Hill 10 through the morning air.

GODDAMN...wish they'd hurry up and cease fire...last thing in the world I need is for the NVA to think Hill 10 is really Khe Sanh.

The ground rumbled again. I was a participant in a Communist sponsored earthquake. Someone jumped into the safety of my fighting hole. Still breathing hard from his dash to safety, he looked at me and asked, "Mind if I hang out here for a while?"

Smiling, I nodded. "And the rent's cheap." Another rocket crashed into the hill. Attempting to ignore the loud concussion of the rockets, I continued, "A real bummer. What do those dudes think they're doin'. At this rate, I'm not goin' to get much sleep tonight."

"Me either...I'm a corpsman."

damn...this dude could be Paul...bro...you'd better not get your ass sent over here...GODDAMN IT.

The corpsman wiped his hands over his sweaty face, telling me how relieved he felt for deciding not to spend the night in Da Nang. "Sitting on this hill right now is a fuckin' bummer, but Da Nang looks like it's gettin' blown to shit...I mean royal!"

"So what were you doin' in Da Nang?"

"Checkin' out a friend at the hospital...some grunt from Charley Company."

"Good old Charley Company. They always seem to run into all the shit."

He agreed and then told me about what had happened several days earlier to a battalion of the 4th Marine Regiment in the vicinity of the Cua Viet River. "Up North the shit's bad...a genuine motherfucker."

Another rocket slammed into our hill. "The 4th Marines. Which battalion?"

"The 2nd...I think. I was reading the KIA roster at the hospital, and all I saw was page after page of names of dudes from that outfit. There had to have been over a hundred and fifty KIAs...and the WIA list was even longer."

I took a deep breath, shaking my head, knowing the people back in the World would never learn about it. "Those dudes had to have been hit by a fuckin' division. Sounds like they got the holy shit kicked out of 'em."

"One of the survivors told me that just about everyone got wounded or killed. The NVA overran 'em."

"Damn, a nineteen-sixty-eight version of Dunkirk."

A fifth and final rocket exploded, like the others, a safe distance from our fighting hole. Now it was the NVA's turn to receive some incoming. Naval gunfire, long-range artillery from the Da Nang area, and the howitzers on our hill poured their garbage into the fleeing NVA.

The NVA attack was over, but the work of the corpsman had just begun. My five-minute-friend disappeared into the night.

Years later, I finally learned the truth about what had happened to Battalion Landing Team 2/4 at the Cua Viet River at the beginning of May in 1968. Having read *The Magnificent Bastards*, a gripping account of the battle, I discovered that the official death toll for 2/4, the specific Marine battalion referred to by the corpsman, was not as great as the corpsman's recollection. During the three-day fight just below the DMZ, the four companies of 2/4 and Bravo Company of 3/1 suffered 81 KIAs and 397 WIAs; however, the total casualty count for all Marines units involved in the fighting was 233 killed and 821 wounded. As I read this account, I realized again how fortunate it was that our battalion had not been sent Up North. Once more, I had been blessed.

Chapter 27
10 May 1968

Outside Of The Killing Radius

Diary entry for my 327th day in Vietnam: *Went to chow; it was pretty bad. Got about 3 hours sleep last night. Supposed to have inspection at 1400. Went on 100% alert. Didn't have inspection. Worked on bunker all day with Kelley. No mail. Paris Peace Talks begin today.*

Chapter 28
17 May 1968

The Iowa-Farm-Boy Methodist

Mike Rae was a Methodist, an Iowa-farm-boy Methodist. Having signed up for a three-year hitch in the Marines, he was amazed when they honored their promise of sending him through Communication School in San Diego. He proved to be a good investment. He could dot-dash-dot with the best of them. Then, he received his WesPac orders. The Nam would be part of his resumé.

He suffered through seasickness and boredom for almost a month before his troop transport ship finally arrived in Vietnam. He was certain the Marine Corps had provided such miserable transportation with a singular purpose in mind: the troops would be so sick of the ship that they would be grateful to finally be in Vietnam. Although it would be a combat zone, at least it would be solid ground.

Shortly after his arrival, be decided that he did not like the place. It was slide show beautiful, but his Scandinavian heart thumped for the cornfields of Iowa. Even slopping the hogs was better, and most certainly safer, than carrying a radio on patrols in the rice paddies southwest of Da Nang. To make matters worse, he was working his trade as a radio operator for an 81s forward observer attached to Charley Company, better known as Suicide Charley. Somehow, whether by skill or luck, he had managed to stay alive for over ten months.

It was the middle of May, and he was glad for that, but August 1968 was his pipe dream. Hot muggy August and flat green Iowa. The war, the rice paddies, the lifers: these he would gladly leave behind. He wanted his three-year enlistment to do him a favor and hurry up. Then, he would return to college.

But Mike Rae was on a hill called 41, an island in a sea of rice paddies between Hill 10 to the north and Charlie Ridge to the south. For this pensive radio operator, there were more than enough lifers to make him want to be a bad Methodist. It was the 17th of May, and in the morning he would be going with Charley Company to find the war. It would be a battalion-sized search and destroy operation for the 1st Battalion, 7th Marines, and Suicide Charley would become the point element. It was always that way.

The force of eight hundred Marines would fight the Communists in a valley that was twenty-five miles southwest of Da Nang. It would definitely be Indian Country. The battalion's objective would be ten miles west of Hill 65, the nearest Marine outpost. The battalion would penetrate deep into a Communist stronghold, where May's extreme heat would be the friendliest thing they'd encounter.

They'd be out in the middle of nowhere, but it would be a somewhere place, a burned-in-the-memory place, where the promise would come true. Some would be given the privilege of doing some bleeding on an airstrip, near a river, by some mountains, for a flag. Mike does not want to be one of the Marines who will get that privilege. He likes the idea of doing a Douglas MacArthur routine back in Iowa, but he is scared.

He is positive the NVA will blow him away; tomorrow, in a week, he isn't sure, but they will kill him, and soon. Fortunately, he is wrong; they will only wound him and seven other Marines with one well-placed mortar round in two days. A piece of shrapnel will miss the femoral artery in his right leg by only a quarter of an inch. Fate will smile on him, but not before he will receive a second Purple Heart in another two months when the six-by truck he's riding in hits a land mine, ejecting him and not so gently dropping him in a rice paddy.

Being in his tent makes him more nervous. It is an upside-down world, and he knows that the smiles of the other Marines in the tent are really frowns. He leaves the tent and its laughter of loneliness. The silver dollar moon goes unnoticed. Mike Rae is hungry for solitude, a rare commodity in the Nam.

He wants to talk to God, but he has never really talked to Him before. He is sure God is ashamed of him for being afraid, for not having faith. He wants to release his fear, but he does not know how. The pain, the guilt, the fear ping-pong through his mind, stretching it, bending it into a pretzel of confusion. Thoughts of the answer gallop away into his night of anarchy. He begs for his justified executioner to allow the guillotine to fulfill itself.

He wipes nervous sweat from his forehead. His knees hurt from kneeling too long, but he does not care. He takes a chance, desperately begging God to forgive him for being like Simon Peter, the denier.

The instant replay of rainbow armies spilling red blood under blue skies is not for him. Then, he tells himself that he will survive. Someone else will have to be the hero fertilizing the green fields for the next battle, for the next blood. He feels braver now.

After four hours, he is too tired to pray. He falls asleep, wondering if tomorrow the clouds will be looking down, laughing.

Chapter 29
18-19 May 1968

Chicken And Noodles With Mortar Round

It was my sister Mary's birthday, and I had remembered to send her a card. It was May 16, 1968, and I had only forty-nine days left of my tour in the Nam.

That afternoon, just before evening chow, we listened, as usual, to the Armed Forces Radio Station. While sitting on my cot, I looked over at Cossack and asked him to turn up the volume on his radio.

"I'm glad my ass isn't out there." Pausing for just a moment, I then continued, "You hear how many NVA got zapped out there...in one day?"

"Thought they said somethin' like a hundred and fifty. Anyway, *boo coo* dudes kicking the shit out of each other."

"That place sounds like a genuine bummer. Too short for that shit. Cossack, did he say who was doin' the ass kicking...the dudes from 2/7 or 3/27?"

"Didn't catch it, but they're duking it out in broad daylight."

daytime...damn...the NVA must have a hell of a lot of dudes out there to take on an entire battalion like that...hell...just like Tet...runnin' around in broad daylight and stomping on everything...crazy...they must be stoned to do crap like that.

Having missed hearing the location of the battle, I asked Cossack if he heard the location that had just been mentioned on the radio. Nodding, he replied, "Sorta south of here about twelve miles...over by Go Noi island. Suppose to be swarmin' with gooks."

Although I was probably aiding and abetting a rumor, I added,

"I've heard the gooks out there stand on top of their bunkers and crank off their AK-47s at our Phantoms when they go in to strafe 'em."

"They're crazier than shit." With his understatement out of the way, he added, " Speakin' of shit...let's head out for chow."

Shortly after returning from evening chow, we received word from the gunny [gunnery sergeant] that he wanted to meet with the section and squad leaders from Bravo and Delta sections. The meeting's purpose became known a half-hour later when our gunny gave us the good news and one day's notice to get squared away. Sugar Bear and I returned to our tent, both of us wishing that our tours of duty were already over.

"Bear, I think we've been screwed. We're too short for this bullshit. You're almost as short as me...right?

"Yeah, August...right after you. What's the story on those guys? They must be crazy. What in the shit are those muthas tryin' to do, anyway? Sendin' us out in the boonies to get our asses kicked...kicked royal! All those NVA that 2nd Battalion blew away...well, if they're sending us out there to take 2/7's place...shit! There's gonna be one hell of a lot of pissed off NVA out there ready to do a number on us...and it's gonna be a numba ten [slang for very bad] job. Fuck this place...too goddamn fuckin' short for this shit."

"This whole goddamn country is numba ten. It's..."

Before I could continue my verbal assault, Sugar Bear interrupted me. "It's just like gravity...it's suckin' wind."

"The way Gunny was talkin'...sounds like this op will be a big ass one. They're sendin' every dude they can get their hands on out there." "Probably have seven or eight hundred of us out chasin' after the goddamn Cong."

"Cong! Don't I wish. We aren't goin' after those dudes. We're goin' after the fucking NVA, and I have a feelin' we'll probably get our asses hit hard compliments of the boys from Up North."

Bear knew I was right, but he wished I wasn't. "I think we've gotten the royal shaft as usual." Agreeing with him, I nodded in silence. Words didn't seem to matter anymore.

We spent all of the following day preparing for the search and destroy operation, which would provide the Jello Squad with a chance to be grunts. For some odd reason someone with more rank, but not necessarily more intelligence, decided that the battalion would not need the services of our highly versatile 81mm mortars. The battalion's eight mortar tubes were to remain on Hill 22, Hill 41, and Hill 10. The good news was that we would not have to lug an extra thirty to fifty pounds of equipment and mortar rounds; the bad news was that our battalion would be lacking the other half of an infantry unit's one-two punch. The ability to respond quickly with deadly effect was crucial for success when battling the NVA, and 81mm mortars had always superbly RSVPed the NVA; however, for this battle we would play role of grunts, so we needed to hastily acquire all the necessary gear for our new job.

Acquiring the appropriate equipment turned into a gargantuan task because Battalion Supply was renowned for its lack of generosity, and this pre-operation day was no exception. That third canteen, so difficult to acquire, became the object of many an equipment-starved Marine, especially our motley crew of ill repute, Bravo 81s.

Ammo magazines for our M16s were even more difficult to commandeer. Getting past first base on a first date with a fifteen-year-old virgin would have been easier. In fact, my being a salty Marine with eleven months of combat under my web belt did not even help. Because stinginess was the order of the day, I decided that begging, although as distasteful to me as Marine Corps chow, would be necessary if I wanted the boys in Supply to be cooperative. Being ill equipped would have been dangerous, and I wanted my survival odds tipped in my favor.

"But...I've got only five magazines of ammo. How 'bout a huss?"

"Sorry about that shit, lance corporal. No breaks today. Our records show that you're checked out for five magazines, and that's all you're s'pose to have," said an unsympathetic voice that was attached to a heartless body. His green utilities, as impeccable as his record keeping, had never smelled of patrol sweat, and he was proud on both accounts. Begging failed, so I shifted gears into the hostile mode.

"You shitting me! You know how long five magazines would last in a firefight?" Asking him such a question was absurd, but I was desperate. Before I could blast the Supply Corporal with a well-deserved barrage of obscenities, he ambushed me.

"I don't give a rat's ass, fuckhead. You're signed out for five magazines, and there's no way you're..."

Forgetting everything that Catholic school had taught me, I angrily blurted, "Forget it, fucker...and you can cram it up your regulation ass, you chicken shit lifer!"

"Lance Corporal, you can't talk that way to..."

"I just hope I don't see your slimy ass on the op!"

"You want to have it out 'round back, asshole?"

"Get fucked...I got better shit to do," I said in matter-of-fact tone as I turned and walked briskly away from the dead-end street disguised as a corporal.

what a maggot...should have kicked his lifer ass...a waste of time...cool it Jello...maintain.

I was still scowling when I entered our tent. Bear, who was filling his rucksack with C-rations, looked up and asked, "Was that idiot at Supply givin' you a bunch of shit?"

"Yeah, he's a real jive ass dude. Did he give you a hard time also?"

"There it is. We should've gone over and stomped all over that motherfucker. Put his ugly face in the hurt locker." I agreed with his suggestion. If the Grim Reaper saw fit to ignore us while we were on the upcoming operation, we could settle our score with the Supply Corporal upon our return, but first we needed to scrounge up the equipment for tomorrow's operation. It took a few hours, but we finally found most of what we needed. We fell asleep, thinking that we were ready for the operation.

Lacking the morning sun's sensible attitude, our battalion was awake two hours before our friend was prepared to show his beaming face. I had nothing against beginning the new day at such an early hour, but it took almost twelve-hours worth of classic Marine Corps hurry-up-and-wait before we began the initial leg of the op. The mid-afternoon was typically Vietnamese, Arizona hot and Okinawa humid, as our convoy of trucks and tanks, devoid of the trademark stealth of NVA sappers, rumbled south for almost eight miles past a litany of villes: La Chau, Duyen Son, Phu Son, An My, and Hoa Duan. Clouds of red clay dust, proof of our passing, settled on each hamlet; seven miles to the west, Hills 310 and 502, home for two battalions from the 31st NVA Regiment, stared silently at each other and at us.

Finally, on the backside of Charlie Ridge, our eight-hundred-man convoy headed west at the juncture with Route 14 rather than east toward Go Noi Island. For three thousand meters, we either stared at the late afternoon sun or absorbed the slideshow beauty of wall-to-wall rice paddies, which owned both the northern and southern sides of the road. To the south, just beyond a ville called Hoa My Trung, rice paddies stretched for several hundred meters until they kissed the banks of the Song Vu Gia as it began its meandering journey west into NVA country. At about four o'clock on that eighteenth afternoon in May of 1968, we finally reached the operation's starting point. Although our battalion was massing at the top of a bunker-infested hill, we stood, abandoned at the base of Hill 65. Neither the burning afternoon sun nor our heartless truck driver cared.

"Cossack. I have nothing against hills, but..."

He nodded in silent agreement, and then blurted out, "Seems ridiculous for us to hoof all the way up this damn hill, seein' how it'll just get us tired before we actually get goin' on this crazy op." He was speaking World logic, but we were in the Nam; Cossack had so much to learn about the Nam.

just like Camp Pendleton's hills...up down up down...LEFT RIGHT LEFT...ONE TWO THREE FOUR WE LOVE THE MARINE CORPS...like shit...FIVE SIX SEVEN EIGHT WE HATE POGEY BAIT...bullshit...boot camp...KILL VC KILL...that crazy ass sign...THE MORE YOU SWEAT IN PEACE THE LESS YOU BLEED IN WAR...sweat sweat sweat...running up and down those mean ass hills everyday for seven weeks.

Upon finally reaching the summit of Hill 65, my curious eyes ignored the swarms of Marines that cluttered the hilltop; instead I scanned the area below us, an artist's dream: cool green countryside and a magical river flowing casually toward the sunset. Although my breathing was labored and my face was a Mekong Delta of sweat, the panoramic view made the trek up the hill worth it; after all, we hadn't been asked to assault the hill while under fire.

Hoping to relax for a moment, Cossack plopped his weary nineteen-year-old body on the ground. Peering up at me, he provided me with a weather report. "There's a pretty decent breeze floatin' around up here. Wow, does it feel good."

"Cossack, groove on that breeze real fast. Looks like we're movin' out...down the hill...the one we just wasted our time walkin' up."

Feeling sorry for ourselves, Cossack and I continued complaining until there was no more hill to descend, only flat land drawing us west into a place called Indian Country. It would be an away game, and the NVA would have home field advantage. Dusk was slipping into the night when the point squad for the battalion drew some automatic, small-arms fire from a dense tree line several hundred meters in front of us. A battalion of easy targets becoming a battalion of ground-huggers hidden in the tall grass. Cossack scooted over toward me.

"Hell, if we had the tube out here, we could..."

"Sure thing, but we don't have it."

My curious nature prompted me to my knees so I could scan the area to our immediate left and right. My quick perusal made me feel uncomfortable about this place. Suddenly I longed for the high ground of Hill 65. I preferred fighting NVA that were exhausted from charging up a hill, but we were on flat ground, and the NVA's best friend, the night, was beginning to say, 'Hello'.

perfect setting for civil war battle...lead flyin' around up front...my luck...stick my dumb head up over this grass and ZAP...hordes of bloodthirsty screaming NVA...stampeding this way...overrun...waxed...creamed...done in royal...green plastic-bag trip...wow...Seventh Regiment...Custer... gobs of Indians...oodles of NVA...forty-seven more days...only forty-seven.

"Lucked out back here. Can't see anything in the area."

"Probably waiting till it gets real dark, and then..."

"Goddamn! Wish those idiots would have a ceasefire on that firefight up there. Picked one hell of a time to fight a war. My bladder's ready to splatter. What a bummer. Can you feature the Tuesday night Huntley and Brinkley news report about a Marine outfit under fire, and up pops this dude takin' a leak. What a hard ass!"

I rolled over and unbuttoned my fly. "Ahhh...that feels *boo coo* better. You should try making a head call sideways...fun. Just make sure the ground slopes away from you." Ignoring the rhythmic sounds of M60 machine-gun fire and the thuds of M79 rounds that were peppering the Communist position, we broke into laughter.

"You're too much."

"Well, what the hell was I supposed to do?"

The firefight lasted only a few minutes. It felt good out numbering the Communists, which was usually not the case. We were on the move again, westward into the sultry May night. At about midnight the battalion was ordered to set up a circular defensive perimeter and to begin digging-in. Because we had announced our presence several hours earlier, the colonel expected an unfriendly visit from the NVA. Digging a fighting hole in ground that seemed harder than concrete was not my idea of how to spend midnight.

Exasperated by my failed efforts to dig a fighting hole, I grumbled, "How the hell do those lifers expect us to dig-in? We'd need a couple of B-52 raids...a little arc-light action on this area before we could dig a fighting hole."

"How about us forgettin' about this digging-in shit? It'd be a waste of time...they'll have us move out as soon as we get dug-in anyway."

Not much made sense in the Nam, but Cossack's analysis seemed logical, so I replied, "If we get our throats cut, we'll never know about it. Screw this cheap shit. Let's catch some zees. If we get overrun, won't make any difference if we're dug-in or not."

"God, I'm beat on my ass! Night."

"Yeah, later."

Our rest was brief: less than two hours. With our options severely limited, we decided to faithfully follow our leader into the dark unknown, into a swamp that lay sandwiched between Route 14 on the south and Charlie Ridge to the north.

sloshing around in nowhere circles...crazy...damn those idiots up front...where the hell are we going...dragging along prisoners...babies crying...shut those brats up...noisy ass place...burrr...cold swampy water...armpit of the world...shit...who gives a shit...like the US Saving Bonds ad...what a fucking joke...BUY US SAVINGS BONDS WHERE YOU WORK...wonder if Cossack wants to buy some Savings Bonds where he works.

Several miles away the NVA slept while we continued snaking our way through the cold, unfriendly water. In most of the swamp, the water was only waist deep, but occasionally it was at shoulder level, which Cossack discovered to his chagrin. "Shit!"

"Hang in there. How's this cesspool taste?"

"Thanks a hell of a lot for not tellin' me that hole was there!"

I wanted to laugh, but Cossack looked so pitiful that I resisted the inclination. Being soaked up the waist was expected, but he was drenched from his helmet to his jungle boots. "Sorry about that. War's hell."

"No kiddin'. Hope someone up front knows where in the hell we're going, Jello."

Looking back at Cossack, I replied in a hushed voice, "Doubt it. Got lifers up there." I paused and then continued in my normal tone of voice, "Keepin' my voice down is a waste of time...they know where we're at."

"No shit. We've been roamin' around this flaky swamp for hours. Thank God the sun'll be up pretty damn quick."

We stomped, sloshed, and wandered until our trek through the swamp finally ended, no thanks to our officers' map-reading skills. Exhausted and drenched, we plopped our gear-laden bodies on a dew-blanketed area at the edge of the swamp. In keeping with tradition, we were graced with a scant one hour's rest as night evaporated into dawn.

Slowly inching up in the east, the morning sun crawled routinely over the horizon. Still wet and cold, we began to move out. It was the morning of May 19, and the sun would work its drying magic on our wet utilities, yet by noon our utilities would be soaked again, this time with our sweat. The power of the sun coming full circle.

"Man, am I beat on my ass!"

Not pausing, I turned around and looked at Pink Rat and said, "You look it."

With a tired voice he asked, "Have any idea when we're supposed to get to that hill?"

I shrugged my aching shoulders, but then I pretend to be a knowledgeable squad leader. "Not sure how long, but it's supposed to be about fifteen hundred meters away."

Too exhausted to have an intelligent conversation, we bantered with each other as we continued our journey to the southwest. "That Cossack...too much...taking a dive in the swamp.

Bad enough smellin' the slime, much less gettin' baptized in the crap."

"You guys bad-mouthin' me?"

"Quit straggling and get your butt up here so we can laugh at your mustached face."

Cossack plunked himself on the ground, set his M16 down next to him and began pulling off his backpack. He sighed, "You know somethin'...."

Peering down at him, I quipped, "A few things. What'd you have in mind?"

"With friends like you, who needs enemies?"

"Can't even take a joke. What the hell you expect this early in the morning. Want bubbling smiles after that abortion of a nature walk through the cesspool last night?"

Pink Rat, deciding that Cossack needed some mothering, consoled him. "Jello says we only have about another mile to go...and then we can rest up some."

I didn't think Cossack needed to be coddled, so I jokingly interjected, "If you're going to be in my squad, you have to be hardcore."

Cossack pulled off his helmet and threw it on the ground. "Yeah, sure. I swear we're luckier than shit to have made it out of that swamp last night. Damn. Unreal...all those VC kids cryin' up a storm. Why the shit did they have to bring the prisoners' kids along anyway? Must a been at least five brats screamin' at the top of their lungs. Can't see as I blame 'em. Would be kind of a bummer being a tee tee babysan [slang for little baby] type and spendin' your good ol' lullaby time gettin' your runty little ass dragged around a smelly rotten ass swamp. What a gross out."

I looked at my exasperated friend. He was a lost puppy dressed in wet jungle utilities. "Makes you kind of feel like we're with the Seventh Marines Baby Sitting Service. Our motto: 'We baby-sit all night, anywhere, and for free,' but we love it."

"One hell of a freak show...that's all I can say."

The people in charge began yelling orders, so Cossack's impromptu rest ended abruptly. As the battalion began moving out again, I looked to the west, noticing a tree line that had ambush site stamped all over it. As tired as I was, my intuition sent up a red star cluster of suspicion. An ominous feeling was rumbling through me.

"You know, I could have sworn we were gonna get ourselves plastered all over the front page last night. All that noise...unreal. Should've sent Ho Chi Minh a personal invite to our little party. Might as well have told the NVA where we were."

Not looking at Cossack, I responded sarcastically, "Wouldn't make much difference...they always know what the fuck we're gonna do before we do."

Within twenty minutes, we approached a hamlet, which was several hundred meter north of the Song Vu Gia, a river running parallel to Highway 4, which would take us to Stanley Looker Special Forces Camp, our ultimate objective. Ha Nha (2) sat at the base of fifty-two meters of crusty earth; pockmarked with a network of fighting holes and bunkers, and salt and peppered with determined soldier from both sides of an ocean, the hill was a pin on a map of opposing generals: this was our first objective, Hill 52.

"Goddamn...actually made it here. Amazin' we're still alive...between the NVA, that swamp, and the lifers."

"Enough amazement, Cossack. Why don't you take someone with you and fill up the canteens? There's supposed to be a river a few hundred meters south of here...on the other side of that hill."

As Pink Rat and Cossack headed toward the river, I yelled, "If you two want to chow down, better haul ass. We could be moving out any minute."

With no intention of getting stranded, Cossack yelled back to me, "Don't worry. We're not going to let you dudes march into glory without us."

Turning toward the other three men in my squad, I said, "If you can hack your C-rats, better chow down. Hell of a way to start the day, but we love it. If it's green, it's groovy."

Responding to my familiar sarcasm, the other Marines in the Jello Squad burst into a chorus of mocking laughter.

starving...growling stomach...glad we stole some extra c-rats before the op...own private stock... the Crotch doesn't take care of you...BATTALION ORDER...FOUR BOXES OF C-RATS...enough for two days...resupply in three...add two days extra for general Marine Corps inefficiency...four to five days in the middle of nowhere with chow for two days...ammo for five minutes...maybe ten...hope new math isn't like Marine math...definitely strange...chicken and noodles...looks delicious...damn spoon you're not supposed to fall on the nasty ass ground...hold on...c-rat can... be back in a....SHIT!

My can of chicken and noodles fell off my knee, which was serving as a breakfast table. When the C-ration can landed face down in the mud, my two-course breakfast had become a three-course meal, and the new combination was less than appealing even though my stomach was growling. I muttered to myself, "Goddamn it. What a bummer. Oh, well. What the hell else can you expect after yesterday and last night."

One hundred meters to the west of us, a single NVA mortar round exploded with its unique and all-too-familiar loud concussion, but I just sat there staring down at my tipped-over can of chicken and noodles. The NVA had ruined my breakfast; I just hoped they wouldn't also ruin lunch. Although I was playing grunt on this operation, the mortarman in me knew why the NVA had fired a single mortar round.

Chapter 30
19 May 1968

The One-O'clock Sun Knew

Two months had passed since the lucky-for-now grunt had vomited the wrong direction on the slopes of Hill 502. He was no longer part of Dale Witzman's 60mm mortar squad. My friend from those zany days of mess duty regretted sending McCallif to a machine-gun section. The NVA had recently sent several machine gunners home early. Replacements were needed. McCallif had the least amount of experience of anyone in Dale's 60mm mortar squad, so he was transferred.

It was May 19th, Ho Chi Minh's birthday, and the sun laughed at the grunts of Charley Company. McCallif and the other one hundred and sixty members of Charley Company were not laughing. They just wanted a fourth canteen of water. Warm or hot, it did not matter: just wet.

The one-o'clock sun knew what was going to happen. It watched as approximately eight hundred of us marched down a narrow dust road in search of an enemy. The Jello Squad was glad we were not part of the point element. It felt so much better having Charley Company in front of us. As war goes, most people in our Headquarters and Services Company were combat grade school dropouts. The grunts of Charley Company had Ph.D.s in the business of war.

Several North Vietnamese soldiers were standing in the tall grass that owned the narrow stretch of land, which was squeezed between the road and the Song Vu Gia to the south. The burning sun, patiently waiting. The Marines, dressed to fight, continued down the road, which clipped the base of a non-Everest hill. Someone shouted orders in Vietnamese. Everyone in Charley

Company was hugging a piece of Vietnam. For several, it was their final lay. Mortar rounds were exploding, sending metal chunks flying everywhere. The perfect ambush. Our battalion's best infantry company was pinned down. The remaining three companies would be next.

The idea of going home alive in another two months was a good one. Dale tucked himself safely behind a two-foot high mound of dirt. Every time he poked up his curious head, a 12.7mm round would slam into his mound and abruptly alter its geography. The NVA were firing the heavy machine gun from a heavily fortified bunker on a hill which was just north of the road. They wanted to keep Dale, the Iowa farmer boy, pinned down for obvious reasons. Setting up his 60mm mortar would change the odds a little. The NVA were stingy. They liked the odds just as they were. Dale decided that being pinned down was better than having his nineteen-year-old-face blown off by a 12.7mm round.

Automatic-weapons fire owned the hot afternoon air. The Communists had a monopoly on the death sounds. A flood of small-arms fire poured relentlessly into the Marines of Charley Company. There was no cover and no shade, just more unanswered NVA 82mm mortar rounds roaming the battlefield. Someone unlucky screaming for help. Clouds of grey-black smoke going to Heaven. Brown chunks of real estate falling hard, spraying the tanned nape of a grunt's neck. No shrapnel, this time. The battle, not over yet. The afternoon, still full of Purple Hearts. The NVA were getting closer. The terse angry sound of chi com grenades exploding too close.

The captain was screaming on his radio that they needed tanks and even jet strikes, and not in ten minutes but now. Ammunition was needed immediately. Their water was gone. One platoon had already been overrun by the NVA. All the wrong things were happening too fast, and all the right things were taking forever.

Dale looked to his left, expecting to see some NVA soldiers charging at him. Instead, only an army of tall grass bending north like a million witnesses pointing accusatory fingers at the hill full of NVA. The breeze coming from waters of the Song Vu Gia was a million-dollar-breeze. It was a raspberry popsicle sliding down his parched throat. It was river cool, and Dale loved it. He wanted to leave the heavy machine gun and its staccato bursts, and the mortar barrage, and the lousy skinny brown road, and Ho Chi Minh's hot birthday sun. He would trade it all for an eyeful of Iowa cornfields. He would even trade his news headlines for the freezing rain of Iowa cutting January's chilled breath. Oh, to be back in Iowa: a leopard-skin of 1923 farm houses, meandering roads, moving rivers that travel their mother's belly, of once-a-day Jack Frost's whine, of winter's slushy back-roads. Yes, Iowa with its cold fronts from Up North that slumber, stammer, stay a while.

But he was in the Nam, and someone firing a heavy machine gun wanted him dead. And a corpsman was desperately stuffing a machine gunner's intestines back where they belonged. The breeze got smart and left. And Dale worked hard at not puking. A few meters away, another Marine lay, his dead eyes staring at the sun. No more sweating for him, just a drying puddle of plum-colored blood.

The 12.7mm heavy machine gun still cranking out its bad medicine. More chi coms and mortar rounds exploding, sending their garbage everywhere. Long bursts of one-sided automatic-weapons fire running wild, celebrating on the survivors of Charley Company.

The corpsman stopped wasting his time on the dead machine gunner. Arched low, the corpsman ran to another Marine ten meters away. He beat the bullets this time. The wounded Marine was thankful for that.

Just then, McCallif crawled over to the dead machine gunner. He grabbed the M60 machine gun and loaded it, the ammunition belt dangling to the ground as he stood up, dangerously tall at six feet.

Dale screamed desperately at McCallif, begging him to get down. Unfortunately, he was on autopilot. McCallif was tired of being pinned down. Someone had to do something. Anything.

The Marine, who was very quiet and very new in the Nam, was fanning his machine gun back and forth, firing several rapid bursts, then one long one; his ammunition belt shrinking quickly.

Dale staring helplessly as the NVA answered with several bursts of machine-gun fire aimed at McCallif's torso, but he was still firing. The force of his own weapon holding him up as NVA machine gun bullets tore into his flak jacket. With the ammunition belt still dangling, his machine gun was still firing as blood flowed from several holes in his back. Out of ammunition, his machine gun finally stopping. He fell back, bullets still riddling his body. Dale, watching McCallif hit the hard ground, begged God for an extra miracle. Maybe God would be listening.

Too many Marines had stopped to die on Ho Chi Minh's birthday. Dale prayed that reincarnation really existed, not for himself but for those ticket holders on the Titanic, the unlucky grunts of Charley Company. They deserved it.

The Jello Squad and the rest of H and S Company [Headquarters and Services] would be next. We were only several hundred meters east of the area that Charley Company was desperately trying to defend. The airstrip, our final objective, was only two hours away, but that would wait. Holding our present position would be difficult enough.

The thought of Headquarters and Services Company joining the battle was a scary one. We were a patchwork of cooks, office clerks, 106mm recoilless riflemen [minus their 106s], other assorted bureaucrats, and four squads of mortarless mortarmen. Most of us were armed with M16s, seven magazines of ammunition, and the belief that we had somehow magically become an infantry company.

Several tanks began rumbling up the road, which was just south of our company's position. They would fire their 90mm cannons at the NVA, but before they could open fire, NVA mortars were exploding all around them. The tanks and a supply truck veered off the road and headed towards us in the hope of escaping the mortar barrage. Two of the tanks and the truck hit land mines. The Communists walked their mortar rounds towards us. Everyone who wanted to get back to the World alive was scampering for cover. Unfortunately, there was none. I just lay there hoping and praying for a miracle. The barrage ended, and I was in love with God.

People in charge were trying to shout over the din; confusion was the order of the day. Officers holding radio handsets listened to the desperate requests for more ammunition and fire support. Crouching nearby, I could hear the screaming and the noise from the battle each time an officer would receive a transmission over a radio. Charley Company's situation was degenerating quickly. Hopefully, their ammunition would last until air strikes could pound the North Vietnamese positions.

Within minutes F-4 Phantoms from Da Nang roared in from the east. Loaded with five-hundred-pound bombs and canisters of napalm, the jets swooped in at tree-top level over our position, finally dumping their arsenals just in front of Charley Company's outer perimeter. The concussion of each bomb, an angry earthquake. Pumping the NVA with 20mm cannon fire, one jet after another roared past us. More bombs exploding. The battlefield shaking. Fiery red clouds billowing up, turning black. The F-4 jets made several more strafing runs and then headed northeast back to Da Nang. These sorties were only the first of 84 that would be used effectively against elements the 31st NVA Regiment during the remaining 23 days of the operation.

With the loud roar of the Phantoms now only a memory, the grunts knew they were on their own. Undeterred, the NVA continued firing their 82mm mortar rounds and tossing their chi-com grenades into Charley Company's lines, The volume of AK-47 and 12.7mm heavy machine-gun fire pouring into the grunts increased once the jets left. The Charley Company had had their tank and air support. Now they were almost out of ammunition.

Our section leader rushed up to me, his eyes bulging and his voice was quivering. "SHIT! Charley Company is getting stomped bad...and they're...they're...almost out of ammo! Collect three or four magazines of ammo from each man in your squad."

I just stood there not believing his words, realizing our fate if the grunts a few hundred meters to the west could not hold against the Communist assault.

"Don't just stand there, goddamn it!"

A few minutes later, I returned with several dozen magazines of M16 ammunition. Our section leader grabbed them and dumped them into an empty ammo box. When the box was filled, two unlucky Marines grabbed the box and scurried in a low crouch toward the deafening noise that was coming from Charley Company's position.

Our section leader turned to me with another order, one I dreaded. "It doesn't look too good up there so...uh...so have your squad dig in over there. Yeah, over there."

The uncertainty in his voice and his choice of locations to defend made me feel uncomfortable and angry. Digging fighting holes in a Vietnamese cemetery was an idea I did not relish.

"Goddamn it! How the fuck do you expect my squad to cover that much area? Shit, we don't even have enough ammo to last us more than a minute! If you want us to cover that much ground, tell those motherfuckin' lifers to get some more men over here! Forget it! You're too tight with those assholes to say anything! Goddamn it. I don't need you getting' my men killed...SHIT! If you got the balls, get those lifers to send some more men over here!"

Before he could answer my incendiary words, a medevac chopper from Da Nang landed in the open area, which our company was responsible for defending. I left him standing there in stunned silence to be in-charge of someone else.

A few seconds later, I joined the other Marines who were carrying wounded grunts on to the chopper. I was on autopilot as I grabbed one wounded grunt after another. One medevac chopper would leave and another would land, each time bringing an unfriendly response from the NVA mortars. Each concussion from the 82mm rounds sent shrapnel and chunks of dirt flying. When they landed too close, I dove for the ground; I hoped the casualty I was carrying would forgive me for dropping him.

Time did not exist as I loaded wounded Marines on the choppers. Images of their faces floated past me; it was safer to sandbag the sight, a Technicolor scene of wall-to-wall wounded: eighteen and nineteen-year-old Marines bleeding, moaning and screaming for help.

After several medevac choppers were filled to capacity, I stopped carrying the wounded to the choppers and shifted gears back to my role as squad leader. Several hundred meters to the west, the battle was still raging, but the noise of automatic-weapons fire was diminishing. It was still midafternoon, and the NVA probably weren't through with us. It was time to dig-in, so I began moving back to my squad, which was positioned near the cemetery to the north. As I fastened my bayonet to my M16 and began walking toward the cemetery, I yelled to the members of my squad to start digging-in. "And make sure you got your rifles on fixed fucking bayonet! Looks like we might need to use 'em."

SHIT...what a drag...something tells me that we're going to be overrun soon...if not now...it'll be tonight...God please let me live...I don't even have two months left in the Corps...I don't want to be dead at twenty.

The burning May sun had beat down on us while exploding mortar rounds peppered the red dirt road and the dry grassy field for over two hours of the longest afternoon of my life. Marines in the open ran for cover, but it was at a premium. Chunks of shrapnel sliced through the 120-degree afternoon air, and the NVA machine guns' death rhythm worked overtime, busily sending Marines home early to mothers with memories of rocking their babies to sleep. Screaming for the corpsman, the wounded hoped for some luck. Some begged for a May miracle, but all they got was a job guarding Heaven's streets. Angry Marines, screaming obscenities, poured bursts of automatic-weapons fire into a hillside, the main source of the NVA ambush. The trapped, drenched in sweat, promised God anything as they muttered at the ground, knowing that their desperate prayers were useless because they had walked into the perfect ambush site in Indian Country, the NVA's turf. The ground didn't have ears, and God, showing more sense than the Marines, usually stayed out of Indian Country. Today was no exception, and the battle noise was deafening, so God probably wouldn't be able to hear the desperate pleas of the wounded and the dying. AK-47 rounds kept ripping through boys who wanted to be men. The pungent smell of smoke roamed the ambush site. Dozens of mortar explosions sent chunks of metal and dry earth in search of a target. In the belly of the beast out by the Song Vu Gia, thirteen Marines slumped over, falling hard as blood-splattered, and their dreams floated away on a hot May breeze. But a steady stream of medevac choppers braved enemy mortar barrages to fly the wounded to the Naval Hospital in Da Nang, and we cheered the F-4 Phantom jets from Da Nang when they roared out of the northern sky, swooping in at tree-top level, but too late to save the dead.

Finally, after more than two hours, the NVA broke off contact with a decimated Charley Company. Most of the day's casualties—13 KIAs, 41 WIAs and several dozen Marines suffering from heat exhaustion—were from Charley Company, which started the day out with 160 men. It made little sense that the NVA had not continued their ambush; for some unknown reason, they did not sweep around Charley Company's right flank and hit H and S Company, the unit my squad was a part of for this operation. Had the NVA outflanked Charley Company, my five-man squad would have taken the brunt of the attack because we had been given the responsibility of defending this area. Had the NVA assaulted us from the north, my order to fix bayonets would have been put to the test. Fighting in close-quarters with a much larger force would not have gone well for my undermanned squad. Fortunately, this scenario never played out, and I was elated for that. With a July flight date on the horizon, I was getting too short in the Nam for the kind of heroics that would have been required. Around 3:30 p.m., the North Vietnamese attack ended. They weren't on the run. They were waiting for another day, another opportunity to send Marines home in body bags, and their patience would be rewarded. By the end of the op on June 12th, 27 Marines and 4 Navy Corpsman would be dead.

Although the main attack was over, the NVA couldn't resist a perfect target: eight Marines bunched up together as they walked up Hill 52. A well-place 82mm mortar round landed in the middle of the group; no one was killed, but all eight Marines were wounded. It was medevac-chopper time for Mike Rae, a radio operator for an FO [forward observer] from mortars. Although he would be out of commission in the Naval Hospital in Da Nang for eleven days, fate had smiled on him. A small piece of shrapnel had missed hitting his femoral artery by a quarter of an inch. When he returned to Hill 41, which was a few miles south of Hill 10, all of his possessions had been thrown away because they thought he had been killed. He was an Iowa-farm-boy Methodist with a to-do-list waiting, and KIA were three letters for which he had no use.

With the day's fighting finished, I glanced over at one of the tanks that had been knocked out. A dead Marine without a shirt, who was stuck in the Nam for one more day, was sprawled on the front of the dead tank. A gaping bullet hole in his side stared at me, sucking my innocence dry. I turned my head abruptly, wishing I had never joined the Marines.

Those of us who were survivors sighed and wondered if the NVA would be back for an encore that night, but some just sat with faces frozen by the heat of battle, their eyes staring out past the moment as hollow seekers of yesterday. The dead Marine on the tank just lay there waiting for tomorrow's chopper to take him home and away from the war.

Chapter 31
19 May 1968

Ponchos Full Of Silence

War is very quiet when you're dead. Ho Chi Minh's birthday was noisy at first, but then a stillness. No bird sounds. The party over. Thirteen silent warriors loitering, their quiet blood flowing. A poncho full of silence is carried away to the place where dead grunts go. It's one hundred and twenty degrees, and the ex-grunt does not care. He just lies there, not needing the shave he needed five minutes earlier.

May 19 was over. It had been the day the alley cat toyed with the wounded bird, the day they killed Camelot. We had been unlucky visitors at a slaughterhouse near a river with a foreign name, by a hill with a number. John Wayne had been AWOL. The brass band never showed up to play the 'Star Spangled Banner.' Thirteen Marines dealing in the futures market, losing the game. The dreams of the dead going off to Limbo. The survivors, zombies, counting their days left in the Nam.

Chapter 32
19 May 1968

Two KIAs And Their Hungry Flies

Cossack wanted to throw up, but there was nothing left. He wanted to cry, but on his tanned and tired face there were only streams of sweat rolling off, tickling his neck, then disappearing into the canvas stretcher. The two Marines on the stretchers to his left could have used the *1812 Overture* and a take-two. They were young, eighteen, except for the fact that they were old, eighteen. They were dead, so it did not really matter. Within hours they would be government inspected, poor brave meat, leaving the sad old war, going home to be planted. Cossack was certain that they were better off. At least they had no pain.

Licking his parched lips, he gulped. Looking up, he hated the burning sun more than the Marine Corps. Sweat kept streaming off his face, and his arms were sticky and caked with hot sand.

Cossack is pissed-off about the two dead Marines. Had he gone to the university, he would call his anger *outrage*. But he is just an eighteen-year-old who quickly lost interest in working at a factory which made fly rings for 750 pound bombs, so he is just a pissed-off two-year Marine from Detroit wondering why his mother is not here comforting her favorite Mad Cossack. Mom, what a beautiful woman, but where is she. Cossack wants her desperately, not the corpsmen who dropped him when they ran for cover during the mortar barrage a few hours earlier; yes, the typically unselfish corpsmen. And he remembers that when the second mortar attack began, they left him and the IV, which dangled from his tired arm. The empty cots and the poor odds: the others left it all. It was so much safer in the fighting holes around the sickbay tent.

Cossack is scared and angry. He reminds himself that it is better to be pissed off than pissed on. He laughs because he knows that someday he will be able to wake up from this nightmare. And he is wondering why the explosions of the mortar rounds around the tent sound quieter than usual. It's the sand. He raises his head and, seeing an empty tent, he wonders where everyone is, but he knows. They are safe, and he is not. Another explosion. This one is louder, killing bits of shrapnel tearing through the canvas of his tent. Bits of instant sunlight. Tiny forever slashes, too high to send Cossack home early. Cossack tells himself that he did not travel ten thousand miles to leave his guts on some beach, which no one ever heard of. It's not even a World-War-II-heroes' beach, just a simple Song-Vu-Gia beach. Die forever? No way. He is sure they would misspell his name on their official letter.

He closed his rawhide eyes, only seeing pink. The sun, still up there mocking him. Finally a big chopper was coming. The Chinook hovered for a moment before making its noisy descent. Bare-chested and suffering from heat exhaustion, Cossack lay helplessly as gusts of wind from the chopper sprayed him with stinging sand and blood from the two dead Marines. A collage: chunks of flesh and bits of dead gut caking his upper body. Splattered with the blood of the dead grunts, his whiskered face and his burning eyelids hated it. Finally, they put him on the chopper. It flew away, first to Hill 55 for Cossack, and then to Da Nang for the two KIAs and their hungry flies.

Chapter 33
19-21 May 1968

Ho Chi Minh's Boys Visit Cossack

They left Cossack in a trench. There were no empty cots for him on Hill 55. The wounded Marines from the operation owned them all. The late afternoon sky had nothing better to do but rain and be grey. Cossack, unconcerned about the trench filling with water, was too busy gobbling up raindrops. His fever seemed to be going away, but the rain, deciding to tease him, stopped within a few minutes, and his fever returned.

The bright moon was staring down at a helpless Cossack, who was resting in his trench. He was unsure if he were dreaming. He was cold. The Nam was supposed to be hot, but he was shivering. And he wished he could be shivering back in Michigan.

No more dreaming for now. The quiet night air was alive, crackling with the all too familiar sound of automatic-weapons fire. A minute later, the eastern end of the hill was receiving incoming 82mm mortar fire from the NVA. Cossack, too exhausted to care, just lay there listening to the roar of the Phantom jets as they strafe the North Vietnamese mortar positions. Canisters of napalm tumbled silently, finally hitting their target, exploding, rolling red and yellow death-fire across the rice paddies. When the jets were finished, a pair of Huey Cobra gunships prowled the unfriendly night skies around Hill 55 in search of the NVA, whom were still pouring machine-gun fire into the western end of the hill.

The jets were not enough to rout the stubborn NVA attackers. As one of the Cobras poured in rocket fire, the other peppered the NVA troop positions with long bursts of machine-gun fire. More white flashes. NVA mortars still firing. One of the Cobras turned and zeroed in, spewing its venom. Tracer rounds, red and graceful, streaking toward the bold flashes below. The mortar fire kept coming. The second gunship stopped circling, and then it shot through the eight o'clock sky, pumping the mortar positions with a steady barrage of M79 rounds. By now the first Cobra was making a strafing run. A volley of rockets raced toward the rice paddies. These explosions muffled the steady sound of machine-gun fire, which the other gunship was spraying on the squad of retreating NVA. The Cobra gunships hovered for a few more minutes and then left the past-tense battle air.

Cossack knows it is not midnight, and he is worried. He is wondering why the NVA attacked so early. They are midnight-to-one-o'clock fighters. They are still out there, and Cossack is positive they will return. It is not snowing, so he should not be shivering, yet he is. He wears his macabre mask of the dead Marines' blood, and he hates the stench of death that owns his face and chest. He wishes the rain would have washed it away, but it has not. He would give anything if he only had his shirt, but he does not have it. He knows that this is the way things go in the Nam, so his eyes give up. He knows that he can escape the Nam for eight hours if he is lucky.

But he hears noises, muffled noises coming from somewhere down the trench line. Then voices, the wrong kind. Footsteps getting louder, coming towards him. Cossack just lying there. No rifle. No bayonet. No flak jacket. Not even a helmet. He is shaking even more. His heart is sprinting double-time. More footsteps, closer this time. Closer. Closer. Cossack peers up. A face grinning down at him. One of Ho Chi Minh's boys. The man is holding a rifle, an AK-47. The trench is shrinking. Then another soldier appears. This one standing by his head. Both soldiers zombie-eyed, staring down at Cossack. Quiet one-sided laughter. Blood dripping from their bayonets, and Cossack has no place to go. Nodding and smiling, they chatter about what to do. Cossack just lies there waiting. He is still shaking. He is afraid and cold. Their eyes light up, burning with hate. A killing scream. They lunge at Cossack with their rifles. His guts their target. Bayonets. Cold killing steel racing closer. Closer. Closer.

The nightmare was over. Cossack was elated that he was shivering and that the blood on his chest belongs to the two dead

Marines. Although exhausted, he will stay awake tonight. It will be safer.

Cossack spent the following day in his trench recouping his strength. His second night on the hill was quiet. The NVA were busy some other place. The next morning Cossack felt strong enough to venture out of his trench. His stomach was finally ready, so he meandered to the mess hall, walked in and stood in line. Dry blood was flaking off his eyelids, and he smelled like he was dead. No one sat at his table. They just stared for a moment, and he just ate.

Chapter 34
22 May 1968

Death Lurks Down By The Water Bo

A fifth day of the operation began, and somehow we managed to be part of it. The North Vietnamese, who had mortared us twice on the third day of Operation Mameluke Thrust, continued to provide the casualty counters with employment for a few more days. Although our mortars were finally delivered to Hill 52 on the day after the ambush, the boys from S-4 [Logistics] seemed to have forgotten to resupplied us with C-rations. Fortunately, some of the South Vietnamese Mike Force Rangers that were helping us man Hill 52 shared their cooked rice, fish heads and assorted greens with us. Although no food was delivered to us, Marine jets delivered a late birthday present to Ho Chi Minh's boys who were entrenched south of us, just across the Song Vu Gia. The sight of the cluster bombs working their deadly magic made me glad I was a spectator and not a recipient.

Unlike conventional bombs, the cluster variety would explode above ground, hurling thousands of grenade-size bomblets over the killing area; because of the expanded killing radius, it was effective against large concentrations of troops. The rapid popping sounds dissipated first, but the massive cloud of dust hovered over the target area long after the final concussion evaporated into the heat of late May.

Many a heat-prostrate Marine missed this and the two NVA mortar barrages on the 20th, the third day of the operation; for Cossack and Rodick, another member of our mortar section, heat exhaustion had been their ticket out of the bush. Their vacation would last only a few days, but any amount of time away from the op was worth a million dollars. Mike Rae, recovering as slowly as possible from his shrapnel wounds, was still in the Naval Hospital in Da Nang and would be until the 30th of May. His days were filled with pain, but he was comforted by nurses and corpsmen, but on the downside, the Communists mortared the hospital once during his stay. Our days and nights were filled with uncertainty, yet there was certainty in one area: we were surrounded by a large, stubborn force of North Vietnamese.

It was the early afternoon and things were unexpectedly quiet. The afternoon's boredom was greatly appreciated. The NVA had called a time-out and were taking a siesta.

I had just finished a letter to my family when Pink Rat stuck his face in the bunker. "Forget your letter writing. Let's go down to the river and splash around. That water looks damn good."

We meandered down the hill. Pink Rat was right. The water looked sinfully inviting. "Well, what are we waiting for, Jello?"

"Nothing. I just hope the NVA company that's supposed to be on the other side of the river doesn't bug our asses."

Two Marines dove into the wet coolness of the Song Vu Gia, but two schoolboys on summer vacation were splashing and dunking one another. The Nam was a million miles away, and we were loving it. "Damn, this water is nice! It sure beats the hell out of sitting on that dusty old hill."

"You can say that again."

Pink Rat pulled away from the excrement that was casually gliding by him. It missed him, and he was glad for that. "That turd's moving right along. What a hard ass...we're swimming in a sewer."

"You should feel at home my Polish friend." I was laughing, but Pink Rat was answering my friendly insult by splashing my face with a deluge of river water.

After a few more minutes of acting like twelve-year-olds, we decided it was time to head back up the hill. Before we did this, we walked across the beach to the artillery positions. We needed to refill our canteens and artillery had a supply of fresh water, which had been brought out to the hill in portable water tanks. The water bo, as we affectionately called such a container, was, like everything else in the Marine Corps, painted green; however, the hot afternoon sun made it easy not to be prejudiced toward the green lady. Fresh water would mean no more purification tablets or dysentery, two of the little pleasures in the war zone.

fresh water finally...thank God arty takes care of their own...won't need those yucky heliozoan tablets now...sure makes the river water taste shitty...no wonder they can kill the crap in the water...we should just put Marine Corps chow in our drinking water...that'd sure kill anything in the water...ah there she is...you beautiful metal lady...water bo you're numba one in this short-timer's book.

The water bo—a 200 gallon metal container on wheels which was used to transport fresh water—was parked about twenty-five meters north of the river. When we reached it, I decided to use the water faucets on the side farthest from the river. Filling the first of the half dozen canteens, I handed it to Pink Rat. His throat was in Paradise when he gulped a swig of water, but I was still on a beach in the Nam filling a second canteen. "Boy, does this taste good! Here, have a..."

An loud explosion. An NVA mortar round exploding several meters on the opposite side of the water bo. Chunks of shrapnel clanking hard against the metal of the water bo.

NIGHTMARE EXPLOSION...BLACK GRAY CLOUD...DIRTY SAND FLYING UP...METAL TO METAL CLANKING...HITTING THE WATER BO...OH FUCK...GET YOUR ASS OUT OF HERE...WE'RE IN THE OPEN...HAUL ASS LICKITY SPLIT.

My heart was running on high, octane adrenaline, and I was in the open. Getting blown away with only about a month left in the Nam was one scenario I was certain I did not want. Six months earlier I would not have cared, but now I wanted be a going-home Marine: the alive version.

Grabbing my M16 and most of the canteens, I bolted, sprinting for the cover of a clump of banana trees near the hill. I never thought that I could have run faster than I had when Chico and I had been chased in LA. I was wrong. The safety of the trees was five-seconds away, and Pink Rat was two feet behind me. "OH FUCK! That was too damn close for me."

Pink Rat and I, crouching behind one of the trees, stared across the river, the source of the enemy mortar rounds. Catching my breath, I sighed heavily and burst out in nervous laughter. My heart was pounding and my hand was shaking as I wiped the sweat from my face. "Too close...too goddamn close."

Pink Rat's answer was held prisoner in his throat. He just kept gulping and nodding. His eyes, signposts of fear. We waited for more explosions, but there were none. I took a deep breath and sighed. "That was a real drag. Do you realize that we almost got our asses waxed royal...I mean royal! That round had our number one it. If the water bo hadn't been there...shit...we would've..."

"Yeah we would've been...canceled. Would a been no Detroit for me and no Arizona for you."

"That fuckin' round landed just on the other side of the water bo...only fifteen or twenty goddamn feet away. Shit...don't want to think about...too fucking short for this shit."

Still attempting to regain his composure, Pink Rat only nodded and wiped the sweat from his forehead.

It had been a successful fire mission for the NVA. They would call it 'Excellent coverage on target: two confirmed kills and two wounded.' We heard that two corpsmen had not been as fortunate as we had been. They had been on the wrong side of the water bo. It had been a strange fate for the corpsmen, who, if they were to die, would have expected death to visit them while they were patching up a wounded Marine during a firefight. A corpsman was one man every Marine appreciated. It was the corpsman's job to make unhealthy Marines healthy and to patch up the shot-up. Unfortunately, corpsmen did more than their fair share of the dying. The two corpsmen, who had just joined the Saigon war statistics, were no exception to this gloomy reality of war in the Nam.

Pink Rat and I drudged our way back up the steep slopes of Hill 52. Rolling down our faces, streams of sweat saturated our jungle utility shirts, turning them dark green; sweating never felt so good.

Paul...better not get your ass sent over here...keep your corpsman's ass back in the World...the Jello Kid's using all our family's luck...SHIT...I ALMOST GOT KILLED.

Chapter 35
23 May 1968

Hold The Paris Peace Talks At Hill 52?

On the sixth day of Operation Mameluke Thrust, it rained, and a large force of North Vietnamese were spotted about 1,500 meters south of the Song Vu Gia. It was from this large sandy area, that the NVA probably had fired the mortar round the previous day that almost killed me when Pink Rat and I were filling up our canteens. The same NVA unit was probably responsible for dropping about twenty-five 82mm mortar rounds on our 105mm and 155mm artillery batteries around midnight. We replied to the NVA mortar fire with air strikes for several hours during the early afternoon.

It was a busy afternoon for us also. We had several fire missions when some Viet Cong were spotted about 2,500 meters east of Hill 52. When those fire missions were over, we also fired at a target on a mountain ridge south of the Song Vu Gia. Once my talents as a mortarman weren't required any longer, I decided to write a letter to Mike Fitz, my across-the-alley friend who was a Marine reservist.

23 May 1968
Hi Mike,
   You'll never guess where I am. No, not the DMZ. We're about 25 or so miles southwest of Da Nang—at a Special Forces outpost on a big operation. Right now I'm in a small but secure bunker, It's about 2 feet high, so I'm squeezed in pretty well—with another dude even! Today is the first time they've allowed us to write since this began. At the present time we are surrounded by a division or

more (3,000 to 5,000 men maybe) of NVA. I don't know if there's really a division of them, but their force was big enough to kick our ass and hold us here for the last four days. What fun! We have one battalion, a battery of 105s and 155s, and some tanks also. We're getting three C-rats meals a day, but for a while we were living on gook food since they couldn't get resupply into us. We get mortared a few times each day, but it's only 5-10 rounds at most each time. Boy, my neck hurts. This bunker just isn't made for a 'tall' Arizonan like myself. Ha Ha! At midnight I'll have 36 days left.

The first few days out here, we got our asses kicked with a capital K. Charley Company was the point for the op. They lost all but 39 people. About 70 heat exhaustion, and the rest got wounded or killed. One platoon was overrun and everyone else was pinned down for 2 hours. This was done by a regiment of NVA. The grunts in Charley Company even ran out of ammo and water. They had air strikes within 500 meters of us. We in mortars lost 25% of our men to dysentery and wounds and had one KIA. Man, what a drag. Oh, yes, I brought JELL-O with me. It helps out when you're tired and hungry. And it's magical.

The first day we were out, we were hit by 20 NVA. No sweat though. Then we set up in a dry ass rice paddy that night. At about 0100 we got up and moved out through a swamp until 0500 in the morning. If they would have hit us, they could have wiped us out. Luckily they didn't. I guess things are looking up for our side.

Hopefully, we should end the operation in another two weeks. Then I'll write you again. Be sure to say hi to Carole and tell her that I'll write when I get a chance. Do the same thing with my family. OK?

The tape I sent you is one of the night our hill and Da Nang were rocketed. Save it! OK? It's gung ho, isn't it! Better go now.
The Jello Kid

P.S. How are the Peace Talks--ha ha--why don't they have them here on Hill 52.

Chapter 36
6-7 June 1968

Someone's Tryin' To Kill Me

The night blanketed the Nam, but our bright, silver-dollar friend was beaming a smile at us. It was one of those rare moments that made it possible to forget that I was in a war zone. Although it felt like a back-home night and nostalgia hung heavily, we were deep in NVA territory on a grassy airstrip out by Stanley Looker Special Forces Camp, our original objective. Nothing much on the operation had gone by plan; day two of the op was our arrival goal, but we arrived seven days later. Additionally, the people at the top decided that 81mm mortar squads should have their mortars, so we were able to retire from our job as grunts, which was perfectly fine with me.

Our sister squad, our companions in this furthermost bastion of Main Street, had decided to forget about the mortar attack earlier in the day. Near their gun pit, which was twenty-five meters from ours, they put on their own drunken version of a USO show. Those back-in-the-World sounds drifting through the bright night were theirs: soul, rock, and country. They were loving it.

The rice wine, acquired illegally from a ville across the river, had taken effect, and wild Irish gigs were danced. Their display of merriment would not have been so dangerous had they only howled and danced. This simple combination meant that the NVA could only hear the ruckus; however, every first rate drinking party must be ornamented with a bonfire. Suddenly, their party fit this category perfectly. Their gun pit was twenty-five meters too close for me.

It was midnight, time for me to wake up Cossack for perimeter watch. A groggy Cossack yawned, rubbed his eyes and complained, "Thanks a hell of a lot. How do you expect me to get my beauty sleep?"

"There aren't enough hours in the night for that. It was either you or Pink Rat, and he is crashed out royal."

"Yeah." He yawned again before continuing, "Our Polish friend needs all the beauty sleep he can get."

We both began chuckling, but Cossack stopped abruptly when he looked over at the other squad's gun pit. In an agitated tone of voice, he blurted, "What the fuck are those dudes doin'? Someone forget to tell 'em were in a fuckin' war zone?"

I was as baffled as Cossack, so I just shrugged my shoulders. "All I have to say is I'm glad I'm just a dumb ass civilian who's just checkin' out this Green Machine. Two years worth, that's all. This kid's getting short. Thirty days and a flight date...then back to the World."

Pausing for a moment, I stared up at the moon and continued, "Actually, Cossack, this place would be kind of nice if everyone would stop stomping on it all the time. Vietnam's as beautiful as they come. It's the Nam and the lifers' bullshit I can't hack."

"Hell, you should be feelin' sorry for me. I've got almost another six months of bullshit like that damn rifle and personnel inspection we had the other day. Can you believe it? Out here in the bush and standing at attention and goin' through all that garrison Mickey Mouse crap."

"The best part was their threat to fine anyone who didn't have a shave. Fifty buck fine. What a hard ass. That's more than a week's wages."

Smiling, Cossack said, "I'm just happy they didn't make me shave my Fu Manchu mustache."

We both laughed, and the night bugs in the rice paddy chattered. I left the laughter and stared up at the moon again.

I'm sick of the biggies not giving a shit about us...it gets old being just a pawn...not just the lifers out here...same thing with those Paris peace talks dudes...worryin' about the shape of the fucking table...too much...have those goddamn talks out here in my gun pit and they'd be settling all sorts of shit damn fast...just one NVA rocket barrage and those dudes would become the biggest peace freaks around...no wonder they picked Paris...it's well out of range...the hell with it all...thank God for the month of July...I'll be legal...finally be 21...out of the Nam...out of my mind probably...and best of all...out of this Green Machine...all I have to do is keep my dumb ass down and everything will be cool...just thirty more days until.

"I see him! A gook!," Cossack yelled. He grabbed his rifle, aiming it at a silhouette standing in the rice paddy directly in front of us. The dark figure was faster than Cossack. There was a flash of light and an explosion. Then another flash, and a second B40 rocket exploded near our sister squad's gun pit.

Just as I dove into a ditch in front of our gun pit, Cossack sprayed the rice paddy in front of us with a burst from his M16.

"Goddamn it, watch out, shithead!"

"Keep your damn head down, Jello. I'm gonna get that fucker!"

NVA mortar rounds began exploding. Then, more B40 rockets and automatic-weapons fire.

"Where's your rifle, Jello?"

I looked back at Cossack, who was hiding in the gun pit. "Where the hell do you think? In my short-timer hands. The NVA aren't getting my ass tonight!"

"Let me have it...can't find my ammo. Goddamn it, there he is again. That son of a bitch. I'm gonna get the fucker this time!"

"Bullshit. Now he knows where we are. I'm getting' too short for this crap!"

"Shit. Can't see him anymore! Fuck!"

"Good, maybe he can't see us!"

The mortar attack stopped, but a few moments later, tracer rounds cut through the night like a high tech laser show gone mad. The automatic-weapons fire was coming from a cornfield south of us. The NVA were all around us.

"Cossack, get some illumination up and fast They've got us pegged!"

"No shit. They're zeroing in..."

"Fuck it. Just fire a round. Get some light up there! Now!"

"What setting?"

"I don't give a damn. Jus' get that fuckin' round down the tube!"

"Fire in the hole!"

Twenty-seconds later, the illumination round popped, spraying it's magical light over the cornfield. I grabbed our mortar and swung it east. Cossack slid another round down the tube. Within a minute, two more illumination rounds were converting the area around us into noontime. Bright was beautiful.

The attack was finished. No human wave assault by thousands of doped-up North Vietnamese. No flame throwers as had been the fashion at Con Thien. No tank assault like the one at the Special Forces camp at Lang Vei. Definitely not a John Wayne scenario, but it was a situation that I did not need.

I decided to stroll over and check on the condition of the other mortar squad. This was the second time on the op that 81s were taking casualties, and I didn't like the feeling of vulnerability that was beginning to gnaw at my well-cultivated sense of invincibility. I was beginning to wonder if the JELL-O magic would hold on long enough for me to escape the clutches of the Nam, but for a brief moment I felt safe and confident. Darkness, the NVA's best friend, had been ushered out by our illumination rounds, which were popping at sixty-second intervals in the night sky. When I reached the other gun pit, people were moaning and cursing.

"Sugar Bear, who got hit?"

"Shit! Got it in my fuckin' arm. Just a small piece of shrapnel, but it hurts like a mutherfucker!"

"Maintain. Just relax. A corpsman should be here pretty damn quick. Be cool. You're gonna skate out of the Nam, yet." I offered him words of consolation, but at the moment he needed a painkiller. Bear grimaced as he kept holding his arm with his hand, which was soaked with blood. I looked over and saw a corpsman working on our section leader. "He looks pretty bad off. What happened?"

Still wincing from his pain, Sugar Bear said, "He's all fucked up. Got it in the neck."

"That sucks. Anyone else get hit?"

"Yeah, two other dudes, but not too bad. Think one of 'em got it in the ass."

"I'm kind of low on dudes, but I'll send a couple over to help man your gun. Okay?"

He nodded, and I turned to walk back to my squad. I felt more than fortunate that nobody in the Jello Squad had been wounded or killed since I became squad leader over five months earlier.

four dudes in 8ls...shit we aren't supposed to get Purps...it's too hairy for me...if this shit keeps up the NVA just might zap my slippery little ass...what in the hell am I doing here...damn glad no one got killed...just don't need that.

Half-way back to our gun pit, I yelled to Cossack to send Pink Rat over to the other squad.

"Sure...what happened over there?"

Continuing to stroll toward Cossack, I explained, "Four wounded...that's all, luckily."

Stopping, I turned and peered back at Sugar Bear. A corpsman was wrapping a large bandage around his arm. He would leave the op for several days, and an officer would give him his first Purple Heart. I was glad his scenario was not mine. I turned and headed back to my gun pit, back to a lucky squad.

Cossack screamed, "The corn field! Tracers!" Before I could dive to the ground, green tracer rounds from a burst of an NVA machine gun cut through the night air just inches from my head; my heart was pounding out of control like it had during the rocket attack on Hill 10 during the Tet Offensive. I scampered on my hands and knees. The safety of our gun pit, my destination.

SHIT...that burst was head level...felt a round whiz by my nose...those goddamn bullets were meant for me...too short for this bullshit.

"Oh shit! Someone's tryin' to kill me!"

Chapter 37
7 June 1968

I Thought We're Supposed To Do The Killing

It had been a forty-eight-hour day. If it had only been a bad dream, yet, this four-act, miniature nightmare reeked with authenticity. Shrapnel real. Agony real.

Unfortunately, my near-miss at being killed and the NVA machine gunner's near confirmed kill were not the final events on the calendar for that night. With the fourth Communist attack at about four that morning, I began to lose faith in certain myths, especially the one about us being the superior force. Although our military prowess had been well advertised at Tripoli, Iwo Jima, and the Frozen Chosin Reservoir, the North Vietnamese Army did not seem to be impressed or intimidated by us; it seemed our PR man had neglected this territory. It was easy to understand why. The Corps may have succeeded in building men, but the NVA intended to bury men, the American brand. They were playing a real and deadly game. It was a bad league in which to be, and unfortunately, it was the only game in town.

The NVA had owned the night. We still owned the abandoned airstrip. And the sun owned the morning sky. We wanted to sleep, but the morning sun was a rude and unpopular alarm clock.

I wanted to be eating breakfast somewhere else and so did Cossack. Even the battalion mess hall was beginning to seem tolerable, but it was twenty forever miles away. It was June 7, 1968, and our continental breakfasts had been canceled due to war. C-rations were the order of the day as usual.

I opened my-box of C-rats, pouring out the contents, hoping for something that my stomach would appreciate. The menu: ham and eggs, canned peaches, crackers and cheese, and cocoa.

Cossack was not as fortunate.

"Goddamn it! Ham and motherfuckers. Yuck. I think my hunger just went AWOL. Come to think of it, I feel like doing the same thing...especially after yesterday and last night."

Cossack was right. The operation, which was in its twenty-first day, was lasting twenty-one days too long for us. There was part of me that envied Mike Rae: not the being wounded part, but the being off the op part. The NVA's bullets and mortars had been missing me for the past three weeks, but they were due to get lucky. I was afraid that their luck would make me a permanent casualty. I would settle for a million dollar wound, one that would send me back to the safety of Da Nang.

"Why the hell didn't those bastards stay home last night with their mamasans? Don't they ever get horny?"

Cossack shrugged his shoulders. "Guess they love abuse a little more than a piece of ass. You'd figure they'd get the message and realize we don't dig them too much. Hell no. They just keep coming back for more. Crazy. Fuckin' crazy!"

I lit a heat tab. My hot cocoa was five minutes away from my lips. "I must agree with you. Those dudes are just a little too persistent for me. Remember, one of them tried to blow me away last night. That's getting too goddamn close for this Jello Kid. As a matter of fact, I've got to get the hell out of this place...and fast! Got any ideas?"

Cossack wore the face of a '*D*' student who did not know the answer to the math teacher's question. "I'll tell you what, if I could figure a safe way out of this hole, I'd send you a letter with the answer in it."

"Thanks, lifer."

"By the way, *your* ham and eggs taste real good. Deee...licious."

"You maggot! Thanks a lot." I looked down at the C-rat can which he had left for me. I was one hundred and fifty pounds of disappointment.

Cossack stopped grinning long enough to laugh about my predicament. "You mean you don't like ham and motherfuckers?"

"Shit! I was going to give you a huss and let you have some of my hot chocolate, but you had to go and be a back-stabber and do a switch."

Cossack interrupted to interject sarcastically, "Oh, you want to be nice to me."

Ignoring his comment, I continued, "Ham and lima beans for breakfast. Gross! Do you realize what you've done to my morale? The troopies are supposed to keep up their morale. We're both troopies, so why are you doing this shit to my stomach and my morale? This war thing...no sleep...crazy people shootin' at you all night long...and almost gettin' choppered into a hot LZ to save Mike or Lima Company's ass the other day. Heard they got mortared for four hours yesterday. The chopper that was supposed to take us in...gettin' all shot up. Damn pilot gettin' hit in the leg. Glad they canceled it. And about two weeks ago, word on the street has it that Bravo Company got hit hard and had 18 KIAs and 60 WIAs. Shit, it's gettin' to be a real drag."

I let out a deep sigh and continued, "Hell, I need a good stiff drink, not that tiger piss, but forget that...the Crotch just didn't get around to settin' up a bar for us out here. The only thing they set up out here was *us*. With my morale in such bad shape, I sure would've appreciated havin' something half-way decent for morning chow."

My cocoa had finally decided to become hot chocolate. The can of ham and lima beans still lay on the ground, unopened and unwanted. I was hungry, but not that hungry. The hot chocolate tasted as good as a French kiss from back in the World, but Cossack would have to imagine. He continued staring at my can of hot chocolate. It was three feet, but a million miles away. It was gold, and I was the banker.

"Forget it, dude. Your lips will never touch this tasty chocolate. You ripped me off and almost got us killed last night. What was the idea of firing at that dude out in the rice paddy in front of our gun pit. You want to be a hero or something? You should know by now that the lifers won't give you a medal for playin' hero. They won't even whip any rank on us. All I can say is that you're goddamn crazy."

Cossack, pretending to look shocked, said, "Me...the Mad Cossack...crazy? You're the one who's insane...joining this green mother when you didn't have to. Strange."

"I may be, but I am gettin' too damn short for your hero shit. I have a flight date coming up in less than a month. In the past week or so Bravo Company has run into some serious shit. A bunch of KIAs. We got it made here compared to those dudes." I took a deep sigh and continued, "And after last night...four dudes in the other squad getting wounded. You know the lifers'll put some incompetent son of bitch in charge of our section now that our section leader went and got himself wounded last night. The NVA are a big enough pain in the ass. We sure as hell don't need some dumb lifer telling us how to run our mortar. I intend to get my civilian ass out of this insane war. I just don't need the bullshit anymore."

Before Cossack could say anything, Pink Rat walked up and interrupted us. "Did you guys hear?"

"Yeah. We used to...that is, before we became mortar men."

Cossack, who liked my play on words, was chuckling his approval, but Pink Rat was not smiling. His face wore a serious mask, and he was impatiently waiting for us to listen to his announcement. We didn't want to overdose on laughter, so we stopped laughing. Pink Rat stood there, looking like an angry father baffled about what to do with his two spoiled children. We liked him, so we looked up at him politely. It was his turn to talk. "Are you guys going to interrupt me again or are you going to let..."

"Yes, I'm going to interrupt you one more time since you interrupted Jello and me while we were indulging in our morning brunch. We were having a quaint little conversation when you butted in. Shall we have this lad thrown into our crocodile infested moat?" I nodded my affirmative vote.

"You guys are unreal."

"What the hell else do you expect? This goddamn place is unreal."

"Is that all you two can do...just joke around all the time? You almost got your asses blown away last night and...DAMN...why don't you shut up for one goddamn minute!"

"Sure thing, my somber and mature friend, but you're the one who's been babbling. So what's this news you have for us...Ho Chi Minh's really a spy for the CIA? God's a Viet Cong? We surrendered, and we're going home? So what's so damn important?"

"Cossack, close your bullshit mouth for a minute, so our

Polish friend will leave us alone."

I guzzled the last bit of my hot chocolate, so I was finally ready to listen to Pink Rat whose voice began to quiver as he said, "Well, it's Bobby Kennedy...yesterday he..." He paused before taking a deep breath.

Before he could continue, I interrupted him. "Kennedy probably won the California primary, right? He's a far out dude. I just might vote for him, but first I have to get my ass out of this place alive. You know it's not safe here. People get killed and stuff."

"Damn it, you two, that's it! I just heard over the radio that some crazy dude blew Kennedy away yesterday. He got wasted."

"Bullshit. No way."

"No bullshit! Straight scoop, Cossack."

There was a triangle of stunned silence. I grabbed the can of ham and lima beans and threw it as hard as I could at the ground.

"Fuck! What a crock of shit! I thought we were supposed to do the killing?"

Chapter 38
10 June 1968

Letters From The World

The NVA mortar men, bored with killing Marines, aimed their 82mm mortars in the direction of the village of Thuong Duc but dropped their barrage on a more valuable target: Stanley Looker Special Forces Camp. Their new target was across one of the tributaries of the Song Vu Gia and was a half-mile west of the grass-covered runway, which had become our home for the previous two weeks. At Stanley Looker, the explosion of the first round of a twenty-round NVA mortar barrage sent the dozen Green Berets and the two hundred South Vietnamese defenders scampering for cover. Having been on the receiving end of seventeen North Vietnamese mortar barrages in the last twenty-four days, it was easy for us to sneak a smile and sigh. Someone else was receiving the Welcome-Wagon treatment from the NVA.

The luxury of giving thanks that we were not on the receiving end lasted only a few seconds because the Green Berets needed immediate support fire to lift the Communist barrage. Within seconds, four silent 81mm mortar tubes were pointing northwest toward the source of the NVA mortar fire. The silence evaporated as the first of ten unfriendly replies slid down our mortar tube. The other three mortars began firing. Within minutes forty mortar rounds were racing toward the suspected enemy mortar position. From a spotter plane, a Forward Air Controller observed the NVA mortar tubes and radioed a location adjustment to us.

"Right two hundred meters. Drop three hundred meters."

Forty-five seconds later, some of the boys from the 31st NVA Regiment were on the run. Those who did not escape the shrapnel of our mortar barrage would become a small part of the sterile statistics in our battalion's command chronology for June 1968. In a subparagraph of a subheading, 112 NVA KIAs and 84 VC KIAs would become characters in the official story of Operation Mameluke Thrust.

"Just got the word. We kicked ass on the gooks and knocked out one of their tubes."

"Far out, Cossack!"

"We kind of lucked out having that spotter plane cruising around up there."

"We lucked out? You mean those dudes at Stanley Looker lucked out."

Cossack nodded his agreement with me, but he had very little sympathy for the Green Berets in the camp across the river. After all, in Cossack eyes, the Green Berets had it made compared to us because they slept under tin roofs, drank cold beer and had steak in their mess hall. Meanwhile, back at the ol' runway, we chomped on our C-rats in the rain, got our asses shot at just about everyday, received mail only once every two weeks, and best of all, we got to deal with mean red ants when we slept on the grassy runway. Cossack referred to our situation as a genuine Marine Corps bummer.

Chuckling, I said, "I get the impression you don't appreciate this little camping trip."

"No shit! I could be back in good ol' Detroit grooving on my chick...but I had to be a dumb ass patriot."

It was a good time to ambush Cossack, so I did. "Look at the bright side...someone else is grooving on your honey back in the World."

"Thanks a hell of a lot."

"You only have six more months left in this suck hole. You're getting short."

"About as short as Wilt Chamberlain. Oh...to be as short as you, Jello."

I replied with a victorious smile, "Twenty-five days and counting."

two-five...beautiful...might make it out of this armpit...back to the World...back to college...oh to have to pull an all-nighter studying instead of doin' fire missions...real people...no lifers...no rifle and personnel inspections...no NVA trying to kill my dumb ass...a decent cup of coffee...real food...a genuine hot shower...eight hours of uninterrupted sleep... seeing movies all the way through...not in reels...no sniper interrupting the movie...no two-beer limit or sandbags to fill...no one trying to kill me...just twenty-five days short.

"If you're going to daydream, you might as well come inside the hooch."

"Sounds like a great idea, Cossack."

"Speaking of great ideas...setting up this hooch was sort of a..."

"Weird idea...dumb idea?"

"Great idea!" Cossack, thinking about what he had just said, paused before editing his statement. "Well...dumber than shit when you think about it."

Surveying our architectural master piece, I snickered sarcastically, "Big Frankie...Frank Lloyd Wright couldn't have done better."

"Maybe, but he wouldn't have been as dumb as us and sleep in this time bomb."

"So what if we're lying on nine damn cases of mortar rounds...not to mention the..." Pausing long enough to count the fifteen wooden ammo cases that formed the walls of our impromptu hooch, I continued, "Why worry? Danger is our business. Action and thrills...we love it!"

I crawled inside and motioned for Cossack to join me. As he stuck his suntanned face inside our shrine to the inventive spirit, he added, "And it keeps the wind out, and the poncho roof keeps us nice and dry."

"Besides, if our hooch is hit, we'll go out with a bang. There'll be little bits of us all over this valley."

"Now that's what I call getting blown away royal!"

Fortunately, our mothers were an ocean away from our conversation. We were drunk with laughter. "Jello, can you dig us being featured on the cover of one of those true adventure magazines. 'Two Combat Marines Sneer at Death As They Sleep On One Thousand Pounds of Explosives.' Growl. Let's eat some nails for lunch."

Rolling off my sarcastic tongue, "We love it!"

"Oh shit! Do you hear what I hear?" Unfortunately, I knew the answer to his question, and I didn't like it.

The haunting sound of death from the skies, the NVA version, was back. The first 82mm mortar round exploded two hundred meters west of our makeshift shanty. The next mortar round burst about one hundred and seventy-five meters west of us. The explosions continued, each about 10 meters directly in front of all the 105mm howitzer positions, each getting uncomfortably closer to us and our high-explosive hooch.

"Shall we exit stage left?"

Bravado coursed through me, so I shook my head. "Not yet. I don't feel like jumping into our muddy ass fighting hole and getting all wet. They'll only drop a few more rounds."

Cossack nodded hopefully, wanting me to be right but the explosions kept coming. Closer each time.

Unfortunately, the decision makers had aligned all the gun positions in a straight line. This textbook military alignment had conveniently simplified this fire mission for the NVA. The Communists gunners, taking advantage of this, exploded a mortar round twenty-five meters directly north of each of our battalion's gun emplacements. The 105s and the 155s had been visited. The four mortar gun pits would be next. Cossack and I were last on their list.

When a mortar round intended for us exploded twenty-five meters too close, we swallowed hard. With the identical question in our bulging eyes, we didn't wait around to answer it or compare notes. "The hell with the mud." I scampered out to the relative safety of a one-man fighting hole, which was only a few feet from our abandoned high explosive bachelor pad.

Because I was the first one in the fighting hole, my face and the front of my jungle utilities was covered with mud. Cossack, who was just a second behind me, landed on top of me.

"Shit! Watch out, fucker!" I was on the wrong side of a Marine-and-mud-sandwich.

"Shut up, short-timer. You're safe. I'm lying on top of you...the shrapnel has to go through me first. You might say, I'm sort of saving you, so maybe I should get a medal," he snickered.

With the front side of me drenched in mud, I found it difficult to appreciate what Cossack was saying. "Gee...thanks," I said sarcastically.

"I hope you didn't want to keep your utilities dry. You don't have a date for tonight, do you?"

I wiped some mud from my mouth. "Well, those are two things I sure don't have to worry about now."

"I think we've been hard-assed."

Cossack was right. Just moments after we jumped into our fighting hole, the NVA ended their barrage. "The NVA are probably sitting around laughing their asses off at us."

mud...Cossack's elbow in my back...pain...at least we're not on choppers flying off to reinforce someone's ass...last week...would a been blown away for sure...a real drag when that chopper landed...one eight-man chopper with machine-gun bullet holes in the windshield...pilot's fresh blood soaking his green pant leg...Jello Squad waiting to board the chopper...tired sun sneaking behind silhouetted ridgeline...sky colors changing...six thousand meters east of us NVA mortars chopping up a Marine company...Phantoms swooping and strafing...dropping napalm and five-hundred-pound bombs...explosions...angry black smoke tumbling and fading into the Confederate sky...a dozen more explosions...smoke billowing...bleeding Marines begging... wanting to be lucky...mortar rounds exploding...machine gun bullets crackling and whizzing...eighteen-year-old grunts with no place to go...order to board the chopper...CANCELED...Jello Squad won't get blown away...lucked out...poor dudes getting hit...glad last week's over...this mud isn't so bad.

Turning my head toward Cossack, I asked, "Well...is it over?"

"Yeah."

"Then get off my bod. This mud is...Goddamn it! You don't have to step on my back."

Cossack's, 'Sorry' was less than sincere.

As I climbed out of the fighting hole, I said, "I'll forgive you on one condition. Since we're so scroungy and muddy now, we might as well get an animal football game going."

"That's cool."

"Let's use this canteen for a ball."

The football game began, but the NVA were not invited. Within ten minutes, raindrops were haphazardly dancing around the already muddy runway. Ten Marines, who thought they were football players, could not be bothered by a few raindrops. They were Christmas presents from Heaven on a sultry June afternoon;

however, fifteen minutes later, the raindrops became rude. It was not raining American-style with the proverbial cats and dogs. It was Vietnamese rain. Tigers and water buffaloes were pouring out of the cloudy sky, an epidemic of grey splotches. The game continued. We wallowed for another hour in the mire that had once been an airstrip. Being on the wrong end of a sixty-to-twelve score, we decided to surrender to the other team.

The deluge stopped as the sun timidly peaked from behind a giant cumulus cloud. To the northeast, we could see the silhouette of a helicopter. Like a water bug, it crawled tenaciously across the grizzled sky. Closer and closer. Finally, a CH-46 resupply chopper hovered above us, descending slowly but landing with a slight bounce. A dozen gawkers were turned into available Marines. Within five minutes, we had unloaded the supplies: cases of C-rations, small arms, mortar and artillery ammunition; and most importantly, yet unexpectedly, a bag of mail. It had been ten days since our last mail from the World. There were two hundred smiles on the airstrip that afternoon.

Cossack had just traded me his C-ration apricots for my cheese and crackers when we heard someone bellow our names. We sprang from our sandbags like track stars. Unfortunately, my just opened can of fruit tumbled from my knee, plopping into the mud. I was unconcerned. It was mail call.

Nine people had cared. I proudly waved my links to sanity. "Far out...nine letters!"

Thumbing through a pile of letters, Cossack said, "Must be a record for you."

"Who cares how many...so long as someone back in the World writes."

"You can say that again."

nine...I love mail call...only good thing about this suck ass place...glad someone gives a shit...wouldn't be able to take this place without mail from the World...the real World...not this lifer-infested cesspool...letters...my link with sanity...love ya mister postman...better than Santa...I'll be home for next Christmas and Thanksgiving...for good...out of the Crotch...no more Marine Corps for me...finally get to see all my crazy friends...FITZ...RIESTER...STEVE PATTON...DAVE ROBERTS... RICK MURRAY...CRAZY RECON DAVE...you better make it the hell out of the Nam also...I'll kick your ass if you don't...guess you're still alive...a letter from you...and FITZIE...CATHY CALL...MOM...wonder if you're still pissed off that I joined the Marines... figured your number-two son would let the NVA blow his beautiful ass away...no way...Jello's coming home...twenty-five days short...only twenty-four days in a few more hours...who else...PAM...don't worry I'm keeping my chin up baby...SHERRI my teeny-bopper lovely...what a good neighbor you are...oh WENDY WENDY what strange off-the-wall letter have you written this time...always grooving on you...never understanding you...more letters...far out...PAUL...about time you wrote...swabby must be too busy being a corpsman...bet you're having fun at the battle of the bedpans...at least you're smart enough to be a reservist...I should have stayed in college like you...damn smart to get yourself a degree and two years of active duty in Massachusetts...opposite direction of this dud war...you ain't dumb like this gung ho little bro of yours...might as well open your letter first...shit I don't believe it...signing up for a third year of active duty...Rota, Spain...why'd you want to go there...I should be talking...ha ha look were I ended up...oh well...Rota, Spain is even farther away from the Nam...at least you'll be safe...and last but not least LIZ...lovely antiwar LIZ...what's new from college...fighting off all those gentlemen from Virginia Military Institute or whatever...you signed it LOVE...wonder what that means...who knows...at least you wrote.

"Jello, why you got that weird look on your face? Is it the ham and motherfuckers?"

"No. It's this letter from Liz...no...it's not that...oh, I don't know. She's such a weird chick. Just don't understand her. Enough of my sorrows. You get one from your chick?"

Cossack, grinning, proudly waved two letters. "Not one...but two."

"Not bad."

"She says that she can't wait 'till I'm home so we can...bleep, bleep, censored...ah..."

"She sounds horny to me. Bet you can't wait to whip some of that mad Cossack love on her luscious body. Do I see lust in your demented eyes?"

"Seven months-worth."

"Speaking of a long time. Do you remember how I finally got Liz to write me a few months ago when I was on mess duty?"

"Yeah...that was a genuine hard ass."

"That chick wouldn't even write my dumb bod for two long-ass months."

"And you were so patient...just waiting round for..."

"For nothin'...until I got creative. On day sixty-four of the drought, a letter shows up.

"Jello, I must admit it was a brilliant idea sending her a stamped self-addressed envelope. Hard to believe such an idea came from a super lifer."

"Super lifer...bullshit! You're just jealous 'cause I'm so damn short. You're talkin' to a civilian who's got nothing else to wear besides this damn hero's costume."

"I love your jungle boots! They are classics!"

"When I get back to the World, I'm gonna bronze these babies."

One adventurous red ant roamed aimlessly over the cracked leather of my left jungle boot. With erratic spurts and pauses, the ant finally found its way to my little toe which was protruding from my leather torn boot. My toe was naked and inviting. Before I was able to inflict the status of KIA on the ant, it deserted my toe. He would live to bite another day. It had spied my apricots ala mud and was off to join a platoon of ants that were overrunning my ex-dessert: my loss, their gain.

"These ants are a drag. Let's get back in our hooch."

"Sounds okay to me."

Thirty minutes of squinting and eight letters remained. The twilight canopy shrouding the valley soon acquiesced to nightfall. The NVA and Viet Cong would certainly be on the move. Hopefully, we would not be on their calendar of events.

"Jello, you gonna catch some zees now?"

"Try...but my utilities are still wet...and these damn ammo boxes aren't the best mattress. I'll work on it. Later, dude."

good night Nam...catch you later...good night Victor Charlie...thanks for letting me and the Jello Squad slide today...good night lifers...yuck...good night President Johnson...never thought a Democrat could be so dumb...good night Cossack...you're so crazy that you're sane...thanks for giving my insanity some company...hope to hell your Fu Manchu face makes it out of this goddamn place...I'll be pissed off royal if you let the Cong get a bead on your skinny ass...if you get zapped I'll never forgive you...you'll go to Hell...it'll be a Marine base and the devil will be a gunnery sergeant...we'll make a man out of you...your enlistment's for eternity or maybe longer...they'll even make you stand in line to get into Hell...so you think the Nam was hot...come this way...HA HA sucker...so you hated lifers...we have ten million lifers for ten million years...field days are everyday...rifle and personnel inspections every hour and even more often when we can squeeze another one in...everything is green...even the flames are Marine-green...son you're in the Marine Corps...HA HA...good night little red ant...you're smart...you enjoy life...my shitty boot and almost my toe and my apricots...you don't let all this bullshit fighting bother you...you just live life...you're okay...just don't take any wooden nickels and don't talk to strangers carrying aerosol cans...especially if it has a picture of one of your cousins on it...peace little red commie ant...good night all you back in the World people...get ready...the Jello Kid is coming home...twenty-five and counting...finally be able to figure out Liz...don't think she knows what's going on over here...war...John Wayne bullshit...the right boyfriend...the right dress and the right lay...spend some time here...there ain't no right this or that...the Nam's a multiple choice test and there are only two choices...ALIVE or DEAD...that's all there is here...death doesn't give a rat's ass who the hell it takes...eighteen-year-olds...little-ass kids just tryin' to be kids...babies...grandmothers...any damn race...NVA and Viet Cong soldiers...ARVN soldiers...papasans...mamasans...Marine grunts...college grads...lieutenants...lifers...shitbirds...pure and simple...ready or not...it's just a taker...DAMN IT...twenty-five damn days short...God...please let me escape this place with my bod in one piece...I'll take care of my mind...just make sure my hundred-and-fifty-pound civilian bod gets back to Tucson...BACK TO THE WORLD .

 Stars everywhere. Cricket chatter. Cold beads of sweat meet my hand as it roams the geography of my face. The thought is back: someone in the darkness wants to kill me. But my heavy eyelids bought a one-way ticket on the Dream Express: my destination, the World. The night went on without me.

Chapter 39
11-12 June 1968

Doc Saves The Jello Kid's Butt

Midway in a blue chunk of sky, the chrome yellow sun glared, staring with me at the Lilliputian army in the valley below. The toy soldiers and the matchbox-size tanks shrinking, becoming smaller. The chopper, with its cargo of twenty Marines, leveled off and headed east. Day twenty-five of Operation Mameluke Thrust would go on without me, and I was just fine with that.

Behind us, the myriad of mountains, painted green with dense jungle, were disguised with a mask of purple shadows. Reaching down, a trio of cotton-candy clouds greeted the dark green silhouette of the ridgeline. Like a stringy scar, the long road into the valley mimicked the journey of the meandering river. Snaking west through the valley, the Song Vu Gia glided casually, finally disappearing, swallowed up by a mountain range. Just north of the dusty road that the map called Route 4, rice paddies, teased by the burning sun, formed a mosaic of glistening window panes. Having left my Kodak Instamatic back at Hill 10, I could only focus the camera of my mind. Click.

down there that scroungy looking Hill 52...road and river winding by it...over there that goddamn swamp...damn big...first night of the op....sloshing around in the swamp...Cossack slipping and going under...nasty tasting swamp water...like Marine Corps soup...VC prisoners... kids crying...eight hundred Marines lost in the swamp...NVA must have been laughing their damn asses off...too funny to attack us...finally at Hill 52...utilities wet...feet aching...yawning...only three mortar rounds exploding...can of chicken and noodles falling...plopping in the mud...never thought I'd appreciate C-rations...out of food after two days...four South

Vietnamese Rangers waving at me and inviting me to eat with them...cooking rice in a helmet...green weed on the side of the hill...ranger reaching over yanking the plant up...dropping it into another helmet...water simmering...fish heads cooking...my stomach growling...finally ready...stuffing my face...fanning my burning mouth...chow damn hot...rangers laughing...Mexican food not spicy compared to Vietnamese chow...windy night on a steep and dusty hill...the screamin' shits...Ho Chi Minh's revenge...burning...stinking...feel sorry for any NVA sappers trying to sneak up on my ass...war's a shitty business...SURE THE HELL IS...Ho Chi Minh's birthday...hell of a birthday party...a real surprise party for us...dud...newspapers probably had us winning...Marines always do...people back in the World...suckers for believing all the battle bullshit...so many Cong been killed...they must be out of dudes by now...we always win...always ten times as many NVA dead...so why did we get stopped on Uncle Ho's birthday...fourteen killed...dead Marines never going home the right way...over eighty guys messed up...Charley Company eaten up...creamed...platoon overrun...goddamn I'm lucky someone up there likes this civilian...twenty-four big ones left for the Jello Kid...maybe I'll be going home alive in one piece.

"You must be in 81s?"

"Yeah."

With the damaged mortar standing upright, secured by my knees, my hands were free to wipe the oily sweat on my faded utility pant legs. The metallic odor still clinging like a glove to my hands. The grunt sitting next to me was trying to make conversation. I was polite but not interested. I glanced quickly at his too young face as he asked, "Goin' home?"

"Yeah."

The grunt replied, "Me too. Flight date in seven days. At least that's what I figure. Never know. Anything can happen. Like this dude in my squad. He was leaving the op on a convoy...got ambushed...jumped off the truck and was deader than shit before he hit the fucking deck. Wife and a kid back in the World. Ain't that the shits?"

"Yeah...sure is."

My head was throbbing, so I ended the conversation abruptly and turned away from the going-home-alive Marine. I was glad he would be going back to the World, glad no one had blown out his twentieth candle. I turned to the window behind me and focused on the National Geographic scene below, which stretched for miles in all directions. Below us, a Marine convoy of tanks and six-by trucks rolled down the now dusty, winding road. Like the grunt next to me, the convoy would be lucky; they would make it through, but there would be a next time: for some, a last time.

beautiful down there...looks like Operation Pecos...my first op...rugged looking mountains...a dud stomping around them but beautiful...damn its been almost a year since the first op...another couple days and it'll be one year in this place...I was crazy before but this place has made me really crazy...always been a little loony...my physical science class with the spacey teacher...she was in the ozone...Swift...Rick Murray...me...all falling out of our desks and rolling around on the floor grunting and laughing...poor teacher...the night we threw water balloons at cars...crazy...first to take off running...laughing so hard and barely able to run...somehow getting away...mud clod fights back in the old neighborhood on Louis Lane...only seven or eight years old...another gang ripping shingles off their roof...flinging them through the air...then a thud...a brick hitting me in the face...my head ringing...throwing more mud clods...laughing and loving it...working at the country club...yes ma'am and yes sir...$1.25 an hour and all the shit you can take... plastic people playing their little rich-people games...aristocrats with master charge cards and bad grammar...care for coffee or Sanka...yes...coffee or Sanka...oh sure...wanting to tell the bitch to open her goddamn ears...I offered you a choice...but not saying anything...really needing the job to help pay for college...BRILLIANT IDEA...the people aren't listening...so why not...sure...with lower class hands gripping pots of coffee and Sanka...politely...ma'am would you care for some shit or piss...yes...thank you boy...wanting to tell her...what's this boy shit...bitch...you're not even listening...ten o'clock at night...party of fifteen hanging around...bullshitting...wish they'd get the hell out of here and go home with each other and try to get laid...probably too drunk for it...forget it...GREAT IDEA...I'll mingle with the crowd...listening to the bullshit...pouring unwanted water in lipstick smudged glasses...I'll blow a silent but deadly fart...floating around in the cigarette smoke air...making the *rounds to each upper-middle class nose...country-club eyes rolling back and forth wondering who's the culprit...casually moving away from their partner in bullshit...suspecting their retreating partner...an ex-student-body-president type of guy suggesting that the socialites call it a night...good night folks...picking up the dirty silverware...I'm grinning victoriously...just like the neighborhood tree climbing contest...the guy back on leave from the army climbing the mulberry tree higher and higher...almost to the top but thin top branches were too weak for his weight...challenging the champion...neighborhood gang below cheering...I'm climbing higher...sixty-three pounds of fifth grade Tarzan Jr. reaching the top...the real top...thin branches...danger and all...hero for a day...haven't changed...Camp Lejeune field maneuvers...camping in a forest of tall pines...up up higher higher...officer below yelling for me to get down immediately...that's an order...nice breeze up here...nice tree over there...this one's a drag...thirty feet up...leaping to the other tree...falling and grasping a pine branch...limb bending fast and breaking...lucky hands grabbing another branch...hugging the tree trunk...sliding down and laughing...angry officer not laughing...if he only knew I have an excuse...I'm crazy...after all I joined the Marines and didn't have to...crazy as going to Virginia for cold weather training in March and getting orders for the Nam in April...ass backwards... no...just normal planning for the Crotch...love this Green Machine...in twenty-four days the Nam and the Crotch can kiss my ass goodbye FOREVER.*

"Far out...it looks like we're just about there."

"Yeah...nice to finally be off that op."

"I second the motion. Being in Charley Company was gettin' to be a real drag."

I nodded. "I can dig it. Charley Company runs into more shit than anybody."

"No shit."

The helicopter hovered a moment and then began its descent to Hill 55, the Seventh Marines' regimental headquarters, which was located about ten miles south of the Da Nang airstrip. It touched down on the LZ with a slight bounce as I was daydreaming about why our battalion commander chose not to let us bring our mortars at the beginning of the operation. I remained baffled by his decision; our mortar fire power might have altered the sad results of our May 19th engagement with the NVA. The tactics on that hot May afternoon made little sense to me. Not using H & S Company to come to the aid of beleaguered Charley Company still haunted me. They needed reinforcements yet we were not utilized. Had our fire power been used to aid Charley Company, there was a high probability that H & S Company would have suffer a number of KIAs and WIAs. I had friends in Charley Company, and that was a risk I was willing to take, but it was time for me to put this conjecture in the *What If* file.

The jolt knocked the mortar bipods loose from my sweaty grip, but I grabbed my ticket off the op before the bipods could hit the deck of the chopper. Clutching their M16s with one hand and their helmets with the other, the passengers from the boondocks scampered out the back of the chopper. The last one off, I clutched my ticket out of the bush. Lugging the soon to be repaired forty-pound bipods had been an inconvenience, but getting off the op made it all worthwhile. My first order of business took me to the regimental armory. With my baby-sitting responsibilities concluded, I set out to find out if the chow hall was still open. Being on the operation for the previous twenty-five days was making mess-hall chow seem inviting.

"Excuse me, doc."

A Navy corpsman, who was walking past the armory, replied, "Yeah...what do you need?"

"You know if the mess hall is still open for lunch?"

"Let's see...1415 hours. No, it closed over an hour ago."

"Bummer! Well, when's it open for evening chow?"

"At 1615. You must be new around here."

"Yeah, but not to the Nam...I'm so short I have to look up at the curb."

"I guess so. I should have looked at your ragged ass boots. Damn...they're sure salty. Your toes are even stickin' out. You must've walked a million miles in 'em."

"Not quite. Catch you later, doc"

"Sure, short-timer...later."

that dude could have been my brother...damn I am glad Paul won't get sent over here...if I make it out of this war I'll have taken up all of our family's damn luck...almost blown away five times...Jello...you want to go to Da Nang with me...no...I'm broke this month...catch you later...six-by truck hitting a land mine...exploding...could have been me...Jello Squad moving to western end of Hill 10...leaving our old tent and gun pit...filling new sandbags for a new gun pit at western end of the hill...bitching and moaning...why our squad...new gun pit still needs three more rows of sandbags to be safe...swooshing sounds racing through the blackest no-moon night...red streaks coming...122mm rockets crashing...one two three four five explosions...five more swooshing in...then more exploding...more...black night...red streaks rushing towards us...Marines yelling...heart's pounding faster and faster...swallowing hard...whispering please dear God let me live...please make them stop...screaming GODDAMN IT... THEY'RE OUT OF OUR MORTAR RANGE...WE'RE SITTING DUCKS...SHIT...five more rockets slamming into the hill...clods of reddish brown earth...shrapnel...chunks of metal flying wildly...black radioman sleeping near our old tent...back of his head ripped off...half of his brains splattered somewhere else...a giant red ink spot soaking into the plywood floor...radio operator going home...integration of the races worked today...applause...a white boy a black boy a brown boy a yellow boy...all got together... equality today...the boys all lay dead...drained of their red blood...free at last...hell...I don't even want to think about that shitty night...no time for this...I'm too goddamn short.

I decided that an afternoon stroll was not what I needed, so I headed for a cluster of lonely benches. The dozen or so wooden benches faced a white sheet, which hung unceremoniously from a square frame constructed of two-by-fours; this served a dual purpose at night: a movie screen for the Marines on Hill 55 and an easy target for Viet Cong snipers.

might as well plop my bod down here...move a couple of benches together and get under them...don't need to sun bathe today...need to relax...my first day in the Nam right here on Hill 55...watching Vic Morrow kicking ass in 'Combat' the TV show...taking a while for them to get the second reel working...watching flicks in reels...what a dud...finally the movie gets going again...three cracking sounds...then more bullets whizzing through the screen...realism in movies is great but this is ridiculous...damn...a year gone by and the Cong still can't zap me...sure am a lucky dude...thanks up there.

The expected refreshing smell of rain was replaced by the unique aroma of Marine Corps chow lurking in the four o'clock air. The anticipated late afternoon rains drenched someone else's jungle utilities. With a relaxed smile, I plopped my helmet on my head, the broken chin-strap dangling as I tilted the helmet back. With the remainder of my gear buckled and fastened, I grabbed my M16 and followed my nose. Arriving at the mess hall within a few minutes, I walked in the barn-like building and stood in the chow line, which had only fifteen or twenty Marines ahead of me. The line moved quickly.

this chow is probably as raunchy as ever...absence makes the heart grow fonder...but the chow always stays the same...must remember tradition...the Crotch has a reputation to maintain...only four more dudes in front of this hungry-ass short-timer...smells like good old shit on a shingle...SOS on toast...at least there aren't any ants to share the chow with...a table to sit at instead of the mud and mosquitoes jiving us...FAR OUT...I'm next...OH SHIT...I don't believe it...ungoddamn believable...what the hell am I going to do now...been out in the bush too damn long...people eat off of trays here...not out of C-rat cans.

"Where the hell you going, Marine? My chow that bad."
suck out dude...watch out who you're callin' Marine...this is the one and only Jello Kid and I'm on my way out of this Green Machine...I don't have time for your dumb ass questions...now where the hell am I going to scrounge up a tray.

The screen door at the rear of the mess hall slammed hard behind my anger. The corpsman who I had met early walked by me unnoticed.

"Slow down, dude. Where the hell you going so damn fast?"

I stopped abruptly, turning to see who was so interested in my anger. "Goddamn it. I'm pissed!"

"You look like a dude who's just found out he really signed up for four years when he thought he signed up for only two. Relax. So what's wrong?"

"I don't fucking believe it. I'm standing in the chow line and finally get to the front...and bigger than shit, there I stand looking dumber than hell without a tray. I'm so damn hungry, and then this. Where in the hell am I supposed to find a tray on this hill? I don't know anyone here."

"Relax, my short-timer friend. We'll go over to my tent, and I'm sure one of the corpsmen that's on duty will be glad to lend you his tray. If we can patch up you crazy Marines, I'm sure we can keep you from starving."

Stunned by his act of kindness, I smiled and said, "Thanks a lot, doc. I really appreciate it."

By the time we returned to the mess hall, the short lines of four o'clock had become typically long. After almost two years in the Marine Corps, I was beginning to believe that *the line*, especially the long version, had been invented by a Marine lifer nearly two centuries ago. Besides providing us with lines in which to stand, the Corps also fed each one of us the manhood line. My being in Vietnam was proof that I had swallowed the proverbial hook, line and sinker.

The line moved slowly, but within twenty minutes we were only a dozen people away from the infamous SOS. "Those dudes up there, sure looks like they're having loads of fun serving that shit."

"Yeah, they definitely look stimulated."

"Mess duty is such a suck ass job. You ever have it?"

"Twice, doc. Two goddamn times too many! Thirty-days' worth back in October and November and a week's worth in Boot Camp. Boot Camp mess duty was kind of a hard ass. They made me a smedley...so I was able to look around during chow."

The corpsman's face pleading ignorance. "What's this smedley thing you're talking about?"

"It's some weird lifer name the Crotch gives to enlisted dudes who make like waiters for the officers and staff. I had to keep about eight DIs happy and find out what they wanted for chow and serve it to 'em. Basically keep them content...which is impossible."

"Sounds like Marine boot camp is as much fun as they say it is."

"Loads of fun. I was pretty lucky since I used to work at a country club as a bus boy before I joined this Green Machine. My brother was a waiter there, so I learned a lot of good waiter stuff from him. He's a corpsman now."

"He over here?"

"No. Thank God. Stationed somewhere in Massachusetts right

now...gonna get transferred to Rota, Spain pretty soon."

"Smart dude."

I agreed and continued with my story about boot camp. "One time this one DI told me what he wanted for chow. Got real specific. 'Two slices of meat...thin not thick and two scoops of mash potatoes with gravy only on the potatoes'. So I went up to the chow line and asked the dude who was serving the chow to give me the food the way the DI wanted it. Well, this maggot decided to be an asshole. He would only give me one scoop of mash potatoes. So I begged him to cut me some slack. He just laughed."

With a subtle smile inching across his face, the corpsman nodded. He knew that the Marine serving mashed potatoes wouldn't be serving any compassion; after all, he had the power, and that was intoxicating.

I continued with my story. "I was ready to shit in my pants. The damn DI would kick my ass for sure. At any rate, when I took the plate back to the DI, he looked at it and then jumped up and started growling in my face. Then he gave me a karate chop to the throat."

"Wow. That sucks."

I nodded and continued. "I thought my throat was going to fall out. He told me I had better come back with the right shit on his plate this time or my ass was grass. Needless to say, I was scared shitless, so I went back to the maggot who jived me before and pleaded with him. He thought it was all kinda funny. I told him again that the DI would kick my ass if I didn't come back with two scoops of mashed potatoes. He said, 'tell that son of a bitch if he doesn't like getting only one scoop of mashed potatoes, he can go to hell'. When the DI asked where his second scoop was, I said, 'Sir, the private was told to tell the son of a bitch that if he doesn't like getting only one scoop, then he can go to hell'. The DI freaked out. When he asked who had said all this, I gladly pointed out the maggot to the DI. He laid so much shit into that dude. Damn, I wanted to laugh so bad... but had to maintain...boot camp and all."

The corpsman joined me in my victorious laughter. "That's great!"

Finally, we became the front of the line. The ground beef and cream-colored gravy, better known as SOS or shit on a shingle, soaked up what had been stale bread. As we walked towards a table with two empty seats, two undisciplined peach-halves sloshed about on my tray. Once seated, I licked the peach syrup which was running down my thumb. Reaching across the table, the corpsman retrieved a pitcher of warm, green Kool-Aid: warm for the Nam, green for the Marine Corps.

fuck...these peas taste like they're left over from the Korean War...mix them with the SOS and maybe that'll kill the taste and not me...I don't believe it...everything around here is green...even the food...don't the lifers ever give up...this stuff still tastes like shit...mixing it up doesn't even help...shut up Jello...chow down and shut up your growling stomach.

With our stomachs pacified, we left the mess hall and joined another line. After a minute's wait, we were dipping our trays into garbage cans full of boiling water; first washing, then rinsing them. With our housekeeping chores out of the way, we walked leisurely back to the corpsman's tent.

"Thanks for everything, doc."

"No big deal."

"Better head on down to the other end of the hill and find me a nice place to crash. Down where they show the flicks looked pretty nice to me. Be seein' you around."

"Hold on." Pausing, the corpsman searched for a solution and then continued, "No need for you to sack out down there. I go on duty in five minutes, so why don't you crash here...I won't need my rack."

Twice in one day I found a reason to smile. Had I been the pope, I would have nominated him for sainthood. Corpsmen always seem to come through for Marines.

"Thanks a lot, doc! It's been almost a month since I've zeed out in a cot. You're okay."

"Well, if I don't see you before you leave tomorrow...good luck."

"Yeah, thanks again. Later."

I was too exhausted to dream, too tired to care. The night noises would be heard by others. When I awoke the next morning, the corpsman had not returned. Still feeling groggy, I dressed slowly. I grabbed my M16 and other equipment, and headed for the mess hall and had a cup of hot coffee. As I was savoring my coffee, I learned that I had slept through a rocket attack on Hill 55.

The NVA had dropped more than a dozen 122mm rockets into the area of the hill where the impromptu theater had been set up.

so that's why the corpsman never made it back this morning...still busy with the wounded...damn I'm lucky that the corpsman let me sleep in his tent...I'd be deader than shit if I had slept down at the theater...getting a little too close for me...the Kid is getting too short for this crap...twenty-three days and counting...twenty-three big ones.

My short-timer's stare shot past the other Marines whom were sitting in the mess hall. I would be going back to the World soon, and the Nam would be theirs until each one of them would escape, one way or another.

Chapter 40
Late June 1968

The Last Shitty Beer

The military called it a Uniform Sierra Oscar show. We called it a USO show. Not exactly Las Vegas, but it would be a taste of home, a morsel to be savored. It would be a back-in-the-World experience. We had been out of circulation for so long that I did not care if our entertainers, a band of Filipinos, were on tour in the Nam because they were number one or because they had been run out of the last dive that had made the mistake of hiring them. All of this was unimportant. After being mortared and shot at by the NVA on an almost daily basis while on Operation Mameluke Thrust, the Marines of Hill 10 were hungry for loud music and not the sounds of war that we had endured for more than three weeks. Although this crew would not be equal to the Rolling Stones or the Beatles, their electric guitars, sax, and drums would do the trick for the entertainment-starved Marines on our hill.

Hopefully, the rumor, that is Rumor Number two hundred ninety-one of the fiscal year, would depart the Realm of Rumor and *Chieu Hoi* [change sides] to the Land of Fact. Would there actually be women on the stage with the band? In one more day, at sixteen hundred hours or four o'clock real time, we would know, but first that nasty night had to do its thing; then, a mere eight to ten hours more of waiting, and we could groove on the imported jams.

Had Ralph Nader been at evening chow with us, a lawsuit, or at least an investigation, would have been forthcoming. Fortunately for him, he missed it. Only one more week of Marine Corps chow was in store for the Jello Kid. Eventually all suffering ends, even in the Nam.

Cossack and I returned to our tent without Pink Rat. "Wish that Polack would hurry up so we can get started on those cases of beer. Been waiting all day to do some serious drinking."

Cossack, frustrated with another unsuccessful battle with evening chow, threw his tray, canteen cup, and eating utensils on his cot. "No, Shit! How's that dude expect us to get smashed tonight if he doesn't hurry up. It's the end of the month and you know the gooks will probably put the whoop on us 'round about midnight. Damn, this war even gets in the way of a good ol' drinkin' party."

"Bitter, bitter. You're just pissed 'cause you have another six months in the suck ass place."

"Stick it, Jello!"

Before I could toy with my friend's frustrations, Pink Rat strolled into the tent. We went unnoticed. His mind was focused on R and R back in the World. Fantasies were such wonderful distractions. "Pink Rat looks like he got himself a cache of love letters from his honey. It's all nice and everything that he writes her everyday...true love and all that shit, but how many different things can you say about this cesspool. This place sucks...period...end of sentence. Shit is shit...no more, no less. How many ways can you spell *shit*, anyway?"

Pretending to take my question seriously, Cossack paused and then randomly picked the number forty-six. "Hold on...I'll check my Marine Corps Manual." Cossack looked under his cot and feigned an attempt at searching for his manual.

"Seems I've misplaced the sacred book."

"Let's ask a lifer. Yeah, we'll ask Pink Rat."

Being referred to as a lifer torpedoed Pink Rat's ship of dreams. His R and R was over. A volley of vigorous denunciations was in order. "You dudes are just calling me a lifer because you're jealous I get so many letters from my girl. If you really want a lifer...well, that boot lieutenant who tried to give us a hard time a couple of weeks ago...that's a genuine lifer."

With a smirk on my face, and my eyes rolling back, I sneered, "What the hell was that dude's problem? We had spent most of that night firin' the holy shit out of our tube. I mean *boo coo* [bastardized version of *beaucoup*, French for *many*] fire missions. Damn NVA were everywhere...even tried to break through the wire down by Motor T. Damn, was it hittin' the fan down by those bunkers. Then I just about shit a brick when the boys in COC [Combat Operations Center] whipped that last fire mission on us. When they called in the elevation for it, I couldn't believe it. The damn tube was pointing almost straight up."

"So why the hell didn't you let me fire the mission, Jello? I may be a mad Russian, but I'm one hell of a gunner."

"Nothing personal, but it was my ass on the line if there was a fuck up. If they wanted us to drop shit on our own damn perimeter, no one but the Jello Kid would be doin' it. That's what a squad leader's for...to take responsibility, even when it sucks. Let me tell you, dude, I was scared shitless that I'd mess up. Man, those were our friends down there. Walking those rounds up and down the perimeter. That was the hardest thing, I've had to do over here. You whipped those rounds down the tube super well. You were a kick ass A-gunner, dude."

Cossack was embarrassed by my compliment, but his eyes telegraphed his appreciation. Our conversation had turned serious; and the awkward silence waited for something to happen. Cossack, impatient with the silent stares, blurted, "Yeah, one hell of a night." Then, he began to chuckle. "There we were after the shit died down...just being squared away Marines, cleaning the area around the gun pit and up pops that skinny-ass, dumb lieutenant. I loved it when you blew his mind, Jello."

Staying out of the conversation was impossible for me. I could not resist doing an instant replay of the scene with the lieutenant. My friends leaned forward, anxiously awaiting my storytelling talent. They were like little children waiting for their favorite bedtime story, and I was their favorite grandfather.

"Up pops this boot-ass lieutenant holdin' the fin assembly to an 81mm mortar, and he wants to know what it is. So I tell him what he already knows. Then he tells me that he found it down by Motor T...inside the wire, even. I know he's gonna try a burn me for droppin' that round too close to our own troopies, so I tell the dude that the Communists can use our 81mm mortar rounds in their 82mm tubes." Cossack nodded, and I continued. "The lieutenant doesn't want to believe me, but he doesn't know what to do since I look like I'm bored with his Perry-Mason routine. Hell, I fire a tough ass mission and some dumb boot lifer has to get all freaked out. Shit, the NVA didn't make it through the wire thanks to our kick ass barrage. Now...that dude was a fuckin' lifer!"

A chorus of laughter. Still laughing, Pink Rat struggled to remind us what had happened several hours after the lieutenant's inquisition. Our barrage of thirty mortar rounds had not only kept the NVA from breaching the barbed wire defenses near Motor Transport, but it had also destroyed the concertina wire. The morning after the attack, I was told to send some of the men in my squad down to Motor T. They were to restring the damaged barbed wire, and Pink Rat had been one of the chosen.

damn that was a bummer night...dropping our own rounds within fifty meters of our gun pit...sure didn't need our own rounds that close...but definitely didn't need a human wave assault that night...sure's a drag when the NVA want to get personal...close even...just like that night a couple of months ago when they opened fire on our gun pit...that damn NVA machine gun pouring all that lead our way...boy was I scared shitless...pinned down outside the gun pit...ten meters to safety...the bullets whizzing just over me...bullets hitting all round me...looking up at the gun pit and seeing Cossack hugging the ground on the wrong side of the gun pit...sand pouring out of the gun pit's sandbag wall...more machine-gun fire...more sand pouring out...Cossack too afraid to breathe...the bullets cutting through the night air a few inches above me...the gun pit ten meters away and I want to dash for it...if I stay I'll be killed...the bullets keep coming...I want to run...I have to make a break for the gun pit...no...can't...I'll be mowed down for sure...run...don't...oh shit...I can't...I have to bolt out of the blocks...the ten meter dash...the winner gets to live...I dive over Cossack and into the safety of the gun pit...OH SHIT...that was too close.

"Jello, come back from the O-zone so we can get this Polack drunk."

As I motioned to Cossack for us to leave, I asked, "Well what are we waiting for? Grab the cases and let's go."

"Still want to go to our underground bunker?"

I nodded my agreement. "Sure. If it rains, we'll worry about that...when and if."

warm...not the best way for beer to be...getting out of the Nam alive...the best way for Jello to be.

The three cases of Miller beer would make it right. Our underground bunker was quickly converted into a non-lifer's cocktail lounge, Nam-style. Pride in the Corps was absent that night, as usual, but our pride in that bunker of bunkers was readily available. In the realm of bunkers, ours was indestructible. We were positive that it would never be destroyed. Hopefully, it would not turn out like the Titanic. Whether with artillery or rockets, we naively believed that there was nothing the North Vietnamese could throw at the bunker to disturb the silent composure of those twelve-foot long railroad ties, which created the ceiling. Sandwiched between the timbered roof and three layers of recently filled sandbags was a layer of dirt-filled ammunition boxes. The bunker's mission in life was noble: stand firm and protect its architects. It must; it served the Jello Squad.

Pink Rat, Cossack and I abandoned the stale dusk heat, which lingered with the half-dozen monologues of the men playing poker at the opposite end of our tent. All this faded away as the cool ebony silence of our bunker greeted us. Partially severed roots haphazardly decorated the earthen walls. The beam from our flashlight caught an earthworm in the act of being an earthworm. In another hour, that earthworm and the Jello Squad would be rapping. A few more beers and the worm would be the newest member in the Jello Squad.

With a jab and a twist, the can of beer surrendered to the pressure from the bayonet. Another hole, one much smaller, was punched and Cossack was the first to guzzle the long anticipated beer. Ten-seconds later, the empty can bounced against the back wall of the bunker. A few seconds later the walls of the bunker echoed his Grade-*A* belch. Our friend, the earthworm, was nowhere to be found.

"Goddamn, what a beast!"

"No shit, Jello...and didn't even give us a chance to have a chugalug contest."

I reached over, and Cossack handed me the flashlight but held the bayonet behind his back. "Thought you were a tough squad leader. Why don't you open the beer can with your teeth like those Korean Marines did at China Beach when you were on R and R?"

"Shut up and give me that goddamn blade."

Cossack tossed his bayonet, which landed between my feet.

"Shit...watch out, you maggot! Didn't say to use me for target practice."

While Cossack laughed, I opened another can of warm beer, chugged it, and belched. Pink Rat was losing patience with our bantering. He just wanted to drink. By the time I handed the bayonet to Pink Rat, Cossack had grabbed two more beers and offered one of them to me. During the next half-hour, the three of us had gone through a dozen more beers. The floor of our bunker was littered with smashed Miller beer cans. Pink Rat was staring at the ceiling of the bunker and was probably daydreaming about his girlfriend back in the World. We loved to give him a hard time about being whipped, but we were actually a bit jealous that he had a good woman waiting for him.

The first hints of sunset were tiptoeing across the June sky when Sugar Bear walked into our bunker turned dive. An Uncle Tom, he was not. Although broad shouldered and well-muscled, he lacked the size for football but not for street survival in the DC ghetto. On his own at fourteen: lonely, angry, and searching. He would leave it all: the tears, sometimes the only running water; the hot anger, sometimes the sole warmth for December's chill. He would escape from the wounded buildings with their rodent-renters. He would do a catch-you-later number on the song of despair that wailed from the already doomed toddlers, too often chewing on pieces of poisoned paint chips. Bear found another merry-go-round four years later. It took him out of one war zone and dumped him into another. Sugar Bear had been given the privilege of doing some bleeding on an airstrip, near a river, by some mountains. It was time to forget all that; beer drinking and rapping with the trio of crazies sounded like a better idea.

"Shee...it! You dudes are crazy ass dooods!" Bear shook his head and chuckled.

"Sugar Bear, what's happenin'?"

"Same old shit. Like you know how this whole jive scene is...a bunch of fuckin' bullshit. Right?"

"Yeah."

"So where's my beer? You dudes too cheap?"

"Shit. No way."

I handed him a beer, and the bayonet went to work. Beer cans popped. Greedy bellies were filled. Empty cans began piling up in one corner. Sugar Bear smiled as I handed him his fifth warm beer, and Pink Rat began sniffing. He was a Polish hound dog in search of an answer.

"Did someone fart?"

"No, Cossack...I smell rain coming."

" Thanks for the weather report. It rains in the Nam?"

Almost done with being sarcastic, Cossack chugged the rest of his beer, and then he belched. "No. Thought we were in the desert."

"Rain. Here? Pink Rat must be deranged."

"Quick, give the Polack another beer or he'll forecast a blizzard."

"Oh shit!"

"It's comin' through the roof."

"Shit...it's leakin' over here, too."

Within ten minutes, we were floundering and splashing in two feet of muddy water. It seemed that the Vietnamese word for summer shower was *deluge*. The clouds had pissed on our parade.

"Let's get the hell out of here. I didn't join the fuckin' Navy!"

Our evening had been sabotaged, and the bunker was a muddy disaster. Fortunately, the June night had not brought the expected NVA attack, and we were glad. The already hot breakfast sun hung low in the eastern sky. The cases of the still-to-be- consumed beer and the afternoon USO show were awaiting us. The new day would be a good one, but best of all, the Jello Kid was one day closer to that flight on the magical silver bird back to the World.

"Pink Rat ... Cossack, get your sorry asses up."

"Buzz off, Jello."

"Come on, let's get some of that good Marine Corps chow."

"Yuck."

"Now that you're up...how about some liquid refreshment instead."

Sitting up in is cot, Cossack rubbed his sleepy eyes and wondered about my statement. "At seven in the morning?"

"Sure. Don't want the beer to get too hot. Besides...don't want some lifer rippin' it off."

Reaching over to Pink Rat, I shook his shoulder until he yelled at me to leave him alone. I ignored his request until he surrendered with an unenthusiastic, "Okay."

Because our tent was on the side of a hill, there was an area beneath it that was a perfect place for our beer drinking. Cossack grabbed the first can. Cold sweat failed to greet his clutching hand. Even the night's rainwater failed to chill the beer cans sufficiently: cool, yes, but cold beers would not be part of our day. We passed the bayonet around, and with a stab and a twist, the cool beer was ready to roll down our anxious throats. With each repetition of the process, the cool blended into warm. Unfortunately, the fifty remaining beers would have that blah nowhere taste. Although quality was lacking, the size of our cache made it made it all worthwhile. Fortunately, we had found an Army grunt in Da Nang who was willing to purchase the beer for us for a mere five dollars. Without his help, we would have been limited to our two-beer limit that was imposed on us on Hill 10.

Pink Rat handed me another beer, and I smiled and said, "This shit sure does the trick."

"You ain't just a bullshittin'."

Pink Rat grabbed another beer and lobbed it at Cossack. A bad throw. The can missed his waiting hands and rolled passed him. I picked it up and handed the can of beer to a thankful Cossack. Before I could warn him to be careful when he opened it, Cossack opened the can of beer, which sprayed me. I laughed.

Cossack lay back, staring at the underside of our tent floor. Someone above him was still attempting to sleep in spite of our party. Cossack made the mistake of trying to drink his beer in the reclining position. Some of the warm beer rolled down his anxious throat; the rest streamed down his chin. Before he could sit up, beer streamed down his tanned chest and was racing for his belly. Pink Rat and I burst out laughing. Cossack wiped the beer off his stomach and then wiped his sticky hands several times on his pants legs. Foam from his beer still covered the left side of his non-regulation Fu Manchu mustache. Cossack began shaking his head, broke a smile and finally joined us in our laughter. I grabbed another beer and handed it to him.

"You guys, did I ever..." I stopped for a moment and then continued with my incoherent thought, "Speakin' of beer and all...I mean...did...did I ever tell you dudes about the time when..."

Cossack shrugged his shoulders but then decided to play

along, pretending to be privy to my story. "Oh, that time. Of course you told us."

"Hold on, folks. You didn't let me finish my...what I was gonna say...anyway, to make a long story short."

Cossack shook his head and said with a dose of sarcasm, "The Jello Kid is going to tell us a *short* story. That'll be a first."

"Yeah, like I was sayin'...to make a short story long...me and these three dudes I was tight with back in the World...well, anyway, us guys..."

Pink Rat picked up two more beers and offered me one. Once I had taken a swig of beer, I proceeded to tell my story.

"So...us dudes...they were humungous ass dudes...like two of them weighed two hundred and fifty and the other dude weighed about two hundred...and there I was with my big ass one hundred and thirty pound bod. These dudes could do some serious drinkin'...like a case each."

"Sounds like these dudes belong in the Crotch." Cossack looked at Pink Rat who was nodding his agreement.

"One of 'em is in the Marine Reserves, and the other two have brains. Like I was saying...we went out drinking one night and did I got so ripped that I wanted to duke it out with the two biggest dudes. Lucky for them they didn't want to fight."

Cossack belched. Pink Rat snickered. They both shook their heads. They were now sure of my insanity. I neglected to inform them that I rarely drank back in the World. The story sounded better if it sounded typical and I embellished a bit.

"Lucky for them? Don't you have that ass-backwards?"

I ignored Cossack's observation and continued, "At any rate, I let them live."

Cossack smiled. "What a big heart!"

"Like I was saying...we went to this ritzy ass party at this country club. When I went to take a leak I didn't cut the john any slack. I mean that john was snazzy...even had shower stalls. I almost busted the shit out of one of them, but my friends stopped me...but they weren't fast enough 'cause I knocked the hell out of this shit-can with my deadly right. It went sailin'. Before they could grab my drunk ass, I was doin' pull-ups on this metal coat hanger bar. It kinda fell down. They got my ass out of the john before this Deputy Sheriff, who was just outside, could do anything. Out by the pool, I started jiving some dude who was just standin' there. Lucky for me, he didn't want to fight. I was so damn plastered. Luckily, my three friends got my ass out there fast this time."

"Boy, when you get ripped, you do it royal!"

just about a year ago...Okinawa...drinking...one...two...five drinks...buzz...nine...mellow yellow...wasted... fifteen...shit...sixteen drinks...someone hold my head...seventeen...stop the merry-go-round...eighteen...zonked...smashed...don't forget...got to be sober by 4 a.m. for the plane...can't miss it...ah...made it...a coastline...oh my head...Da Nang down there...my head throbbing and pounding...shit...eighteen drinks...my poor head...runway...707 jet landing...Vietnam...June '67...runway pavement...my head's throbbing...damn...where did they put the air...hotter than shit.

"Wow! It just flashed on me that I've been in this sorry ass-place for just over a year."

"Hate to remind you guys but you've got another six month in the Nam. I actually feel sorry for you. Really."

Just before Pink Rat left to make a head call, he said, "Thanks for reminding us." When he returned, he turned and pointed toward the armor, which was only thirty or forty feet away and pointed out that was a small group of Marines standing in line next to it.

"Check it out, Jello. Those dudes over there are genuine boots. They make Cossack look like the saltiest 0341 in the Nam."

"Yeah, they're just a bunch of candy ass Boy Scouts. I even look older than them."

Armed with our brew, we staggered several yards toward the armory. The glare of the adolescent sun bounced off its corrugated tin roof. The armory's plywood walls wore last July's olive green canvas. The monsoon rains and the searing heat had left their faded mark on this canvas visitor from the West. A dozen Don Quixotes leaned unMarine-like against the weathered canvas. Their freshly starched utilities would become like the canvas, faded and limp. So, too, these eager boots-at-life would be changed forever. Their dreams of glory would soon explode in a nightmare-of-hate-and-blood. Fear would be conquered with the right number of tokes from a joint. The rifle each was being issued would soon bring a strange, awesome power. With it, a suspect could be killed, and it would be all right because Vietnamese would become gooks. And altar boys would trade in their Latin phases for their Nam mantras: their Kyrie-eleisons would run for cover, replaced by a barrage of 'Fuck you, gooks.' Death would dance in their schoolboy-eyes. And they would know that hollow, silent stare, going nowhere yet everywhere. Mumbles of what went wrong out there would dribble from their stone lips; their faces, statues of silence; their eyes frozen in time, forever prisoners of that terrible moment. Vietnam would become the Nam. These boots-at-life would become seasoned warriors, some as casualty figures to be played with by the Pentagon, the rest as survivors, always remembering, always changed.

"Hey, any of you dudes want a beer?"

A dozen confused faces staring back at us. "What? This early?"

"Forget it then. Guess you boots can't handle it. Give you a few weeks in this shithole, and you'll take us up on it. You guys know yet who you're supposed to be assigned to?"

"I think we're supposed to go to Charley Company."

The three of us grabbed our stomachs in unison, fell to the ground, and Cossack dropped his beer can. Drunken laughter bellowed from our shaking bodies. "Charley Company! Did you hear that, Jello?"

"Yeah, 'fraid so. Charley Company is..."

My hesitation was followed immediately by a nervous question from one of the cherries. "Is what? What's wrong with Charley Company?"

"Boot, if you got life insurance, good possibility someone back in the World is gonna be *boo coo* rich when they collect it."

"But, I..."

"Well, you might luck out and just get wounded two or three times. One thing for sure, you'll run into major fuckin' shit in Charley Company."

Pink Rat half grinned, and Cossack nodded in agreement as he interrupted me, "And my friend ain't bullshittin' you."

"Like I said...everybody in Charley Company gets a couple a Purps or gets zapped." We left these new replacements with an idea of the brutal reality of life as a grunt in Charley Company, and they stood in stunned silence.

As morning mellowed into afternoon, we mellowed into

oblivion. When we saw the armory move for the fifth time, we knew we were in no condition to do anything of importance, so we kept drinking.

"Goddamn, this beer tastes like shit!"

"More like piss."

"But it sure does the trick. We should be in great shape for the USO show."

I had just successfully opened my fifteenth beer when our section leader brought us unwanted news.

"Jello, you under the tent?"

"Yeah, what you want?"

"It's about the USO show...your squad has to stay here with the gun in case we get any fire missions called in over the radio."

"Shit! Why can't the other squad stay? We..."

"Sorry, but..." The decision had been made, so our section leader walked off. With our stomachs full of beer, it made it easier for us to feel sorry for ourselves.

"Goddamn it! Give me that last shitty beer."

Chapter 41
Late June 1968

The Downside Of Being A Short-Timer

At four o'clock, 1600 as the lifers liked to call it, the USO show began: girls, band and frenzied Marines were all there, but the Jello Squad was absent.

"That's a great idea, Jello."

"Well, what are we waiting for? Grab the radio and let's get our asses up to the mess hall and check out the USO show."

Grinning, Cossack, Pink Rat and I attempted to navigate the quarter mile to the mess hall. Our meandering and staggering brought chuckles from the other three members of the Jello Squad, the sober ones. Ten minutes, a dozen stumbles, and a volley of belches later, we completed our mission.

Because we weren't honored guests, just a squad of mostly drunk Marines, the show had not waited for us. The music blared, the go-go girls shook their most inviting shakables, and the sea of green was loving it. Because we had arrived late, we were at the back of the mess hall, and the throng of bobbing heads were boring. The stage at the far end of the mess hall lured us and our radio on, so we pushed our way up a narrow aisle, which bordered the northern wall of the building. Once we reached the front row, we plopped our inebriated bodies on the unfriendly concrete floor. Although the corrugated tin walls offered us uncomfortable back support, we didn't complain. We were only a few feet away from the stage, and we were intoxicatingly happy.

The music ping-ponged throughout the building. As was usual, the officers had the best of everything; these chessmen in green occupied the front row: their king, straddled by bishops, knights, and rooks with gold bars and oak leaves. Their clean-shaven profiles took second place to the happenings on the stage.

Cossack nudged me and pointed toward the stage. "Look at that dumb shit. That major's a genuine wimp."

"The major's tryin' to twist. Hell, I'll get up there and show that lifer. I'll do the gator and freak this place out of its gourd."

"Hold on, you drunk son of a bitch. Jello, cool it. The colonel's checkin' us out."

Ignoring Cossack, I blurted, "Hey, colonel, you maggot lifer!"

"Shut up! He might hear you."

"Where's my flight date, you sorry ass jerk? Corporal Jello wants his flight...so you better give it..."

"Goddamn, shut your crazy mouth and fast."

"Okay. That guy's not worth it."

Our radio blared. "Whiskey Bravo...Whiskey Bravo...this is Handworth Whiskey...over."

"Shit, damn radio." Grabbing the handset, I keyed down and slurred, "Hamworth Wizkey...yeah...yeah...this is Wizkey Bravo...ah...over."

"Whiskey Bravo...radio check...how copy? Over."

"Wizkey Bravo...Wizkey...Hamworth Wizkey...we're doin' jus' fine...so's our radio...how's you dudes up there?...over an' out...roger dodger."

"Whiskey Bravo, this is Handworth Whiskey. Procedure...and turn down music. Over."

"What music?...roger dodger...Wizkey...catch you later...how copy?...under and out... Bravo Wizkey."

The colonel's glaring eyes left the merriment on the stage and targeted in on us. Although I was drunk, I realized that the show was over, at least for us.

"So much for the old USO show."

"Yeah, partin' is such sweet sorrow. Let's part an' fast."

"*Adios*, super lifer. Later."

Having escaped from our favorite battalion commander, we proudly weaved our way back to our tent. The clouds were bouncing around in the late afternoon sky. At least we thought they were. Cossack had been sober enough to remember to bring the radio back with him, but drunk enough to wear a permanent grin. Maybe he was glad that I was about to escape the Nam as a survivor, but probably he was cheesing it in an attempt to forget that he still had six months remaining of his tour in the war zone.

I was mesmerized by the plywood buildings, which lined the path back to our tent. The buildings themselves weren't interesting, but I was amazed that they swayed so much. Cossack's sole interest was the ground. It kept moving in spite of his threats and was not impressed at all with Cossack's foul-mouthed abuse of it. The ground did not care. The buildings did not care. We did not care. We just wanted more beer.

When we arrived back at our tent, Cossack tossed the radio towards his cot. It missed and bounced on the plywood floor.

"Smooth move."

"So what do you expect from a drunk Russian warrior?"

Cossack decided to lie back on his cot. Before he could close his eyes, I was lifting up the end of his cot.

"What the shit you think you're..." Thud. His cot bounced, and he lay on the floor.

"Come on, dude...no time to be playing Sleeping Beauty. God knows you're too ugly for that role."

Cossack jumped up and swayed for a moment. When he regained his balance, he flipped me the bird and told me that I was jealous of his beautiful mustache. "Bullshit!"

"Then you're jealous since I get to stay and fight the NVA hordes from Up North. Poor you...got to go home to all the chicks and put up with them attackin' your bod."

"Yeah, sure's gonna be rough...I'll be a nice guy and drop you a line and tell you about all the hand to hand combat I'll be doin' to protect my sexy bod from them."

I attempted to give equal time to seriousness. "You may be a drunk kid just doin' some hard time in the Crotch...but you're okay in spite of that Fu Manchu mustache that's hangin' on your strange face. And if you decide to get your ass out of this crazy ass war alive, I might even check you out back in Detroit."

"Don't worry about this dude. I'm on top of the situation. I am goin' to escape out of the Nam early. Just you wait and see."

"You just might pull it off, but this dude's not gonna hang around in this arm pit to find out. I may not have a flight date yet, but the Jello Kid ain't gonna be here much longer...one way or another. If I have to, I'll swim back to the World."

My last statement proved to Cossack that I was definitely

drunk. He was right. Cossack continued to babble at me as I walked over to my cot. I stood on it and unbuttoned my fly. Cossack started laughing. "What the fuck you think you're doin'!"

"Pissin'! It's a two-count exercise. Ready, piss!"

By this time, the three other Marines in the tent had joined Cossack in his laughter.

"I can understand the need for takin' a leak, but why are you pissin' on your cot?"

I was too drunk and Cossack was too good a friend for me to become embarrassed. "So I missed my target. It's my cot, so... Ah! Relief's just a piss away."

I failed at my attempt to button up my fly, so I gave up and sat on my cot. Somehow, in spite of his drunken state, a lucid thought snuck into Cossack's mind. He decided we were too drunk to be useful as mortarmen, so he suggested that we sober up. "Maybe a shower would do the trick."

I turned away from him and spied our gun pit, which was filled with a foot of water. Like Ford Motors, I had a better idea.

"Gorget a shower. Let's go swimmin' in our gun pit."

Cossack's eyes lit up. "Outstanding idea."

After we had splashed around in the gun pit for five minutes, we realized that it was more fun being drunk than wet. We staggered back to the tent and put on some dry utilities and decided to avoid evening chow. The combination of a day's worth of drinking and the quality of food at the mess hall would be too confusing for our stomachs.

Cossack gave up on his attempt at letter writing and had passed out, so I decide to go up to the other end of the hill and visit my friend Mike Rae, a radio operator for 81s. During the past year, we had spent several evenings together discussing non-Marine topics, intelligent topics. We both had spent some time in college before joining the Marines, and we both appreciated the chance to talk about all the ideas that liberal arts students discussed in university cafeterias.

When I stumbled into his tent, Mike was working on a correspondence course, which he had been trying to complete for the previous six months. The war kept getting in his way.

"Hey, school boy, what's happenin'?"

"Nothin' much. Just a little homework. Have to keep my brain from getting too rusty."

"I don't have to worry about my brain gettin' rusty. It's numb. A case of beer does wonders for your brain-housing-group."

He offered me a seat. Missing his cot, I landed on the floor. We both laughed. The second time, I succeeded on sitting next to him on his cot. Closing his English literature workbook, he set it on the floor. Flipping open his Zippo, he lit up a Marlboro. After savoring two drags from his cigarette, he paused for a moment. Mike, realizing that I was too drunk for a meaningful conversation, looked in his file marked *conversations with drunk people*: do small-talk. Then he said, "You must be gettin' pretty short, Jello."

The aimless smoke from his cigarette, like a fog bank, rolled toward me. I was too inebriated to notice or care.

"Short, but no goddamn flight date."

"Typical. I sure hope they don't mess with my head when it comes time for my flight date. Should be about a month away."

"Damn! Mike, didn't realize you had that much time left. Can't feature puttin' up with this suck hole for another month. Days...that's all I have left, and it's really startin' to freak me out."

I sat there silently staring at nothing; then, I sat mute like a just developed photograph, a catatonic casualty only capable of a simple hollow stare that shot beyond Mike, his smoke, his eyes, his voice; they all vanished. There was only the silence. Closing my eyes as if to surrender, I mumbled something indiscernible, and then the silence returned.

it's the end of the month...I know those goddamn NVA are goin' to attack the hill...it's due...they're so predicable that way...don't want to be part of all that shitty grief...that damn siren going off...INCOMING...NVA mortar tubes popping...flashes of light...death from the skies...explosions getting closer...louder...red star clusters popping in the black night...contact with the NVA all around our hill...a million trace rounds racing to our hill...none going out to answer them...NVA sappers slicing the throats of everyone on bunker watch...I'm firing mortar rounds north...south...north again...mortars needed to the east...flames shooting out of the mortar tube...smoke crawling over the hill...San Francisco fog with the wrong kind of smell...the guy next to me dropping his last mortar round as machine gun bullets rip through him...blood splattering everywhere...still firing mortar rounds with red dripping-wet hands...popping illumination rounds so we can see the NVA charging...they're through the wire...screaming like a lynch mob...but there's no sound...hate burning in their eyes...a thousand bayonets dripping bright red...my heart pumping like a jackhammer...grabbing my rifle...jamming on my bayonet...firing a quick burst at the line of NVA getting closer...grabbing a hand grenade...my hand shaking...finally pulling the pin...throwing it...five NVA screaming...others still charging...firing and screaming in silence...shoving another magazine of ammo into my M16...no time to fire it...they're at the gun pit...swinging my rifle...bashing the side of an NVA's face with a home-run-swing...kill kill kill...the instructor bellowing...another NVA soldier lunging at me with an empty AK-47...I'm firing a ten round burst into his young face that's exploding into bits and pieces...bloody chunks splattering...a third NVA screaming and swinging his knife...leaping into the air...landing in the gun pit...grabbing me and yanking me down hard...rolling on the ground...wrestling...knocking the knife loose...my sweaty hands grabbing it...swinging the knife down hard...the NVA's eyes filled with terror are staring up at me.

Tears sliding down my face. I was still in my trance. The fear of dying catching up with me; my imagination was out of control. I had been too lucky.

"They're gonna overrun the hill. We've skated too long."

Mike leaned over and hugged me. "No sweat. No one's going to kill you, Jello. You deserve to go home. God isn't that shitty."

My raindrops still were trickling down my face as I stared at the plywood floor of the tent, which was beginning to spin out of control. I was too drunk to believe Mike as I mumbled, "Goddamn it. Enough dudes have died. I jus' want my chance to live...jus' want to make it to age twenty-one. God, let me slide. Please."

I fell back on the cot and passed out, wondering if God listened to drunk Marines.

Chapter 42
Summer 1968

The Nam Without JELL-O's Magic

Although it took me nine years to find out, I, unfortunately, discovered that when I left the Nam on July 4, 1968, I had taken the magic of JELL-O with me back to Arizona. With my departure, the Jello Squad no longer existed. Our squad's luck ran out when Cossack and Sugar Bear decided to *borrow* a jeep for a joy ride to Da Nang. Upon their return trip to Hill 10, a land mine sent them and the jeep hurling through the air, wounding both of them. This was Sugar Bear's second Purple Heart; he had received his first one when he became squad leader of other squad in Bravo Section. All good things eventually come to an end; the Jello Squad's record of zero KIAs and no WIAs had truly been remarkable especially when considering the number of Marines killed during the three hundred eighty-two days of my tour of duty in Vietnam: 5,321 of my Marine brothers had paid the ultimate price, yet I had been blessed with the gift of life. In fact, during the horrific month of May when our battalion had sustained heavy casualties, 806 Marines were killed throughout Vietnam .

Cossack hates the idea of being wounded, but he is. WIA are three letters be does not want in the alphabet of his life. The chopper begins rising, then tilting. The two-year Marine lying helplessly on a stretcher which is sliding, and Cossack hates Newton's law of gravity because the rear of the medevac chopper is still open. His stretcher becoming a casket, sliding closer. The neon-lights-of-his-mind flashing *HELP*. Canceled forever, one hundred feet below. He is still sliding closer. The pilot forgetting to push the magic button. A few more inches to a forever-goodbye. CLANK.

A sigh as huge as Alaska. The rear door finally shutting. No more sliding. If the pain weren't so intense, he would be beaming a smile. Buddy Rich is banging away on Cossack's nineteen year old heart. Obscenities and 'thank-yous' are prisoners in his dry, silent throat. The chopper leveling off and turning northeast.

Those nightmarish hundred feet are gone, but always there. For a brief moment, the door-gunner next to him taking his eyes away from the ocean of rice paddies below. He smiles at Cossack and is glad that the wounded Marine will leave the Nam alive and early. His eyes are smiling, but he is unaware that Cossack has screamed at him in desperate silence for two minutes, a lifetime, earlier. But Cossack knows. The medevac chopper finally landing at the Naval Hospital in Da Nang.

The room is both empty and dark. Cossack, the unwanted cargo and newest member of the Purple Heart gang, is left on a plywood table, his right leg dangling off the side of it. He wants to scoot himself into a more comfortable position, but his legs don't hear him. He only feels the pain, which is running wild in his body. The two corpsmen, who brought him in on a stretcher, are gone.

He is a misplaced Marine. No one comes to see him for hours. He hates the voices outside his room. He wants them to become doctors and nurses standing by him. He hates the Marine Corps because they always make you wait, even when you're wounded. Like a hungry rat, the pain is gnawing at his spine. Cossack wishing he were dead, lying in a green plastic bag with the other casualty figures waiting for the plane ride home.

WAITING. They would even make you wait if you're dead, but Cossack's alive, so in an attempt at escaping his prison, he thinks about last summer with his high school girlfriend. Juiced up, the clock clocked, and two people peopled. A thought, a laugh, a smile, a touch, a look, a kiss and now is then. But he is in the Nam, and the clock on the wall is ticking military time, Nam-time.

Five hours: the waiting is finally over. The noises in the hallway are entering his room, carrying a stretcher full of a wounded fighter pilot. The corpsmen place him on the table next to Cossack. The room is quiet again. The population of Cossack's Nam, increasing by one. Cossack listening to the jet pilot's story of how he was hurt when he ejected from his plane over the South China Sea. The pain in the pilot's collarbone and in his left arm are telling him that they are probably broken.

Although it is the first time he has been shot down, the fighter pilot knows he is fortunate. This time his jet won't be racing back to his base, and a cold Budweiser won't be waiting for him. Although he had been lucky thirty-two times before, he is no longer the successful arsonist flying his Phantom jet, cruising the skyscape, gliding like a hungry white shark, the smell of a meal below. The supersonic death-jockey hawking his prey in the naked blue sky. Blurry becoming clear, clear becomes crystal. Enemy soldiers scurry like ants with no place to go. Napalm canisters tumbling gracefully. The angry jungle burning, exploding like a Fourth-of-July celebration. The jungle stinking with the broiled flesh of the boys from Up North. The pilot only seeing, but never smelling the forever-smell of napalm-consumed flesh.

Cossack remembers being on Hill 10, watching the jets racing toward their targets to the west. And of course, the-never-to-be-forgotten roar of the jets swooping in on the NVA out by the Song Vu Gia, a river of death, on May 19th. Like the stink of a skunk, some memories just don't fade away. The wounded pilot next to him, not wearing a wedding ring. He must be a bachelor pilot, always swooping below the tree line to strafe his target. Disappearing below tree lines finally catching up with him. Cossack wishing he is on the hill, watching a bombing run, and guessing the marital status of the jet pilots.

Five minutes later a nurse walks into their room. She is yelling at a corpsman because Cossack has been forgotten. Cossack wants to kiss her. She is right; five hours it too long to wait.

i was sir gawain
  your green knight
  the jousts were fought in your name

i was sir gawain
  your red white and blue knight
  the medals you gave showed your thanks

i was sir gawain
  my red knight
  the shrapnel mangled me in tones of crimson pain

i was sir gawain
  my returning knight
  your hospitals found no time for my cries

i am sir gawain
  my angry knight
  you wish i would disappear
    but
  i never will
i am your sir gawain
    and
  for you
i ride forever in my wheelchair

Chapter 43
September 1969

Mike Rae's "Corpsman-Up" Moment

It had been over a year since one of my friends from Iowa, a radio operator for 81s, had left Vietnam with two Purple Hearts. Mike Rae and I had kept in touch. When the Marine Corps discharged him from active duty in the summer of 1969, he moved to Tucson, became my roommate and attended the University of Arizona.

The previous year, I had failed miserably at being a model fraternity brother; the eighteen-year-olds in my pledge class were not only three years my junior, but they had been at their senior prom while the NVA had celebrated Ho Chi Minh's birthday on us out by the Song Vu Gia. For my fraternity brothers, losing their innocence meant getting drunk or getting laid; my innocence died with the first NVA I blew to shreds with one of my well-directed 81mm mortar rounds, aka *Death from the skies.*

They drank because that was what frats did; for me, it wasn't part of a rite of passage; I drank because I wanted to numb my emotional pain. My life back in the World lacked adrenaline surges that were commonplace in the Nam, so I felt like a bungee jumper who had been condemned to a knitting class. The frat brotherhood could never compete with the unique camaraderie that existed with the Marines with whom I served. My combat experiences had created a bond which Shakespeare aptly referred to as "We few, we happy few, we band of brothers." In the summer or 1968, Shakespeare's reference to *happy* didn't fit me as well as *angry* did, but those with whom I served—especially those in the Jello Squad—were definitely a band of brothers. I was a Nam vet, and vets needed to stick together.

It was a hot September night, and our apartment was quiet. Mike, who usually spent his evenings drinking beer while he read, had disappeared an hour earlier. I set an empty bottle of eighty-nine-cent-screw-the-metal-top-off wine on the floor by the couch, which even the Salvation Army would have rejected and classified as 4-F. As I leaned back, I stared at a psychedelic poster on the wall in front of me. The alcohol was winning. Mesmerized, my mind floated away helplessly like a leaf on a windy day.

floors reflect shine clean but dirt still...our society gleams in wealth murky reflections mirrored in our trashed ghettos...shouts of thunder anguish despair disgust...canker sore of the white body...fire cleanses...purifies the soul...destroys the body...crashing gashing ripping into the callous heart of our land of freedom...now must fall prey to the justified executioner...death brings life...tell...speak painting on the blah walls...walls around with mistletoe and lights...their energy paid to the company...lips of fiery orange plastered on the poster body...below...green dying tree of His birth...each winter celebrated...He saved us...but we...the saved...still in our winter...when will our spring be.

I grabbed a pencil and piece of paper and wrote my thoughts down. Another poem with an audience of one.

Wondering where Mike was, I left the apartment to see if he was visiting Rick Murray, a friend from high school, whom also lived in the complex. He was not at Rick's, but as I returned to my apartment, I noticed Mike sitting alone in the desert which bordered our apartment building. Unnoticed, I walked towards him. His mind had left Tucson for other places. His head was bent, and he was muttering his regrets at the ground.

My intuition sent me a telegram. Visions of the Nam, a double feature playing on the silver screen of Mike's mind. It was apparent that he wasn't doing well, so I inquired if everything was okay.

He looked up at me, and mumbled, "Yeah," but the tears on his face were feeble proof that everything was fine. He remained looking up at the intruder, wiping the evidence from his face.

"Mind if I pull up a piece of desert?" He nodded, so I sat down and asked, "So what's bummin' you out?" Silence. A buddy from the Nam and a canvas full of stars still waiting. "If you don't feel like rapping, that's cool." I began to stand up.

"Don't go. Thanks for givin' a shit, but I don't know if you need to listen to all my grief."

In a calm and reassuring voice, I said, "I don't need to. I want to. We went through the same shit together and we're friends." I sat back down and continued to explain to him how important our friendship was for me. "I hate to use the Marine Corps' term, *Semper Fidelis*, but when it comes to friends, I mean it. I'll always be there to listen when you need it. That's what it's all about."

Mike paused; staring at me, his eyes saying, 'thank you'. With more than a hint of hesitation in his voice, Mike asked, "So you want to know what's buggin' me? The Nam, the Marine Corps, the whole fucking country. God, was I a sucker. Just a starry-eyed, nineteen-year-old farm boy from Iowa thinkin' I should do my part and go off and fight for democracy and all that good shit they poured on us in school. What a fucking waste of three years. Semper Fi, do or die, gung ho, fuck no! That's where the hell I'm at. I hate it all. I got ripped off. So many people got ripped off. That son of a bitch LBJ...took us to the cleaners. And what's worse, the people were stupid enough to let Nixon take his place."

I nodded my agreement, and Mike continued with his dissertation of anger, "And what really pisses me off is the CIA sending me that letter, asking if I would be interested in maybe working for 'em. I enjoyed tellin' those motherfuckers that I didn't want to have anything to do with their kind of bullshit. I had a lifetime's worth of that kind of garbage in the Nam. The best part of my letter back to those jerks was signing it, *Very Unpatriotically Yours*...sons of bitches!"

I smiled, and added, "One thing for sure, those fuckers don't like your ass...as a matter of fact, your *fan* club is getting real small. The Marine Corps doesn't dig you either. You blew their mind when you burned that questionnaire they sent you...and then mailed the ashes back to them. You're a real popular guy with the US government."

Anger and resentment, buried too long, begged for an escape. It was time to spew. Keeping his myriad of emotions internalized hurt too much. "I don't give a shit. I hope those bastards burn in hell. They send us through boot camp, brainwashin' you...makin' you think stupid things. 'Yea, though I walk through the valley of the shadow of death, I will fear no evil, for I am the baddest motherfucker in the valley.' Give me a fucking break."

Mike's pent up anger had a sympathetic audience, so he continued, "They forgot to tell us the NVA sat in the same valley, thinking the same bullshit. There were a lot of bad motherfuckers who just died in the valley. Dumb kids blown away for what. The bummer about that war is that you'll never forget the shit. It likes to sneak up and ambush your ass. Like tonight, I just started thinkin' about the day the six-by I was ridin' in hit a box mine. God...was that a nightmare. Fucked! I think it was just a couple of days after you left the Nam. Early July. We were bouncing down the road to Da Nang, and my friend and I were just standin' in back of the cab, staring at the sky that kept bouncing. The next thing I knew..."

Mike was being sucked through a time warp back to the Nam. He gulped and sighed twice; the wound was rawer than he realized. He was in Purgatory, but he needed to finish his story if he were ever to heal his pain. He mustered up the will to continue. He winced as he said, "I was slammed to my knees and the truck was swerving all over the road. People were bouncin' up against me. We were tumblin' around in the back of the truck. I tried to open my eyes, but I couldn't. There was too much dust and smoke and shit. People were screamin'. The truck finally rolled off the road and stopped in a rice field. I jumped out immediately. My knees felt like someone had broken them, but I didn't give a shit. I figured the VC would be ambushing us, but they didn't. The first thing I did was look inside the cab to see what happened to the driver. I wanted to throw up. Raw flesh was hanging from the bone of his upper right arm. He was goin' into shock, so a couple of other Marines took care of him. Then it hit me that my friend wasn't around, so I started yellin' for him, but he didn't answer. I was scared shitless for him. I looked down the road and saw him lying there about twenty or thirty meters away. I ran up to him, and he was laying on his back, and he wasn't movin'. It looked like he was tryin' to breathe, tryin' to suck in air, but it wasn't working."

Pausing, Mike closed his eyes for a moment and let out a pair of deep sighs. Then, he continued, "I rolled him over, and blood poured out of his mouth. He started to breathe better, but his head was fucked up bad also...looked hopeless. Looked like my friend would die, so I grabbed the Saint Christopher medal that he was wearin' and held it and prayed for him. That was only the second time I prayed in the Nam. I was so scared for him. A chopper finally landed and picked him and the other wounded guy up. They took them to Da Nang. When he was at the hospital in Da Nang, he was pronounced dead. They pulled a sheet over him and were about ready to leave the room when a doctor noticed a slight movement under the sheet. That goddamn dude was too stubborn to die in the fucking armpit of the world, so they started pounding on his heart and doin' all that emergency shit and that brought him around. After that, they flew him to Japan for some operations. He spent the next year having at least five operations done to his head. He is walking around now with a skull that's partially stainless steel. He lost all sense of smell and has no feeling in part of his face."

Mike's story, disturbing as it was, begged to be told, begged to be heard. Although I wanted to listen to Mike, I did not want to hear the story. Hearing the details of his story made me remember the place I thought I had escaped from a year earlier. I was feeling like a corpsman, running into the thick of a firefight to help a wounded Marine. When he had said that he needed to talk, that was the equivalent of 'corpsman up, I've been hit'. Like the corpsman's response, mine could only be identical. After all, two guys from the Nam owed it to each other: it was an automatic, pure and simple. "Wow, that's a bummer. I almost feel guilty since I skated through the Nam without getting wounded."

"You know..." Mike paused and then continued, "I'm glad you were here to listen. This is the first time I've been able to talk about this shit with someone."

I nodded. "Keepin' garbage inside of you can really do a number on your head. A year is just too long."

"I really appreciate you listening, but it sure would be nice if I had a chick who would listen and not expect to hear all sorts of plastic crap." I continued listening, agreeing with his words. "It seems that the only kind of chicks that go to the university are shallow bitches. Just a bunch of sorority girls looking for the right guy, with the right car, with the right everything." My sentiments were dittos of his.

"I get so pissed off thinking about all the games these chicks play. I feel like being an asshole to them." I looked at Mike and interjected, "You might say we've both been a couple of shit heads a time or two with the chicks we've gone out with. My time in the Nam made me not want to put up with any phony bullshit. Just doesn't work for me."

Mike nodded and emphatically crushed out his cigarette as he gazed up at the ceiling of stars that owned Tucson's late September night. "It's so quiet and beautiful up there. Those same stars stared at us in the Nam. They laughed at us over there, and I'm sure they're laughing at us now. They just spend their time twinkling, and we spend ours playing games. God, it's got to get better, but I am sure it will get worse first."

"Maybe so, but I'd like to believe that we have some control over the situation. I've been spending this last year back in the World doing some serious thinking. I would like to believe that life is beautiful because of us or is ugly because of us...goddamn it, because of us, dude, us!"

There was no reply to my dime's-worth of philosophical insight. Mike only staring, remembering a thousand yesterdays: strike the rhythm, Death Drum, beat your cadence clear; your drummer so handsome, stern, straight, has no fear; sound the Battle Bugle, excite the soldiers' pride; no time for battle's lull, courage we must abide; but crashing mortar shells, singing through once-musiqued air, sound a hundred death-knells, and yet we wander unaware.

war is not so bad when you're in it
 but don't think about it
 that's when fear sneaks up on you
war is not so bad when you're home from it
 but don't think about it
 that's when all your ghosts sneak up on you
war is not so bad when you're dead
 you don't have to think about it ANYMORE
  and
 you don't have to cry
dead people don't have tears or memories.

Chapter 44
September 1969

The Overpaid Marine

It had been a month since my last letter from the Marine Corps. For almost a year, they had been reminding me that I had been overpaid. As my stack of mostly unanswered letters from Marine Corps grew taller, my hair grew longer, my mustache grew fuller, and my sideburns inched down the side of my face. It had taken a bit more than a year, but I almost looked the part of a college student; I was definitely non-regulation and proud of it. Like James Dean, I was a now a rebel, but I was a rebel with a cause, so, borrowing a page from the Viet Cong play book, I applied guerrilla warfare tactics to the Marine Corps that had mistakenly paid me for being a corporal for two months, which was one month's extra pay which I was not entitled to because the Marine Corps released me from active duty early.

Because I had acquired the rank of a corporal only a month before leaving active duty, the Marine Corps wanted me to repay the sixty-four-dollars-and-forty-eight-cents they had mistakenly paid me. The military was spending approximately an equal amount of money each time they fired a single mortar round in Vietnam. I had probably fired at least a thousand mortar rounds, which always seemed to be readily available. I thought it was humorous that the Marine Corps had become so frugal and was now interested in being reimbursed so they could fire one more mortar round in their multi-billion-dollar war. During a one-year period, an array of lieutenants, captains and majors had sent their threatening letters. Guilt had been the order of the day.

During the middle of September, the Marine Corps decided to pull rank. The doorbell rang. It was the postman with a certified letter. I signed a card acknowledging receipt. The Marine Corps' desperation at balancing their books was costing them more than their overpayment to me. The Marine Corps Finance Center was in Kansas City, and I knew that the officers who had written to me were too far away to order me to do push ups or pick up cigarette butts for my sins.

I was laughing as I pulled their letter from the envelope and read it:

MARINE CORPS FINANCE CENTER
Kansas City, Missouri 64197
EX7-3A-oms
5890/2315404
10 Sep 1969

Mr. Peter M. Bourret
5320 E. Linden Place
Tucson, AZ 85716
AMOUNT DUE: $14.48
Dear Mr. Bourret:

You have failed to respond to prior correspondence concerning your indebtedness to the United States Government. This indicates a complete disregard of this obligation on your part. You were provided a complete explanation of the indebtedness and were tendered an opportunity to repay the debt by reasonable installments. Accordingly, you are hereby advised that a satisfactory resolution of this matter must be effected immediately.

With respect to your liability for the amount of the indebtedness, the Comptroller General of the United States has stated the following:

"The recipient of an erroneous payment resulting from a mistake by public official must in equity make restitution, as restitution results in no loss to him, he having received something for nothing, and even financial hardship which might result from collections cannot stand against the injustice of keeping that which never belonged to him at all."

The Marine Corps is now in the position of being unable to spend further efforts to gain your voluntary liquidation of the amount you owe. Thus, if you do not respond to this letter within 30 days, we will be forced to declare this debt "UNCOLLECTIBLE." The failure to liquidate this debt will become a permanent part of your service record and could be detrimental to your credit standing.

Make your check or money order payable to: MARINE CORPS DISBURSING OFFICER. Mail your remittance to: Marine Corps Finance Center, Examination Division, Kansas City, MO 64197.

Sincerely yours,
C. S. MC NEILL
Lieutenant Colonel, U.S. Marine Corps
Read, Examination Division, Marine Corps Finance Center

I was still chuckling when I finished reading their letter. My mom walked into the room and asked me why I was laughing.

"It's the Marine Corps again," I replied.

She sat down at the table with me and lit up a cigarette. She set her cigarette lighter down next to her half-filled ashtray and asked, "Are they still trying to get that money from you?"

Grinning, I nodded my agreement. "I think they're finally going to give up. I guess a year of my harassment is enough for 'em. All those officers probably got in trouble because they could only get fifty bucks out of me. One thing for sure, the colonel who wrote me this letter will never see the remaining fourteen dollars and forty-eight big cents. Who does he think he is...tryin' to lay a guilt trip on me?"

My mom stared at me with a smile; her face, a portrait of approval. She had been a life-long Democrat, and her love for the Marine Corps was only equaled by her *affection* for President Nixon. I was a tenacious fighter, and for that she was proud. "You probably should never have paid them any of that money. We do not need to have more of our money spent on destroying Vietnam."

"You don't have to twist my arm about that. The military

needs more money...I doubt it. What a joke...and besides, have you ever heard of an overpaid Marine?"

She didn't answer my question. She just smiled gently at her Jello Kid. Behind her dark-blue eyes and buried deep in her heart, her pain and her joy danced quietly together. She did not speak to me of the overwhelming mother's fear that had owned her while I was in Vietnam, nor did she dance a jubilant Irish jig when I returned from the war alive. My return had been a non-event. Through the years, I had learned to understand my mother through her gentle yet sad Irish eyes, and as usual, there was much sadness, but today I saw the joy of a woman who had escaped a mother's greatest fear: the loss of a child, an experience she did not want to repeat. Even in 1969, my mother had yet to process her grief over the loss of my baby sister eighteen years earlier.

My mother had been spared the anguish of losing a second child because I had somehow survived the Nam. Three months later, the Rolling Stones sang their prophetic lyrics about not always getting what you want, and unfortunately, within a little more than a year, Bessie Smith would be singin' the Blues, and Elisabeth Kubler-Ross would be knocking on my parents' door.

Chapter 45
Autumn 1970

Fate, Guilt And Growth

Paul is coming home. His tour of duty as a corpsman in Rota, Spain ends one week early. He leaves the Navy with full military honors.

The October night is brisk. People who care fill the Catholic church. All of his friends have come to his ceremony. The once-upon-a-time altar boy, the big brother, the almost-sixth-grade teacher, the corpsman who wanted to become a doctor is home.

A folk group from the parish is singing the Peter, Paul and Mary song, "The Day is Done." When it ends, the music of Simon and Garfunkel owns the church. Their song tells us not to worry because 'there is a bridge over troubled water.'

A priest with an Irish brogue finishes his sermon. Knowing that I've asked to speak to the congregation, he invites me to the altar. As I walk past the flag-draped casket, I am filled with fear and apprehension. I desperately want the courage to say that which I must to honor and eulogize my older brother. As I am walking with trepidation toward the altar, my hands are trembling, and the paper on which I have written a poem soaks up my perspiration. My heart is pounding to the cadence of my fear, and my throat is begging for a glass of water, but as I turn around to face my audience, complete tranquility washes over me. My mind is an empty desert: no thoughts, no words, but the fear is gone. At this transformative moment, I am at complete peace as I take the microphone and, shifting into a spontaneous gear, the perfect words begin to flow freely as I tell the mourners about Paul:

I am Pete Bourret, Paul's brother. It is interesting to note that when someone passes away, we appreciate that person and all his accomplishments. I wish, and am sure Paul, too, would like each one of us to not wait for such a sorrowful moment as this to appreciate someone. Appreciate the person next to you, the person you will know someday. Try to appreciate them while they are alive. The time to do it is now. I am sure this world we live in would be a beautiful place if we would at least all try. The word is try.

But, sadly enough, this world is a hateful place, and we tread on and mock the people who are good. We have seen this in the past, we see it now, and we will see it in the future. I guess it is just part of our human condition. So, rather than mourn his death, though we have lost a real human being, we should—we must—rejoice that Paul has found peace. And that is PEACE spelled in capital letters. He is now free from this hassle on earth.

Paul was 25 years old when he died. Paul wanted to teach sixth grade. Paul was against the war in Vietnam, but Paul still did his part. He did it by being a Navy hospital corpsman, a person who helps others in need. Two and a half years ago, in 1967 and 1968, I, without consent from my brother Paul, was with the Marines in Vietnam.

But I was different. I went to a combat area. He went to a place called Rota, Spain, where there was no combat, but the big difference was that I came home alive. If anyone should have died, it should have been me. But we're here inside a church—and I guess we all believe in something—if we don't now, I sure hope we start believing and having faith. God does work in strange ways and does strange things, strange because we don't understand them. If we would only try to understand a few more things in this life and accept a few more people who are different from us, maybe this would be a much better place in which to live.

My being alive, and my brother's death, have perplexed me. I've wondered, and it still perplexes me.

One other thing: my brother wanted to help people, but by dying, he was stopped short of his goal. Let's not let his death stop his work. There are a lot of people here who can continue it. Even if you do just a little bit, it's a damn good way to give a memorial and to eulogize him.

On those cards that were handed out to you, it says when he was born and when he died, and on the back there is a poem that I wrote while I was in Vietnam. I will not read it to you, but I want you to read it. And I think that if you read that poem, this casket here is not going to hurt you as much, and it won't be as sorrowful because it all will seem to make a lot more sense. Being alive doesn't just mean existing. It means that someday we will have to die also. That's part of the whole thing. How we live is the important thing.

So, out of my condition of perplexity and sorrow, I wrote another poem. It will never win a Pulitzer Prize or anything like that, but that doesn't matter. It's for my brother Paul. It's called "Paul's Poem":

He's comin' home—
yes, it's true, she said
true it is; he's comin' home.
Gonna see him again—
yes, I am; been a long while, such a long time.
We'll be five to say goodbye—
yes, adios, farewell;
at Mass we'll be to set him free.
This Mass'll mean so much—
yes, more than any other;
will be the last time,
the last time as six.
And then the prayers are said—
yes, prayers and silent songs;
many goodbyes for that man,
and so many questions why.
He was good—
yes, I'm sure it's true;
is it fair to take away?

where is this justice?
So it's happened—
yes, it is now done.
PEACE, he lived for here,
but had to leave this place to find it.
—The Beginning—

And the last sentence is very important because Paul Bourret didn't begin twenty-five-and-a-half years ago. He began on the 14th of October of 1970.

With all my words for Paul spent, I stare at the congregation for a moment and wonder if they are only being polite. Bowing my head slightly, I begin my walk back to the pew where the rest of our family is sitting. As I pass the casket, I halt momentarily; I kiss my right hand and reach out to touch Paul's flag-draped casket. The words 'Goodbye, I'll miss you' dribble from my trembling lips; as I clench my teeth, my eyes well up. I am changed forever.

Eager to truly understand my loss, so overwhelming, I hunger to heal, yet the grief process seems deaf to my impatience. Sitting in the pew next to Paul's casket, I seek solace in a poem, which I wrote while staring out into the South China Sea while in Vietnam. Believing my poem had a fitting message, my family put it on the *In Memoriam* card for my brother's funeral. as "The Third Day."

The stereo beachcomber throws his pebbles
    to the sea...
As he gazes at the waves, they crash,
    then ooze toward their destiny.
In Neptune's cycle of the sea, detect a view
    of man's odyssey;
So too, an image or even a caricature.
When waves are still within the sea,
—remaining so powerful and pure—
Christen them with majesty.
Yet, as these waters escape the bearing womb,
They shrink to nothingness on the sandy beach,
Greeted by the desolation of an empty tomb.
Yet, for this dampness once so proud,
There is hope—for Neptune cries aloud:

"Return and share in my majesty;
Your dwelling place, the eternal sea."

In spite of my best attempts at moving on, I am predictably stuck. A few weeks after we bury Paul in a family plot near San Francisco, I want to meet God down at the neighborhood park so I can kick His butt for betraying me, for tricking me, for letting me live yet allowing Paul, a corpsman, to died in a car accident in Spain only one week prior to his discharge from the Navy.

Screaming at God, I inform Him that He could have at least allowed Paul die while saving a Marine in the Nam. God ignores me as the days glide by like wind-blown clouds, sometimes strolling across the blue skyscape, but today the November wind howls, sending the white puffs racing across the horizon. The trees, like timid children, cling desperately to their mother, and wind gusts rip spring's leaves from branches made naked by the roaring bully called November. Nervous tree shadows dance wildly on the concrete walls of the buildings, and when the sun escapes in the west, the black blanket called night is thrown over the town, and the woodpile will shrink just a bit, and the popping sounds from the fireplace will once again chatter, and bare feet will dance around the house made a home on a November night. Outside, the wind rushes through the blackness of sleep time, and the home is a place for cuddling. But I do not feel the warmth of the fire. I only feel the emptiness in a sorrowful place in my heart, and the night is dark.

Four months after my brother's death on October 14, 1970, my wife Barbara gives birth to a boy. We name him Paul.

I will toss seven calendars into the trash before I tell the new people in my life that I had an older brother. Unfortunately, the pain of my grief outweighs my pride for having Paul as my older brother.

When I begin my teaching career two years after my brother's death, I decide to eulogize him by dedicating my teaching career to him. His opportunity to make the world a better place is gone, so I choose to influence the world in a positive manner through my teaching as my way of honoring him. The healing begins.

Chapter 46
Winter 1970

The Question

"You were in Vietnam!"

Their faces, always question marks and exclamation points.

"Yes."

"But you're so young looking, so how could you've been in the war?"

He wants to be rude and sarcastic and say something like, "I look young. No shit. I am. Haven't you heard? They haven't been sendin' the old folks to war in a few years. Kids... that's who goes to fight for all that bullshit." He could get nasty, but he decides against that.

Then, he has second thoughts when the conversation continues: "Did you kill anyone over there?"

Once again, he wants to be rude and say something raunchy like, "Have you had sex with your sister?"

He could be semi-crude and say, "It's none of your goddamn business, asshole!" But he refrains. Instead he always say, "What do you think people do in wars?" This is not appreciated, so a, "Well, did you?" usually follows. The script, always the same.

Rather than ask him how the war affected him or if he gained any insights from his experience, he usually is asked *how many* people he killed. He always wonders if people want to be impressed or horrified by the answer that he might give.

Chapter 47
Summer 1977

The Jello Kid Goes To Michigan

The flight from Tucson had taken nine years, but just below us was Lansing, Michigan. When I had called Cossack earlier that day, he informed me that he was teaching school, so his wife would be picking me up. Since she had not been part of my past, she would not recognize me, so I told him to have her look for a long-haired thirty-year-old who looked twenty-four. The plane was an hour late, but my instructions were perfect. During the thirty-minute car ride to their home, we shared stories about our common bond, Cossack. She needed to return to her job at the veterinary hospital, so I relaxed on their overstuffed couch and dozed off for about an hour.

A kitchen door slammed. Cossack was home. Still groggy, I stood up and stared across the living room. Just then, my friend from nine years ago walked into the room. He still wore his dual trade marks: an impish grin and a Fu Manchu mustache. His electric eyes bulging with the excitement of a four-year-old on Christmas morning. "HOW THE FUCK YOU BEEN?"

"Okay, dude, okay!" After we hugged each other like we had been the other's Prodigal-son-come-home, we sat down. At that moment, the Nam was just yesterday. We had known each other for only six months, yet we knew we had become friends forever. All the anticipation disappeared. The flight to Michigan had been worth it.

"So what have you been up to, Jello? You ever marry that chick...Wendy...wasn't that her name?"

I chuckled, shaking my head the opposite way he expected. "No way! This kid sobered up back in the World. Her trip was too strange for me. I ended up falling in love with four or five other chicks before I met my wife Barbara."

"What about that chick who was goin' to college in Virginia, the one who had such a hard time getting' around to writin' you when we were in the Nam?"

"Good old Liz. Nice, but things just didn't work out. Even went back to visit her a few months after I got out of the Nam." I spent the next few minutes explaining what had happened with my litany of ex-girlfriends. "Cossack, speaking of women, what ever happened to your chick from Ohio...the one we wrote that bullshit letter to."

Cossack, struggling through his laughter, told me that she was cute, but he had wanted her to be beautiful. Their relationship had died of terminal boredom. He was a Russian Prince, a Cossack warrior. He wanted to file a lawsuit against her for not being Sleeping Beauty.

He laughed and then asked, "Have you and your wife had any little Jello Kids?"

"Two. Paul...he is six, and Jeremy's almost three. They're a real trip." After I had shown him pictures of my wife Barbara and my two boys, Cossack offered me a beer. I gladly accepted his offer. A six-pack of empty cans later, his wife returned home. Out of beer and hungry for a steak, I offered to take them out to dinner.

We returned from the restaurant and prepared to share another six-pack of beer. Cossack's wife gave him a kiss and went to bed. It was a time for drinking, a time for remembering. I was the first to offer memories, the humorous ones. He choked on his beer when I reminded him about the night we had been mortared and someone had dropped an Oreo Cookie down one of the mortar tubes, which prevented the mortar round from being fired. With a little detective work, the problem was solved but not before the fire mission was over.

"What do you expect from a bunch of stoned Marines?"

"How about the time we H.A.ed [hard assed / pulled a prank on] Pink Rat?"

Cossack interrupted me with his own question. "Which time? We played lots of tricks on him."

"Remember when he came back from guard duty ready as shit to catch some zees and wammo...he shits a brick! We have his cot suspended four feet off the floor."

Cossack, laughing, interrupted my story. "And his footlocker dangling up there under his cot like some sort of magician's trick."

"Boy, was he pissed."

"That Pink Rat was no dummy. We didn't even fake him out by pretending like we were asleep. All he did was scream at us to fix his cot. He didn't even fall for our who-us? routine."

"We were kind of mean since he wasn't a lifer."

"Yeah, but it was fun."

The memory train was rolling with two passengers from the Nam. "I still can't believe we didn't get sent home on a Section Eight...especially you, Cossack. Jumping around the tent acting like a bunch of monkeys should've done the trick. You'd figure the lifers would be freaked out when you'd hang upside-down from the tent rafters letting out your signature , and ngiant eagle calls. No way. They figured we were crazy...no favors, no early flight date out of the Nam. After all, the Nam was an insane place, so why not keep the crazy people there."

"We messed up by only doing this shit for the benefit of second lieutenants and NCOs."

I disagreed with him, reminding him that in my last days with him in Vietnam, we had provided several senior grade officers proof of our insanity. While on a sandbag filling detail at the battalion command bunker, we sacrilegiously, and off key, sang the "Star Spangled Banner" and the "Marine Corps Hymn." They did not appreciate it, but they liked the idea that we were adding a fourth layer of sandbags to the roof of their bunker.

The conversation halted for a moment, Cossack staring at the ceiling. "You remember your first day in the Nam?" I nodded and told him of my disappointment at not being assigned to a line company. I had an insatiable appetite for becoming a grunt in an authentic war. The Marine Corps and fate had conspired to make me an 81mm mortarman instead. "Looking back on it, I should count my blessings. I was one lucky dude. If I had become a grunt, I probably would have had my legs blown off or been blown away. Do you realize that for the six months that I was the squad leader of the Jello Squad, no one in our squad got wounded or killed? Must have been the magical power of all the JELL-O we ate.

Lucky. Damn lucky."

"I got news for you...a month after you left, the Jello Squad's luck ran out..."

I sat up abruptly, my ears ready for stories I did not want to hear. I wished this conversation was just a nightmare that I could wake up from, but this was Michigan, not dreamland.

Cossack rambled on about how he and Sugar Bear had stolen a jeep and had gone to Da Nang to party. On the way back to Hill 10, their jeep spent most of the time swerving back and forth on the dirt road. Cossack and Sugar Bear were stoned, laughing on full-automatic. Three Vietnamese kids sprinted across the road. There was an explosion. Being stoned did not help Cossack when he landed with a hard thud on the dirt road. Sugar Bear, crawling out of the rice paddies that bordered the road, staggered past the mangled Jeep which was on its side in the rice paddy: just another casualty figure in the war. The road was littered with dozens of beer cans made useless by the attack. The beer-run had ended the wrong way. Cossack lay there wondering why God was making it so difficult for him to breathe. Maybe he was dead and was in Hell. He felt like concrete, and the August sky was spinning.

I sat there not wanting to believe the words I was hearing, but Cossack rambled on. "It gets worse. As you can tell, I wasn't killed, but the Marine Corps did there damnedest to drop my wounded ass out of the medevac chopper. There I was lyin' on this stretcher. The chopper taking off, tilting...and bigger than shit...I am slidin' towards the open door. That damn law of gravity is a bitch. Just as the stretcher was about to slide out, the back door finally closed. Damn, I almost shit a brick."

"No kidding! That would have freaked me out too."

Cossack got up and went to the kitchen. He played bartender and assumed I wanted another beer. I did not need one, but I liked what the beer was doing. Having set his unopened beer can down on the rug in front of his chair, he weaved his way to the bathroom. "Wait until you hear about all the bullshit I went through in Japan...a genuine bummer!"

When he returned, he told me about his adventures at the naval hospital in Japan. Cossack had never been impressed by a person's rank. He also believed in speaking his mind. Being egalitarian and honest had gotten him in trouble once again.

The duty nurse on Cossack's ward scolded him for leaving the ward without her permission. She did not appreciate it when Cossack flipped her the middle finger. He was not satisfied with offering only this silent gesture of contempt, so he told her where she could stick it. The base commander was less than thrilled by Cossack's brash actions, so he threatened to send him to Okinawa, which meant that the insubordinate Marine would certainly be given the opportunity of revisiting Vietnam. With some help from his congressman, the commander's threats never became reality.

After he was shipped back to the World, he spent his last months stationed at Camp Pendleton working as an instructor at the rifle range. He enjoyed his job for two reasons: first, he got stoned every day, and secondly, he had authority over the DIs who brought their recruits to his rifle range.

I sat there sipping one-too-many beers. My blank face staring silently. Cossack continued, "When I finally got out of the Crotch, I went to Michigan State for a year. That is when my back was all fucked up. Boy, was I hurtin'. I even limped a little. I was livin' in this two-story duplex, and it was a real drag. I would black out and stay on the couch for a couple of days. I got tired of crawling up and down those stairs. I cut a milk carton in half and would piss in it. It just hurt too much to get to the john."

I sat in stunned silence as I listened to the beginning of Cossack's nightmare experience, but he had just begun. He continued, "Luckily, I was getting the GI Bill or I wouldn't have been able to survive. The next year, I transferred to Wayne State. I remember on my birthday I couldn't get out of bed. Finally, after a week I was able to sit up, but I couldn't walk, so I just crawled to the bathroom. It was twenty painful feet away. Intense is the word for it. So after a few days of this bullshit, I got an appointment at the VA Hospital. Gettin' there was a real drag. I had to crawl through the snow to get to my car...but it sure felt good drivin' there. It was the first time I had relaxed in over a week and a half. I had to sit there waitin' for over five hours for some dumb shit doctor to see me. This son of a bitch had to be at least seventy, and he was definitely not with the program. Check this out. This dude who's supposed to examine me comes cruisin' down the hall towards me. Just before he gets to me, he makes a right turn into what he thinks is his office. This old fart walks smack dab into the wall. He told me that I would be okay, but if my spine hurts too much, I was supposed to take *Seconal*. Over the next couple of months, I got hooked on 'em. They gave me that shit like they were jelly beans."

"What a bunch of shit."

Cossack was staring at the ceiling again. His silence lasting for only a few seconds, and then he threw his empty beer can towards a trashcan. It missed, but Cossack did not care. His voice was steeped in anger as he recounted memories he wished would disappear. "Those sons of bitches! You know what they tried to do to me? If you can believe this...they were givin' me just over twenty-three fucking dollars a month for my disability. They said it was only a ten-percent disability. I tried tellin' that to my lower back and legs, but my legs just didn't understand. So when I tried to get the VA to change my disability to sixty percent, they not only turned me down, they actually tried to take away my ten percent...and if that isn't bad enough, the government decided to cut off my monthly disability check until I paid back the GI Bill money, which they had been sendin' me when I was goin' to Michigan State. They thought that I was tryin' to defraud them because I was receivin' GI Bill checks but wasn't goin' to classes at the university. I tried to tell 'em that my back was too messed up, and I couldn't work, much less, go to school. They gave a rat's ass and put the word on me that I wouldn't get any shitty disability checks until the GI Bill money had been repaid."

"What a crock of shit! Aren't you glad this damn country appreciated us so much." Cossack was getting drunk enough to want to cry, but no tears. He just sat, staring nowhere, wondering a thousand whys.

Two days later, two friends from the Nam hugged each other at the airport. Saying goodbye in the World was so much sweeter than our last goodbye. The sun in the Michigan sky looking down, smiling.

Chapter 48
Winter 1977

Eddie Plays Socrates

I'm looking outside through a large window...a man standing in my backyard...looking like he knows what he's doing...a crew of six men carrying corpses...dead men dressed in green combat uniforms...no helmets...the work detail brings three four five bodies...two corpses already thrown in a hole...a grave large enough for a half-dozen men...three four and five piled on top of the first two...the crew walking away...the man in charge staring at the hole and the grey cream-colored faces of the dead soldiers...the face of the man-in-charge turning away from his business...he is staring at the window and at me...leaving my concrete house I begin to walk towards him...I don't want to shake his hand...his cold eyes staring at me...staring past me...he does not shake my hand...I ask him what's going on...we're burying these casualties...but this is my backyard...we stop talking...two workmen carrying a sixth dead man...then a seventh dead man...two swings and a thud...a hole full of dead men with cold grey faces staring up at us...two workmen drinking coffee...the man in charge grabbing a shovel and telling me to cover up the grave...taking it...shoveling...dirt covering up the pile of dead men wearing faded green fatigues...MARINES FROM THE NAM...shoveling faster FASTER FASTER...the grave now covered...sweat rolling off my forehead...looking up...the six crewmen are gone...the man in charge telling me that I've done it all wrong...I don't understand...you can't just fill up the hole and expect people not to know that you have a grave in YOUR backyard and it's impossible to fill in the hole without creating a mound of dirt on top of it...the man nods his head but tells me to make this grave look like a hole and not like a grave for seven dead men if I know what's good for me...grabbing the shovel again...digging and clearing away the mound of dirt...the man in charge disappearing...the mound almost cleared away...my shovel hitting something...the grey face of the seventh dead Marine getting in the way of my shovel...brushing the soil from his nose and his cold cheeks...finding his stiff hands...clutching them...pulling the seventh dead Marine up and out of his grave...the six others pulled out and piled next to the hole...then...back in the hole...a tighter fit this time...all seven will fit in...no mound this time...no crew of six workmen who drink steaming coffee when they can't bury dead Marines in a vet's backyard...this time it'll be done right...this time only a hole filled with dirt...FINISHED...the man in charge walking up to me and looking at me as I lean on my shovel...we don't shake hands...we turn toward the hole that I have filled in...but piles of dirt are around the hole...and it is an empty hole without the bodies of seven dead Marines from the Nam...not a grave but just a hole in my backyard...screaming at the man in charge WHERE THE HELL DID YOU PUT THE BODIES...what bodies...please calm yourself...WHY ARE YOU DOING THIS...I just have a job to do...tell me where you put the SEVEN dead Marines...there weren't any corpses here in this hole...DAMN IT their faces stared at me and they didn't say too much if you know what I mean...don't worry about this incident since it didn't really happen...BUT THOSE GUYS WERE REALLY DEADER THAN SHIT and don't try to tell me otherwise because I know what dead looks like...let's not talk about this any further...WHAT...please come with me for a moment so I can show you something I think you'll be interested in...both of us walking to my concrete walled house and entering and walking to a small barren room...the man in charge pointing to a plaque on the grey wall...one word...DEATH.

I woke up and stared at the ceiling for a moment. It was not concrete, and I sighed. I rolled over and curled up to Barbara's warm, sleepy body. It felt so much better than the cold, grey, dead flesh of my nightmare.

The clock next to our bed was my friend. 5:30 a.m. looking so good. Twenty minutes later the alarm fulfilled its mission in life once more. A moment later, an obnoxious disk jockey said something stupid. Ten minutes before six was as good a time as any to say those kinds of absurdities. He either forgot to accurately check his own clock, or he was in another time zone. "It's ten big minutes to seven." Having bungled his way into our bedroom full of yawns, he introduced a hit song that rhymed well but said absolutely nothing meaningful. I made a joke about the deep social commentary in the song. My wife grinned politely.

Our three-year-old son Jeremy, still playing the role of a sleepyhead perfectly, staggered into our bedroom. Having yawned and rubbed his eyes, he proudly announced his accomplishment, "Mommy and Daddy, me did not go potty in my pants."

"Very good, Jeremy You're such a good little son."

I had said the wrong thing, and Jeremy quickly straightened me out. "Me not Daddy's little son. Me Barbara's big son."

Paul, our oldest son, was typically still in bed staring at the Batman kite, which hung from the ceiling.

"Morning, Paul. It's 6:30, so you better start getting dressed now."

"But Dad, my legs don't want to get up yet."

"You'd better have a talk with your legs before your mother has a talk with your butt. You're almost seven, so I think you could convince your legs to get up and put on some trousers."

I handed him a color-coordinated outfit. Although I was smiling, he knew that the excuse-well had run dry. Before I could leave his room, he wanted to know if I knew the answer to forty-nine plus forty-seven. Giving him a chance to answer his own question, I pleaded ignorance. A smile ran wild across his gentle face as he proudly told me the answer.

"Did you know that you're a very smart almost-seven-year-old."

Paul's eyes were electric. He nodded, still brimming with an embarrassed yet proud smile.

"Do you know why I know the answer? It's because my brain told me the answer. That's what brains are for, right?"

There was nothing I could say. I hugged him and reminded him about getting dressed. In between making some bland cheese sandwiches for Barbara's and Paul's lunches, I managed to gulp down my yeast drink. It provided me with a heavy dose of energy, which was an absolute necessity if I were interested in surviving a grueling day as a junior high school teacher. I was armed with my yeast, a sense of humor, and my Marine Corps training: my trio of secret weapons.

After six years of teaching social studies at the junior-high-school level, I still enjoyed myself, probably because I was zanier than the students. I doubt if they really believed me when I informed them that teachers were not born in the classroom, but many of us had actually gone to school in the olden days. Yes, many of us had been children once, but life had been more difficult on us as back during the dinosaur days.

As usual, the people in my first period class enthusiastically worked on their slave diaries. The six people who had gone to the library returned with almost finished reports about various famous black leaders. Laura and Mary Ann giggled because they thought Jimmy Hernandez was so cute. As usual, Michael wore his coat all period. Sitting alone and saying nothing, he filled most of his paper with the second and third entries of his slave diary. Jodi McDorman, my student assistant who was a ninth grader, collected all the papers when the dismissal bell rang. Rusty, who was repeating the eighth grade, remained after class to find out how he was doing. He had been absent for almost a week and wanted to get caught up.

"You don't have anything to worry about if you care enough to talk to me about it. Tomorrow, either Jodi or I will work with you on getting caught up on the slave diary. Okay?"

Rusty smiled and sighed. "So, I'm doing okay then."

"Are you learning anything in here, and are you doing your best possible work?"

He nodded his agreement.

"Then I can't expect anymore than that. Hang in there, okay."

"Thanks, sir."

yuck...why do kids always have to call me SIR...I sure hope Rusty doesn't drop out like his brother and sister...what will they be able to do with a lousy eighth grade education...hell...they didn't even have that...could barely read so what else is new...big ass classes...so what can you expect...I couldn't believe it when they sent the withdrawal paperwork around to his brother's teachers...Reason For Withdrawal: Discontinuation of his studies...what a bunch of crap...why didn't they just say it...DROPPED OUT OF SCHOOL AND IS ON A FIELD TRIP IN THE STREETS...NO...wouldn't want to admit that...and then to top it all off...CITIZENSHIP...GOOD...BAD...hell no...I'll mess with the form and put United States citizen...everyone has given him an F for a grade...why not write down an A...it makes no difference...so who cares...he sure didn't.

"Mr. Bourret, could you answer a question for me before I go to science class?"

"Sure, Jodi."

I began writing her a pass to her science class because she would be a few minutes late, and her teacher had a strict tardy policy.

"Last night we were talkin' at home, and my father said that he thought that children had to be controlled and would only do good things if they got a reward. I disagreed with him. I said that *all* children were not the same and that some children took responsibility for their actions. Then he told me to check with my teachers, and see if they agreed with him. He was certain they would all go along with what he had said. So what do you think about all that?"

I looked up at the clock, and then back at Jodi's questioning face. I knew that Jean-Paul Sartre, the famous existential philosopher, would have been proud of her, especially since she was a philosopher at the tender age of fifteen.

"There's one thing your father was wrong about. You found one teacher who disagrees with his theory. I can still understand why he said all those things. He's coming from a different place than you. He's had different experiences than you. The important thing is not to worry who is right or wrong, but rather to understand how your father acquired his theory. You brought up some excellent points when you talked about personal responsibility and how every child isn't the same. If we keep talking about this, we could be here for a long time...I don't want you to get hassled for being late."

Because I had second period off, I locked the door, and we left the hum of the fluorescent lights behind us.

"Isn't it amazing that I'm going to science class when I could be continuing a really great discussion. Something's wrong if that's what school is all about."

"I'm afraid you're right. Smile, it could be worse. You could have lunch duty like Mr. Dedicated."

Jodi laughed, but a bit of sadness tiptoed across her eyes.

"We'll continue this discussion while I'm on lunch duty trying to catch all the tricky boys and girls who will try to take cuts in the lunch line." We both laughed.

"Thanks. Bye."

My second period planning time was spent in our teacher planning area, which housed the desks of most of our eighty-member teaching staff. Students were not permitted in this room, much less were they allowed to peer into our inner sanctum of insanity.

Mike Levy was sitting at his desk in the back of the TPA [Teacher Planning Area] when I walked in. He swung his chair around, tilted his head to the left and rolled his eyes erratically. He was not officially crazy. He just acted that way.

Before I could sit at my desk, which was next to his, Mike began rambling on about one of the students in his first period math class. This boy was in the process of causing Mike's curly dark hair to stand straight up.

I felt sorry for him, especially since my first period class was so enjoyable to work with. When he told me that Eddie was the cause of his anguish, I stopped feeling sympathy for Mike. I began feeling sorry for myself. I had the same boy in my third period class. When I told him this, Mike chuckled. Suffering seemed to be more tolerable when it was a shared experience. Not being a selfish person, Mike was overjoyed to share.

Third period was not as bad as it could have been. The boy Mike had anguished over was mild mannered throughout most of class. I was happy. The class was happy, but the boy was not. His acting like a schoolboy was out character for him. He had a reputation to uphold, and today he was failing miserably at it. He probably had been busted during his second period class and was beginning to realize the precariousness of his situation. He would return to jive around another day.

The dismissal bell rang, and half the people in class left their slave diaries on their desks. Eddie, who usually exploded out of the room like a greyhound at the dog track, walked casually to my desk.

"Sir, what'll you give me if I pick up the papers?"

Andres Burrola, my student assistant for third period, shook his head and snickered as he picked up the papers that Eddie was negotiating about.

"Nothing."

"What a dud, sir."

After Andres finished collecting the papers, he placed them on my desk and waved as he left the classroom.

Eddie gazed up at the ceiling for a moment and then began rattling questions at me about the war. When he had first discovered that I had been to Vietnam, he was most interested to know if I had killed anybody. That had been several months ago, but now his questions were back.

"Sir, you're Catholic, right?"

"Yes, why?"

"Well, when you were in the war, you killed people...didn't you?"

I hesitated and cleared my throat since I could not think of anything better to do at that uncomfortable moment. Eddie, still anticipating my reply, looked at me.

what's the story with this dude...why does he have to be so damn interested in this stuff...if he only knew about killing...so what else is new...can't really expect him to understand... especially with John Wayne movies and all that glory bullshit.

Eddie Leon, the curious twelve-year-old with the uncomfortable question, was still staring, still waiting.

There were no choppers to evacuate me from this hot LZ. His simple question ambushed me, hitting me like a perfectly aimed B40 rocket. My only escape was to play teacher. "Mr. Leon, did you get all your work finished today? You should be up to entry number five in your slave diary."

"Uhhuh, sir. So if you killed people, did you go to confession and tell the priest what you did? Well, sir?"

The bell rang. It meant that Eddie would be late for his fourth period class. I nervously scribbled out a tardy pass for him. Having handed his paper to me, he stared at me for a moment, realizing that I would not answer his question.

Eddie left the room, but his question lingered.

Chapter 49
1978-1979

Jack Daniels, Guns And Backgammon

"First off, put the gun down," I said with a calm yet firm voice. Obviously, she needed to know that I was serious.

"Okay, but...my...." With a current of fear coursing through her hesitant reply, she obediently followed my instructions. Unfortunately, the College of Education neglected to prepare me for such a scenario. Meanwhile back in my eighth-grade American history classroom, my students were either dutifully working on their assignment or were involved in a spit-wad war. Because they were thirteen-year-olds, either situation could be happening; that was the nature this age group: saints one day, sinners the next. Regardless of their choice of activity, I was on the phone in the Teacher Planning Area.

The urgency of the situation dictated that I needed to have great faith that my classroom would still be there when I would return. Having weighed the damage capacity of a .357 Magnum compared to a well-thrown spit wad, I knew I needed to be on the telephone. I only hoped that I possessed the right answers.

Remaining nervous, she stumbled though her words as she sobbed, "But my dad'll be so mad at me if he finds his gun out. It's cocked...and I'm not sure how to uncock it. I feel so stupid. He'll be so mad at me."

Being as reassuring as I knew how, I replied, "Everything's gonna be okay. Just follow my instructions, and you'll be able to uncock the gun...then you can put it away."

Having taken a deep breath, I let it out slowly as I waited for her to tell me some good news.

"I did it."

"Excellent, I knew you could. Now...I want you to put it away."

After she agreed, I asked her why she was so afraid of her father. She would only tell me that she had been bad. She wouldn't explain the details, but she promised me that she wouldn't try to kill herself again. Although the causes of her suicide attempt had remained locked up in the vault of her emotional hell, she had at least reached out for some help. I only hoped that talking with her counselor would help her resolve her deep-seated pain.

Unlike the fifteen-year-old eighth-grader who killed himself in 1972 during my first year of teaching, she was alive; she would graduate from junior high school. But the memory of that boy was brought front and center on the parade deck of my mind by my phone conversation with this thirteen-year-old girl. He, on the other hand, had been a student who didn't stay around long enough for me to even learn his name. When he died, he was only a name neatly printed on a seating chart for my first period American History class.

Unfortunately, in the earlier chapters of the novella that would be his young life, he had been one of those adolescent corpses, yawning in the sterile graveyard where the fluorescent lights hum overhead and the grave digger points his stuttering finger at the sloucher, who sits in his appointed desk a safe distance away; and there is the joy of turning to page ninety-seven, maybe for others but not for this boy, who is really in Pago Pago or at the park by his house; and the truth merchant says that the boy is failing geography, but the dreamer can't hear him; the waves, crashing hard against the outrigger. And possibly he had been a daydreamer, who peers through his window, seeing an orange tree obeying the wind: that tree, a perfect partner in the ballet: rhythmic dancing, accepting God's breath, not wondering, just being. Maybe he wanted desperately to be that tree but didn't know how.

And so on a Monday morning in early 1972, I marked him absent; and as it turned out, he would be absent forever because he planted that final needle in his arm and sent the white death to his soul; fifteen years wandering, now an eternity, buried in that hole. And I never discovered why he thought it was necessary to drink a fifth of Jack Daniels and shoot up heroin for homework. My classroom was far from a sterile graveyard, and I wasn't a grave digger pointing a stuttering finger at my students, but that was of little solace for the boy who decided to drop out completely.

The eighth-grade girl who had called me attended class the next day. After school, she told me the cause of her pain: her father had just taken an interest in her younger sister, and she knew that she was powerless to prevent him from exploiting her. And she knew her mother would do nothing, just as she had failed to act when she had learned years earlier that her husband was having sex with his oldest daughter, the girl who had phoned me. Her childhood, a bastion of innocence for most, had been compromised by her father's betrayal; hurt, fear, rage, depression, guilt, helplessness and loneliness were the shock troops of parental betrayal that overran her emotional landscape, which now was littered with the rotting corpses of her dreams. Sadly, the attitudes of 1970s were not on the side of children; they were still *to be seen and not heard*. Parents had a monopoly on the truth.

Two eighth-graders: one buried and one battered. As I sat patiently, listening to the words that my principal used in my evaluation to describe my teaching abilities, I was like the sloucher who was really in Pago Pago or at the park by my house; I was like the dreamer who couldn't hear my principle as she told me that 'I, although effective with students, failed to follow the state adopted curriculum,' and the waves crashing hard against an outrigger evaporated because I only saw an empty desk, as vacant as the fifteen-year-old boy's heart, and I only heard the sobbing sounds of a thirteen-year-old girl who hated being daddy's little girl.

A month before I ended my tour of duty as a junior high school teacher, three of my Hispanic students came to class wearing oversized, knee-length winter coats, which was a bit peculiar because April in Tucson, Arizona has never been cold, much less cool. Although such behavior seemed strange, my seven years of teaching experience had taught me that early adolescents viewed the world in their own unique way. Their world-view could change as quickly as a new pimple might grace their foreheads.

For the past eight months, I had been running a program for at-risk-students. Having volunteered to work with these students, I was promised complete support for the program. I unfortunately had forgotten some of the lessons from my Vietnam experience. I was promised no more than twelve students for my afternoon program; I received twenty-four students: twenty-three of them had probation officers. I was promised that I would receive specific books by the beginning of the school year; I received only a few of them, and they showed up during the middle of the second semester. I was told to use whatever methods worked with these *incorrigible* students, and so I did.

There was one unifying characteristic that all my at-risk-students possessed: school was synonymous with failure; for this reason, being on suspension was as normal for them as studying for a test was for an *A* student. In the geometry of their lives, they would never have to concern themselves with going from point *B* to point *A*: they were at point *F*, so all those other letters just didn't matter. They weren't *schoolboys* or *schoolgirls*, both pejorative terms in their world; they were at-risk-students, but that was just a fancy new term for *losers*: tomorrow's prison inmates and welfare recipients.

Fortunately, some of them recognized something in me that was different: I had not given up on them even though some in the class had stopped living and were only existing, surviving day to day on the high which one too many joints would give them. Whereas successful students have resumés, these children of the barrio were the proud owners of rap sheets—not the musical kind. They were better acquainted with the cops than with their teachers. Stealing, drinking whatever was available, smoking dope and dealing grass were their extracurricular activities. School was just something that the law required, which they would resist until they were sixteen years old; for most in my class, their battle with the school system would rage on for another three or four years.

It took awhile before many of the at-risk-students realized that I also thought the school system was flawed. They had been casualties of a system that usually failed to appreciate square pegs because they resisted too much when they were forced into round holes; using the hammer had not been beneficial for either. Traditional methods had failed to achieve positive results, so I opted for a more creative approach; teach them the thinking process through the game of backgammon. Having learned the value of guerrilla warfare tactics from the Viet Cong, I decided to trick them into using their most dangerous weapon, their mind.

They needed to discover that it was learning, not school, that was most important.

Sadly, at this juncture in their young lives, they had yet to learn that some hope still glimmered for them. Getting wasted on some *good shit*, as they put it, was not their only option. There would be no miracle cures, only an ounce of hope to possibly replace an ounce of marijuana. And so, my platoon of square pegs and I set out on *Operation, The Brain Is A Dangerous Weapon.*

On the day following the winter-coat-athon, one of the students, this time without his coat, sauntered up to my desk as only a thirteen-year-old gangbanger could. With arms folded across his chest, his coolness oozed from every pore, and his head, attached to a cocky sneer, bobbed rhythmically as he measured the words to his terse question, "So...do you know why me and my boys wore coats yesterday?"

I look up at him and smiled, hinting that I knew some secret that he wasn't privy to.

"Well, I thought it was a bit odd that you'd want to wear coats in April, but what the heck...maybe you were makin' a fashion statement." Although I chuckled, he didn't.

With a serious tone in his vice, he asked, "You don't know why, do you, sir?"

"No, but I think you want to tell me...Right?"

He nodded, and then informed me that he and his boys, as he liked to refer to them, had been packing handguns under their coats the previous day. He stood there waiting for my mouth to drop at his news flash. My jaw stayed in place, but his face slowly became a portrait of bewilderment as he scrunched up his young eyebrows in disbelief. His teacher was neither shocked nor trembling with trepidation. I only sat there, peering up at him as I said, "Oh."

The calm in my voice and my matter-of-fact attitude were disarming; his ambush had been ambushed, but he quickly regrouped, replying, "Well, sir, aren't you afraid of me and my boys...we could've taken out our pieces and blown you away...well?"

Before I answered him, I found a comfortable spot in my chair, and leaning back, I tilted my head, cupping it in the palm of my right hand. I paused a moment as I mulled over my response. When I was ready to descend into the hot LZ, I slowly leaned forward and spoke deliberately, "No and no."

Baffled by my reply, he repeated what I had said, possibly because he wanted clarification or maybe because he was in shock at my response. Then, I repeated, "No and no" as he squinted and his face became contorted.

He was bewildered, so I thought some explanation was in order. "Do you guys think that I'd let a couple of junior high guys waste me? When I was in the Nam, the NVA...they were the bad guys...and they had bigger weapons than you guys could ever dream of havin', and there were thousands of them. They tried to blow me away many times...came close, but they couldn't get me...so think about it...why would I let you guys waste me after surviving all that?"

By now his tough-guy look had left town, and the kid hiding behind the mask timidly began to peer over the wall that he had built so many years earlier. He wanted to say something, anything, but there were no words, only stunned silence.

"No, I'm not afraid of you because I know that you're not stupid...I'm probably the only adult in your life that really gives a damn about you...and you know that...so why in the hell would you want to do somethin' dumb like blowin' away someone who cares about you?"

My words made sense to him, but he could only muster up a one-word response. "Oh." He only nodded as he turned and walked over to a table where his boys were sitting. They huddled together as he tried to explain his conversation with his teacher.

Although I hadn't specifically told the gangster wanna-be that guns would not be tolerated in my classroom, he was beginning to realize that his teacher needed to be taken seriously and guns would not be tolerated, but more importantly, he understood that his teacher cared about him and had his best interests in mind.

One week later, I was called into the principal's office and was informed that the parent of one of my at-risk-students was unhappy with my teaching techniques; he wanted spelling tests and all those educational strategies that had failed to help his son in the past. He also didn't seem want to accept that his fourteen-year-old son had a serious drinking problem. Denial was alive and well in the desert, and unfortunately, my principal chose to cave in to the parent's demands.

The traditional classroom was what they wanted, so my principal informed me that I must obey his edict, but, in all good conscience, I knew that I would not run my classroom in such a manner: these students deserved more. Therefore, I told him that I would resign at the end of the school year which was only a month away. My sense of betrayal brought me to tears as I told the principal that his lack of support reminded me of my Vietnam experience. I had been a character in that chapter before; I didn't relish the feeling of betrayal. I only wanted the principal's support, but I was once again expendable, once again cannon fodder. I hated being reminded of those Nam feelings from yesteryear.

On the following day, I informed my at-risk-students that there would no longer be backgammon games, which were considered mortal sins under the new rules of the program. Schools were supposed to be about textbooks, tests, homework and order; this had been the recipe for years. Backgammon, like the students in my program, simply didn't belong. Unfortunately, I had failed to convince the power brokers that *thinking* was a key ingredient in the educational mix. Once again I was at odds with the supporters of the status quo.

Because my at-risk-students needed to acquire a taste of accomplishment and success in their lives, I had taught them how to play backgammon, a game that requires intelligence as well as several positive aspects. By utilizing a hands-on approach, the students rapidly discovered the need for long-term strategies; such a concept was both novel and foreign to most of them because they came from families that had failed to model such ideas. In the same vein, they learned that consequences existed for their choices on the backgammon board; they would have to pay for a poorly thought out move, and likewise, they would be rewarded for a thoughtful decision. In fact, their mistakes even taught them to come up with a Plan *B*, something most of them had never implemented.

The concept of students learning from their mistakes was an idea that many of my peers had failed to embrace and recognize as having value. They had never been in my classroom, watching as students calculated the odds of making one move as opposed to another. They had never heard our conversations as I played the role of a surrogate parent, offering insight, but more importantly, just listening to these emotionally starved children who were experiencing something new: an adult authority figure who didn't yell at them or hit them when they made a mistake on the backgammon board. It was safe for them to be human, to both succeed and fail.

Finally, they were discovering that a consequence doesn't always need to be a punishment. When the roll of a pair of dice gave them a poor combination, they didn't sport their victim hats, but rather they suffered the consequence, and eventually, either bounced back or fell short. In either case, they were learning that life requires resilience, and that, although they might fail, they weren't failures.

Life for these children was looking up; after all, if they conceived a well-thought out strategy, they could defeat their teacher, a man with a master's degree. Such a delicious victory brought smiles and cheers, and my outstretched hand, offering congratulations to the eighth-grade victor. They were finally beginning to smell the aroma of hope, which permeated our portable classroom, which was isolated a safe distance away from the *regular* students.

With a heavy heart, I explained to my students that the new edict had banned the playing of backgammon. Until the end of school, we would act like a *normal* classroom, one without the benefits of backgammon. When I told my students that I had chosen to resign in protest at the end of the school year, several students volunteered to 'take care of' the principal's car. "Damn, Sir. *Eso vale verga.* If we slice up his tires, he won't be goin' anywhere...That'll teach him."

Smiling because I appreciated their sense of loyalty, I agreed with their Spanish expletive and replied, "Yes, it sucks, but if you want to teach the principal a real lesson, beat the odds and graduate from high school. The house's money is on you guys not makin' it through school, but those folks don't really know you. My money's on you hangin' in there. Whatever happens, no one can take it away from you that you learned how to beat your teacher at backgammon...if you're stoned because your life sucks, you don't have chance at beatin' your three-year-old brother at the game, much less me. Figure it out, or you can prove all those who wrote you off to be right. I lost this battle, but I'm a survivor...are you?"

Thoughts of retaliation and revenge had evaporated; the principal's tires would survive, dying a slow and mundane death at somewhere around 50,000 miles. There was only pensive silence and an illegal backgammon board slowly collecting dust and waiting patiently and hopefully for Godot.

Chapter 50
December 1979

A Kubler-Ross Moment

Standing there, smoking my third nervous cigarette, I keep interrupting my speech with visits to the bathroom: the toilet, my ashtray. I am back with more angry words for her. I am tired of keeping it all inside of me. Politeness is past; the time for sharing who I am, who I'm becoming, is here. I can still remember our 'good-nights' that took two hours; but that was ten years earlier. Since 1970, much has changed. The decade is dying, and our marriage is also ready for a funeral.

Wearing a stunned look, she sits on the brown-leather couch staring at me, wondering what my next words will be. For the past ten years she has heard my anger, one of her reasons for wanting out of the marriage, yet now she sits and listens to my words as if possibly there is something different in them.

"I'm fed up with everyone else fucking with my life. Goddamn it, I'm sick of...!"

Tired of biting her lip, she interrupts my tirade with her first salvo. "See, there you go. You're still pissed off at the world. For seven years, I listened to you complain about the pay you got for teaching. Last year you made thirteen thousand dollars. I know someone from work whose husband just got a teaching job. They're religious and are perfectly happy to be making that kind of money."

Still leaning on the bookcase, I stand at a distance from her. Shaking my head, I reply, "What the hell does religion have to do with all of this? I got news for you, give that dude a few years in the teaching business, and he'll be as angry as I was."

Shaking her head back and forth, her body language provides

ample proof that I have failed to offer enough evidence to make my case, so I fire away, "I hope you realize that Jesus even got pissed off when the people in the Temple were missin' the boat. And besides that, at least I had the balls to get the hell out of teaching when I realized that I was too angry to do a good job at it. SHIT! At least I didn't hang around pretending like everything was okay when it wasn't."

"But..."

"Hold on...goddamn it! I'm not finished." Pausing a moment to take another drag off my half-finished cigarette, I continue, "I've spent most of my life keepin' my anger inside me. I never really dealt with it. I think that's my real problem. I guess I just give too much of a damn to sit back and say, 'Oh that's just wonderful,' when I know things aren't really that way. Maybe my only crime is that I give a shit! I care, so what's so fucking terrible about that?"

Unimpressed by my impassioned words, she replies, "See, there you go again. You're still angry at the world."

Glaring, I fire back without hesitation, "You bet I am. This year's been the pits. Everything's hit me all at once. Even Vietnam wasn't this fucked up!"

I stand silently, keenly aware that her thoughts on the matter are just seconds away. Because I feel like a tired, spent volcano, I don't want to hear or discuss her opinions. Again she reminds me that she is fed up with my constant anger. Although I want out of the ring, my impatience knocks my self-control to the canvas, so I throw a verbal jab at her. "I know I have disillusioned you. When we first met, I was so nice and optimistic, but then you found out that I was just a pissed-off Nam vet. Yeah, just like everyone else, you couldn't handle my anger. You must have wanted a phony asshole, a character from a Disney movie who just smiled all the goddamn time...well, forget it!"

I desperately want to hurl an ashtray across the room, but fortunately for the living room wall there is no ashtray available. The thought feels good, but it is a fantasy that needs to die at birth.

"I just don't want to live with all your anger. I'm negative enough as it is, and I don't need any more garbage in my life."

"So you tell me to get lost, and you find yourself a lover boy, and everything's rosy...nice and superficial. Shit! What ever happened to workin' at somethin' important. Whatever happened to marriage vows. It's just a bunch of hypocritical bullshit. Love, honor and cherish just as long as one of the two people doesn't get bored or wants to do their own thing. So who said that marriage was going to be easy and without mistakes. Maybe my mistake in marrying you was that I forgot to ask you what the conditions for divorce would be. Maybe you should've told me from the start that if I made three mistakes and was an angry person, you'd leave me. Maybe then I would've decided to get mellow and learn to deal with all the anger inside me. You ripped me off, goddamn it! I'm sort of old-fashioned...I actually believed that we'd be married forever. Nowadays *forever* doesn't mean shit!"

"But..."

Exasperated, I interject, "I am not through yet, thank you!"

She gets up and walks toward the bathroom. "If you want to talk, I'll still listen. We tried three times, and it didn't work out. Aren't three separations enough?"

"Yeah, if you aren't into workin' at somethin' that's important to you."

"What did you say?"

I raise my voice and repeat myself before I add, "When you were a baby how many times did you try to walk before you finally pulled it off. Three? I doubt it. Walking was important to you, so you worked at it. If it hadn't been important, you'd still be crawlin' around on your hands and knees."

When she returns to the living room, she finds a spot at the far end of the couch and sits down. She pauses for a moment before she tells me in a soft but firm voice that it is time for me to leave.

I realize the futility of continuing the conversation. Before I make my move toward the door, I walk over to her and stop. Leaning over, I kiss her on the cheek, and then I stand back.

"You know..." I pause before continuing, "I think I'll take your suggestion and set aside a day so that I can spend some time with the kids. They deserve it. And as far as my anger goes, I know that learning to accept both the good and the bad is important for me. I'm still going to have my anger, but I'm learning to put it into perspective. Recently I've been trying to figure out the lesson...what I can learn from all of this. See, I am growing, even if you don't believe me."

I turn away from her and walk to the door. I open it, and as I begin to walk out, I toss my dead cigarette butt onto the front porch. I hesitate and then turn around, and looking directly at her, I say, "One thing all this garbage has taught me is that I am going to make it in what ever the hell I do. Business...writing...life, no matter what I do, I'm going to succeed. Maybe someday you'll realize I was worth a fourth try, and that my anger only meant that I am a real human being who cares enough to give a damn. Thanks for the motivation. Goodbye."

There are no tears, only my campaign promises for my future. Because the present moment hurts too much, I board the Einstein Express. Time travel to the future is so much safer; and outside, the Tucson sky is ripening as the Earth spins, and the sun is gliding casually down, beginning its foreplay with a first kiss: another Arizona sunset smiling across the city, but this one goes unseen.

The door shuts hard behind me. My epistle to the world evaporates into the past. When ten years of making love is just a memory, a corpse on the last plane out of yesteryear, what else is there to say: only goodbye as I walk out into my tomorrow.

The ex-Marine and the ex-teacher becoming an ex-husband, but there is no winner in this game of tic-tac-toe. With my goodbye behind me, I sit on my back porch in silence on the swing with its creaking, and my thoughts are trapped, swaying back and forth. The vacant spot to my right waiting to be filled with a voice that will muffle this sad song of the swing's creaking.

Chapter 51
January 1980

The Five-Year-Old Magician

My five-year-old son points out that special star in the sky and tells me that he wants to be Santa Claus when he grows up. He's certain that Santa Claus will need someone to take over his job when he dies. If Santa Claus decides to live forever, my son will become the Candy Man when he learns to ride his bicycle, but his bicycle will wait. The magic tree outside the kitchen window is filled with my son Jeremy, a five-year-old tree climber, just waiting to grow up.

Jeremy is concerned about his dad. Somehow this five-year-old's sonar has detected a sadness in me. I am sitting on a secondhand couch with an early Salvation Army motif when he walks up to me. I am smoking another unnecessary cigarette, and he is wearing a metallic green hat with the words HAPPY NEW YEAR stapled to the front of it.

"When is the divorce, Dad?"

I hesitate a moment, and then tell him that it will be tomorrow. He pulls two pink balloons and one yellow balloon from behind his back. Holding them out, he asks which color I prefer.

"Yellow."

The two unwanted pink balloons disappear quickly behind his back. "Dad, you can take this balloon to the divorce if you want."

I smile at him. "Thanks, Jeremy...but why do you want me to take it to the divorce?"

He peers at me with a look of bewilderment; his dad should know the answer, so why is he asking such a foolish question. After all, although he is only a five-year-old, he knows the reason. He is puzzled because it should be obvious why he has given his father the gift of a yellow balloon.

There are three reasons why his dad should understand: his dad is thirty-two years old, and old people are supposed to know these types of things; his dad has been a teacher, and teachers are supposed to be very smart; and lastly, a boy's very own dad is supposed to possess great wisdom and understanding concerning the crucial issues in life. This is one of those times when a dad is supposed to know, so why is his hero asking such a silly question. Maybe he is joking with his little boy again. He likes it when his dad jokes with him, but if he wants the conversation to continue, he will need to be the one answering his father's question.

"Since you like yellow balloons, it will make your sadness go away, and you'll feel happy when you go to the divorce."

I want to tell him that it will take much more than a single yellow balloon to make me feel happy about the divorce, but I am silent because he doesn't deserve such a response like that. Instead I just smile and thank him for being so considerate. His dark blue eyes becoming oceans of joy, but this poster-child for a Norman Rockwell painting is not finished with his generosity. Pulling the gaudy party-hat from his head, he offers it to me.

"It's a Happy-New-Year's hat, and you can have it so you can be happy tomorrow."

I accept his gift. Smiling, I lean over to hug my five-year-old magician. So simple yet so powerful, a five-year-old boy's tender magic turning the night before a divorce into Valentine's Day.

My son Jeremy.

"So simple yet so powerful, a five-year-old boy's tender magic turning the night before a divorce into Valentine's Day."

EPILOGUE

"the catechism of killing"

war is deceptively simple
when the bullets are whizzing by
and shrapnel is racing for its finish line
war isn't complicated until you get home

War is profound on so many levels. To call it a life-changing event is an understatement. For the unfortunate, war alters their existence completely; death stops being a word in the d-section of the dictionary, but rather, death becomes the door to eternity for boys who sought to be men, or what they thought men should be. For the survivors, war sticks to them like skunk juice. War becomes an indelible thread that runs through the souls of the survivors. In 1968, some people misunderstood veterans and treated us poorly; today many people feel warm and fuzzy when they say, "Thank you for your service," but many who offer this salutation are void of understanding. They feel good, but we live with the angst of PTSD and the ominous threat of Agent Orange: both constant reminders of what our service gave us.

Time does not heal all wounds by itself. The wounded must be active participants in their healing process. A decade after my return from the Nam, I had yet to learn some of the key tenets of the emotional healing process. During the late 1980s and the 1990s, PTSD reared its vile and insidious head, yet it ironically presented me with opportunities—more than I wanted—to discover my true essence as a person. It was during this time that I began to realize that if I fell on my face on my journey home, I needed to, as the song says, "pick myself up, dust myself off," forgive myself for not being perfect, reach deep into my heart and find the courage to put one foot in front of the other and move toward healing.

Although resilience would become my weapon of choice in my battle with PTSD, I was a slow learner, remaining in the angry gear for many years after my returned to the World. While in the

Nam, I had set myself up to be disappointed when I returned from my tour of duty. While there, we dreamed of how fantastic it would be back in the World. Unmet expectations fed my anger. But there was some good news about being back in the World, which I realized my first night back in Tucson. As I was about to fall asleep, I looked at the window in my childhood bedroom and thought: "Wow, tonight no one is going to try to kill me." This awareness felt good, but I didn't feel connected; I felt alienated. There were few who understood—or cared about—my experience, and most who inquired about my war experience had an agenda, listening only when it suited their particular political perspective. Whether they were pro-war or anti-war, I felt used. No one asked how the war had affected me; it was always about politics.

As time marched on, like so many Vietnam vets, I began to bury my emotional pain during the 1970s and the early 1980s; I had yet to learn one of life's most valuable lessons: if I bury my pain, my pain will bury me. Eventually, I would discover that I would never drown from my tears but would drown from my unshed tears. Likewise, I ever so slowly began processing my grief which I had denied during the 1970s. My innocence had become a casualty of war. Survivor's guilt was my approach to grieving the loss of my fellow Marines who had died. Eventually, I would find a more fitting way to deal with their untimely loss. We are built to heal, but I would need to wait until 1990 for that catalyst to enter my life. My plane from the Nam had yet to touch down on the tarmac called Home. The Rolling Stones were so right when they sang, "You can't always get what you want / But if you try sometime you find / You get what you need."

When I write, I let you peek behind killing's curtain. My words leave footprints on the long road home as I search for the beauty of this world that was murdered so long ago. I write my story to remember, to share, to teach, to heal, to finally come home.

I hope to meet you in my sequel as I discover that war gets complicated when I get home. The odyssey of healing continues…

Peter M. Bourret, aka The Jello Kid

PHOTOS

The Jello Kid in Ohio in 1951

"Four-year-old tree climbers grow up."

Private Peter Bourret, USMC 1966

"Some of them become Marines going off to war."

LIFE WITH 1/7 IN 1967-1968 & MORE

Walt Kolomyjec, aka Cossack (right) & I taking a break on Hill 10

Michael Oleniacz, aka Pink Rat (left) & I on Hill 10

Front: l-r Waggoner &Mainville
Rear: l-r Jerome Cockerhan, aka Sugar Bear, Aaron C. Legget & States

l to r: Boksa and Paul Ignash filling sandbags

The Jello Kid circa late '67 going on a patrol

The Jello Kid: squad leader in mid '68

'Ski', an 81s FO for Bravo Co. in 1967

l to r: Boksa, Waggoner, Sgt. King?, Mainville, Ignash, & Oleniacz, aka Pink Rat

Me in mortar gun pit

Nguyen Ngoc Dahn, 12. I sponsored him through Save The Children Foundation.

Dale Witzman 60mm mortars Charley Co. 1/7

My John Wayne pose

Front to rear: Cossack and Kelley

Andy relaxing by my gun pit

Villagers returning from market

Rice paddies near Hill 10

Mountains west of Hill 10: NVA country

Marine tank just north of Hill 10

Da Nang in the distance: NVA's favorite target

105mm howitzer on Hill 10

A hamlet about a mile east of Hill 10

At west end of Hill 10, we built new gun pit 2 days before hill was hit with 25 122mm rockets.

Going out on Operation Pecos in July '67

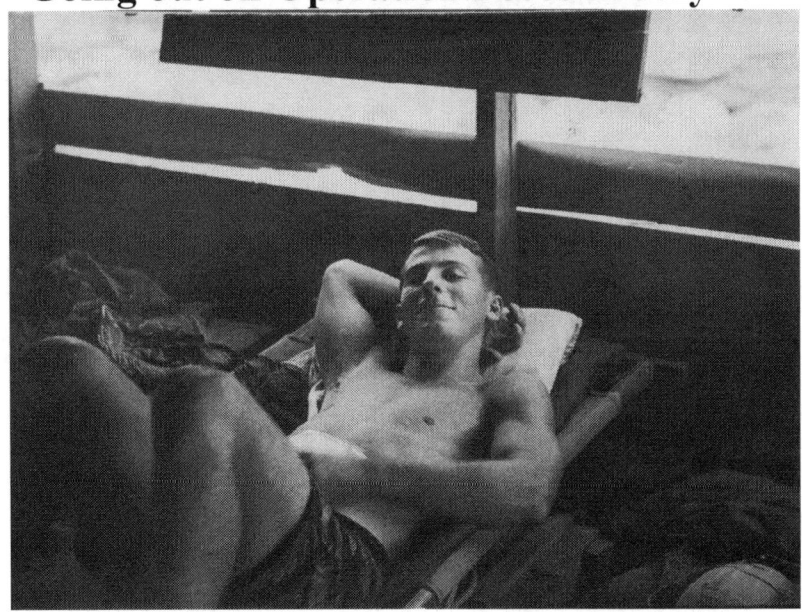

I'm relaxing in our tent on Hill 10.

The Jello Kid wondering how many days he has left in the Nam.

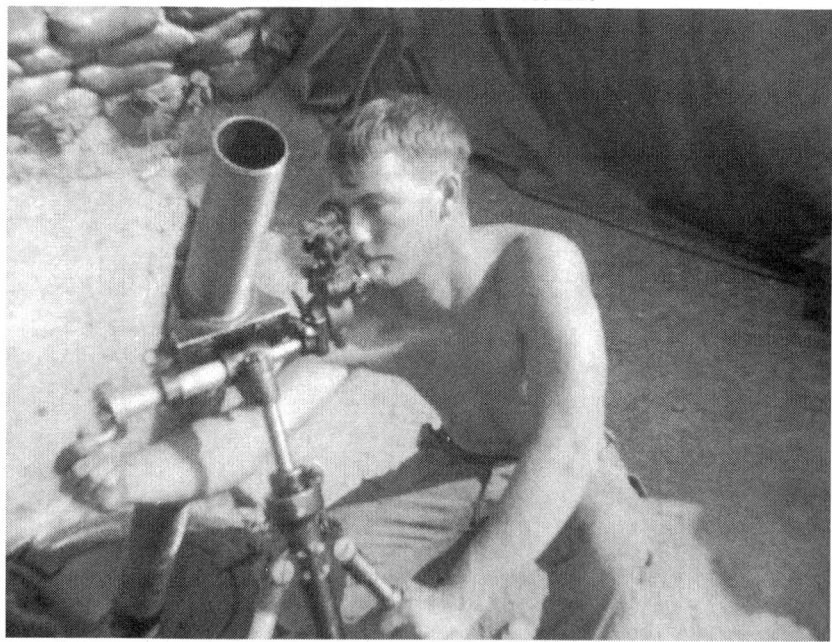

Setting up a fire mission

Gun pit with aiming stakes in the background

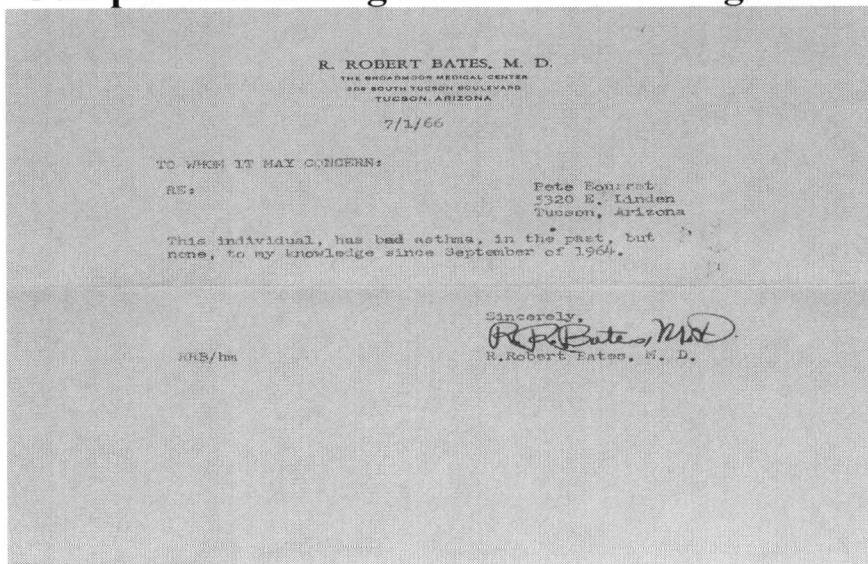

My doctor's note which caused the Marines to reject me until I got creative, aka lied a little

My older brother Paul, the Navy Corpsman

Right to left: Paul (5), Barbara (ex-wife), Jeremy (almost 2), and me, circa 1976.

Liz at Mary Washington College

My non-Marine look as a social studies teacher in the mid-1970s

PETER M. BOURRET

ABOUT THE AUTHOR

Born in New York City, Peter Bourret has lived in Tucson, Arizona for sixty-five years, where he attended twelve years of Catholic school, graduating from Salpointe Catholic in 1965. After serving with the 1st Battalion, 7th Marine Regiment as an 81mm mortarman in Vietnam during 1967 and 1968, he graduated from the University of Arizona in 1971 and received a Masters Degree from the U of A in 1974. Prior to the start of his teaching career, Bourret volunteered with a local adult education program for several years; then, he taught social studies for seven years at Apollo Middle School and also taught English for eighteen years, seventeen of them at Sahuaro High School.

Currently retired, Bourret has volunteered in the local public schools, teaching writing to second and tenth graders; he has volunteered for the past three years at the VA where he helps teach a class about PTSD. In addition to being a guest speaker for over a quarter century in high school American history classes, he speaks to classes at the University of Arizona College of Nursing about how to best serve the needs of patients with PTSD. For the past five years he has been a guest speaker/teacher in the Creative Writing classes at Salpointe Catholic High School.

Bourrert received a First Place medal for "Alone with *it* on Veterans Day" in the personal experience category at the 2014 National Veterans Creative Arts Festival; additionally, in 2015 and in 2017, he also was awarded First Place medals for two other pieces of writing.

War: a memoir was published online in 2014 by The Writers' Circle, Inc. @ www.riwriterscircle.com . Bourret has also published three books of poetry: *The Physics of War: Poems of War and Healing* (2015), and *Land of Loud Noises and Vacant Stares* (2015), and *Snowflakes From the Other Side of the Universe* (2015). *Three Joss Sticks In The Rain*, his first novel, was published in 2016. *Jello's Nam: A Memoir* was published in July 2018; he is in the process of finishing the second installment of his memoir.

Book Availability - Frequently Asked Questions

By going to the Amazon site, search for books and enter the title. Amazon offers the kindle version first and from there you can go to the book sections. As gifts, they can be shipped directly to the person.

Other Books By Peter M. Bourret

The Physics of War – Poems of War and Healing
By Peter M. Bourret

Bourret reaches deep within his personal war experience as a Marine and shares with the reader a glimpse of the true nature of war and its long term consequences. His observations and insights will profoundly impact the way the reader views war.
ISBN-10: 1502471973
ISBN-13: 978-1502471970
Regular Price: Book $15.00

Land of Loud Noises and Vacant Stares
By Peter M. Bourret

Bourret shares the profound impact of war on a twenty-year-old who discovered the horrors of war, letting the reader peek behind killing's curtain. This fasten-your- seat-belt experience will show what General Sherman meant when he referred to war as Hell, a view into PTSD and its insidious nature, the impact of war on the families at home and the arduous healing process. Combat veterans will easily recognize the topics about which Bourret writes, and those who have never known the war experience will possess a better understanding of the phrase "Thank you for your service."

ISBN-10: 1507715315
ISBN-13: 978-1507715314
Regular Price: Book $15.00

Snowflakes From The Other Side Of The Universe
By Peter M. Bourret

How are the Ah! Ha! moments created? Where do they come from? Bourret shows they are snowflakes found in the universe and connected. He creates poems from them and tells you how he did it.

ISBN-10: 1515028844
ISBN-13: 978-1515028840
Regular Price: Book $15.00

Three Joss Sticks In The Rain
By Peter M. Bourret

An ambush near a village goes badly wrong. It echoes through three decades seen from the viewpoints of who were there. Courage, loss, transformation and redemption develop over those years.

ISBN–10: 1516952278
ISBN-13: 978-1516952274
Regular Price: Book $21.95

Books By Friends Of The Author
Old Eyes, Grey Souls By Bill Black

Veterans are often heard to say "You wouldn't understand, you haven't been there." What are these images and memories that can be so misunderstood? Through poems that explore a veteran's soul, you are shown what these veterans wish families and friends could understand. Wars have colors, smells and images which can quickly and involuntarily summoned. To remember brings pain but to forget betrays wounded and dead fellow soldiers. These small groups of tormented people shape our world even though most people never know them.

ISBN-13: 978-1500886325   **ISBN-10:** 1500886327
Regular Price: Book - $15.00

Cattlemen At The Cantina By Bill Black

Bill said, "These are collected poems from my shows and recordings of over two decades for those who want to see what the poems look like. Most have never been in print other than as a script in my pocket. I also give some notes on performing poetry shows. These poems have been edited and polished in shows and recording studios. They bring laughs, sighs, a few tears and moments you will want to share aloud. This collection is the majority of three CDs and an audio book contribution set s from 2002 to 2012."

ISBN-13: 978-1503223615   **ISBN-10:** 1503223612
Regular Price: Book - $16.00

A Cowboy Walked Into A Bar: The Monologue Show By Bill Black

Bill Black presents an entire theatrically based monologue show using his own poetry. It was written and developed as an expanded show he presented to audiences in the Southwest. He then presents details on how a monologue show like this is created. This section is a short history of oral performance as well as a detailed analysis of this specific show. There is also varied selection of other performance poems he wrote during the same time he was developing the show. While many monologue shows have been developed, few writers have been as candid as Black on how the show is made to work. He brings over a half century of writing and performing experience into this play and its analysis.

ISBN-10: 1514798794
ISBN-13: 978-1514798799
Regular Price: Book - $19.50

Sea Song By Bill Black

Those raised by the sea are marked in ways beyond water stains and sun-colored skin. It is a life and culture that stays even when removed from the sea side. As Black moved away, memories of the shores never left him as he explored new places, people and stories. This is the fourth book of his story poems.

ISBN-10: 1534613994
ISBN-13: 978-1534613997
Regular Price: Book - $21.50

To Go With A Drink By Bill Black

Matt, an old bartender, reflects on his life in tales shared during the twilight of his life. For the young, many of the stories are of a world now gone. For some older audiences, Matt is reflecting times they lived through without noticing the changes.

His tales may take place in a few towns, but Matt is distinctly non-Metro-centric in his world view. Depending on your point of view, Matt may be either one of the last honest chronicler of his era or the personification of the unreliable narrator. His tales are, by turns, eclectic, esoteric, exotic, enigmatic, chimeric, almost erotic and mystical, with slanted glances to a fickle view of karma. Detectives, dancers and doves share pages with con men, warriors, and mud wrestlers. What could go wrong?

As with most stories told by bartenders, they are "To Go With A Drink."

ISBN-10: 1544874944   **ISBN-13**: 978-1544874944
Regular Price: Book - $21.50

In Search Of Jolie Blon By Bill Black

Black illustrates what happens when you live by the stories from songs listed on old jukeboxes found in the types of places your mother warned you about, religions moralize against, politicians hit for donations and everyone else says, "Damn, I wish I could have been there!"

The poem stories explore the murky boundaries of meanings of morality, ethics and legality, of shadow realms between the world of known science and almost forgotten myths. He taps into chords almost 4000 years old and as recent as yesterday afternoon. Is it a realm of venal and deadly sins? Well, maybe, but only if done correctly.

ISBN-10: 1544874812   **ISBN-13**: 978-1544874814
Regular Price: Book - $21.50

Seedlings: Stories of Relationships
By Ethel Lee-Miller

We are defined by our relationships. From seven-second meetings with strangers to lifelong bonds among family members, relationships nurture, challenge and teach us not to take ourselves so seriously. *Seedlings* pays tribute to those connections, honoring those who bring meaning to our lives.

ISBN-10: 1627870474   **ISBN-13:** 978-1627870474

Thinking of Miller Place: A Memoir of Summer Comfort
By Ethel Lee-Miller

Relive the magic of childhood in stories of summers spent Miller Place, a town on the northeastern end of Long Island. Ethel and her identical twin enjoy carefree days diving in the waters of the Long Island Sound and nights chasing fireflies. Coupled with the twins adventures are the wondrous people of the area. With her "Finn" always by her side, Ethel savors childhood innocence while coming of age and forming secure, lasting ideals about beauty, home, and family. Even today, Ethel has only to think of Miller Place to claim a sense of comfort, serenity, and belonging.

ISBN-10: 1627872949   **ISBN-13:** 978-1627872942

Prospect For Murder
By Jeanne Burrows-Johnson
After envisioning her grandniece's body draped over a vintage Mustang, writer Natalie Seachrist investigates the Honolulu foothills apartment where Ariel died. Discovering the Shànghǎi origins of the complex's owners…and considerable discord…Natalie wonders if she can solve the riddle of the unexplained death before the murderer kills again to hide their secret.

Hardcover Book	ISBN 978-1-932926-45-3
9-CD Audio Book	ISBN 978-1-932926-46-0
Downloads :	
E-book	ISBN 978-1-932926-47-7
Audio Book	ISBN 978-1-932926-48-4

These authors were working from the Southern Arizona area at the time of publication of the works listed here. There are multitudes more writing and publishing in the area. See the back pages of future books from Bill Black to learn of new books by these authors and other new authors.

Made in the USA
Columbia, SC
28 July 2018